D1543197

CARS
of THE CENTURY

TODTRI

Cars of the Century has been originated, designed and produced by Nordbok International, Gothenburg, Sweden.

WORLD COPYRIGHT © 1998
Nordbok International, P.O. Box 7095, 402 32 Gothenburg, Sweden.

This edition published in 2002 by TODRI Book Publishers, 254 West 31st Street, New York, NY 10001-2813.
Fax: (212) 695-6984,
E-Mail: info@todri.com.
Visit us on the web!
www.todri.com

ISBN: 1-577717-318-X

EDITOR
Anna Cerps.

TEXT CARS
Christer Glenning, Bengt Ason Holm.

TEXT HISTORY
Lennart Haajanen.

GRAPHIC DESIGN
Claes Franzén, Mixgruppen, Gothenburg.

TYPESETTING
Kajsa Andersson, Mixgruppen, Gothenburg.

TRANSLATOR
Jon van Leuven.

Printed in Spain 2002

PHOTOGRAPHY
Neill Bruce Motoring Photolibrary, England, Bengt Ason Holm and Nordbok International, Sweden, unless otherwise stated.

CARS
of THE CENTURY

TODTRI

Contents

In this book – CARS OF THE CENTURY – we have tried to give a technical summary as well as a historical view of the motor car during the past hundred years. It all began in 1885, but it was not until the middle of the twentieth century that the automobile really spread worldwide.

Our aim has been to reflect the roots, the excitement and the achievements of motoring, yet also the mistakes that happened along the way. Included, too, are people and personalities who have contributed to making the car what it is today. These pages are a cavalcade of great moments in automotive history.

CARS OF THE CENTURY is divided into ten chapters, each of which marks a decade. Every decade begins with a general survey of life around the world at that time. In each chapter, we have highlighted important cars which, for different reasons, made history. Some of them were not important when they first appeared, because they were so advanced that the public rejected them. Many of those innovations we take for granted today.

In the text, you may find a few old stories and anecdotes that are questionable. Such information can never be checked for accuracy because the individuals who once told the tale are long gone. Still, we have done our best to report the truth and hope that we are as close to it as possible.

CHRISTER GLENNING   BENGT ASON HOLM

1886

−1910

The first F.I.A.T. car, resembling a scaled-down Benz, had a horizontal two-cylinder engine of 697 cc with automatic inlet valves, mounted in the rear of a simple steel-reinforced wooden frame. Its shifter-gear box was inspired by the Levassor and had three forward speeds, but no reverse until 1900, and then only optionally. All the mechanical parts were made in the factory, while the above *vis-à-vis* carriage came from Alessio in Turin. Only eight examples of this 1899 model were produced.

DURING THE LAST HALF OF THE 19TH CENTURY, LARGE factories and industries get their power mostly from steam engines, which are huge, heavy and clumsy machines. For minor workshops, mills, printers, bakeries and the like, small internal combustion engines are used. Such engines run on city gas, i.e. the gas that is being distributed to the lamps in homes and for street lighting. Canals and waterways are still used for long-distance transportation, but even here the steam engine is taking over in the form of locomotives that pull railway trains. Short-range conveyance is dominated by diverse horse-drawn wagons, but also hand-carts are still being used.

Combining a wagon with a stationary engine to make a "self-propelled" vehicle would seem natural enough, but is practically impossible; the existing engines are too heavy and inefficient. Neither can city gas be carried in a wagon. Widespread experiments are being conducted, primarily in Central

Benz's first car with four wheels, called the Patent-Motorwagen Benz "Victoria", appeared in 1892 and was manufactured until 1900. Another model, the "Velo", was made between 1894 and 1900. In the latter year, both models were replaced by the "Comfortable", which is shown here. This had a one-cylinder engine of 1045 cc, generating 3 horsepower at 700 rpm. Its price in 1901 was just 2,500 marks (equivalent to around 9 times as much today), but the model was made for only two years.

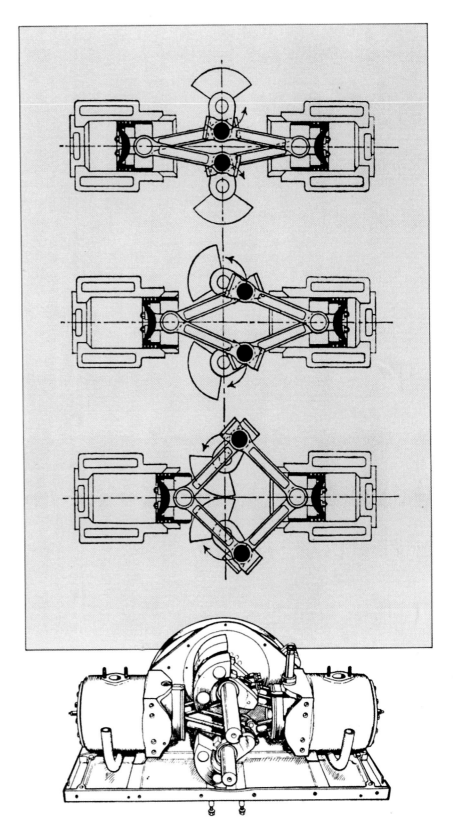

Three phases in the working cycle of the Lanchester engine, a two-cylinder almost vibrationless "boxer". Its two crankshafts, rotating in opposition, were connected to the two pistons by as many as six rods. This kind of engine was used in the 1897 Lanchester prototype, and in all two-cylinder production cars during 1900–05.

Europe, with smaller engines – and different kinds of fuels such as liquid chemicals. One of them is ligroin, a petrol-like hydrocarbon based on naphtha, used chiefly as a solvent.

The mid-1880s are not only interesting in terms of technology. Franz Joseph I rules the dual monarchy of Austria-Hungary, as emperor of the former and king of the latter country, each with its own parliament and government, but sharing defence, diplomatic corps and foreign policy. While industrialism is speeding up and railways expand, the region remains solidly agricultural, its principal means of transportation being the river Danube. By contrast, Denmark is a colonial power that possesses Iceland, Greenland, and three islands in the West Indies. Great Britain is clearly the global giant, and the land of progress at this time, with colonies on every continent and – thanks to many important inventions – a flourishing industrial economy. Scientific successes are frequent news. Machine-made products emerged in England already during the 1700s, enabling Great Britain to become the centre of world trade in the 1800s. London has 3.9 million inhabitants, New York 1.3 million, and Tokyo 900,000.

Germany is a federation of states ruled by eight kings, eight princes, two grand dukes and four dukes, each ruling his own territory. In addition, three cities are independent and have their own senates. There is also Alsace-Lorraine, the Alsace part of which was re-united with Lorraine, Germany having

Together with the Benz, these three cars represented the leading ideas in design at the end of the 1800s. The Peugeot (*right*) replaced its Daimler-type engines in 1897 with a horizontal two-cylinder engine built by Gratien Michaux. This was mounted in back, the cylinders pointing forward. Peugeot kept the rear engine longer than most other companies; the first front-engine car appeared only in 1900, and rear-engine "town broughams" still existed in 1905. Models in 1897 had a conventional radiator, instead of circulating the cooling water through the tubes of the frame. The 1897 English Daimler (*opposite page*) and the 1899 Panhard (*below*) both had a vertical two-cylinder engine in front, and hot-tube ignition. Being two years younger, the Panhard could boast a steering wheel – but the older Daimlers were often modified with a steering wheel by diverse English firms. One was Frank Morris in Kings Lynn, the self-appointed "Repairer of King Edward VII's motorcars".

Edward Butler has been unfairly treated by automobile historians. His 1888 Petrol Cycle had Ackermann steering, a jet carburettor, and mechanically operated inlet valves. This drawing shows the car in its original form, with the rollers for lifting the rear wheel off the ground when starting the engine.

won the 1870–71 war against France in 1871, and whose regent is another prince. The Chancellor and coordinator for the entire Federal State is Otto von Bismarck – and Germany is seething with activity. Not least in the Ruhr district, industries thrive, and social classes come into increasing conflict, giving rise to a great movement of workers. German socialism begins to play a leading role in the ideas and practices of inter-national socialism. The Social Democratic party's programme serves as a model for similar programmes all over Europe, notably in Scandinavia. During the same period, China has an emperor of the Ching dynasty, a religious life full of Confucian morality and Buddhist wisdom, but few signs of political or economic development.

Carl Benz in Mannheim has test-driven his three-wheeled

The Locomobile, also built under the name Mobile, was typical of the light steam carriages made in the USA at the turn of the century. This 1899 two-seater, called the "Spindle Seat Runabout", had 3.5 horsepower and a top speed around 25 mph (40 km/h). The fuel tank lay beneath the floor, and the water tank – with a recess holding the boiler – stretched across the rear end. A chain drove the rear axle at its middle (*above*). To avoid violating the Locomobile's patent, the Stanley brothers let their horizontal two-cylinder engine drive the rear axle directly.

Motorwagen several times. For fuel, he feeds it ligroin, bought at the pharmacy. In January 1886 he acquires a German patent for his Motorwagen. The automobile is born! From the engine to the chassis and body, Benz's car is designed as an organic unit. No parts are borrowed, for example, from horse-drawn carriages. Even the elegant wire-spoked wheels are made in his own workshop. That year, too, Gottlieb Daimler in Cannstatt presents a car, resembling a horse-drawn carriage on four wheels, with central pivot steering (which turns the whole front axle) and an engine built by Wilhelm Maybach. Many people have long tried to create self-powered vehicles, but the achievements of Benz and Daimler *mark the year 1886 as the date of origin for practicable motorcars.*

The Mercedes 60PS, built during 1902–05, was the model that brought the make into the limelight. It married power and flexibility with fine quality. In America it was produced by the Daimler Manufacturing Company in Long Island City, a subsidiary of the famous piano firm William Steinway. It also became an ideal for many designers on both sides of the Atlantic, who more or less closely imitated it.

Technical improvements soon follow, at first mainly in France, whose roads are better and more numerous than anywhere else in Europe. Hence the market for engines is in that country, so Benz and Daimler export their internal combustion engines mostly to French automobile makers, among them Peugeot and Panhard & Levassor. Immediately the bold French start to test their cars by holding speed races and hill climbs. Suspension, wheels, and other chassis parts – as well as engines, eventually – are thus developed fastest in France. The motorcar is still a very rare and expensive artefact only available to the wealthy,

Of the 1904 Rolls-Royce, superbly constructed by Henry Royce with 10 horsepower, only sixteen examples were sold before the company turned to larger cars. A chassis without a body cost 395 pounds, so it was not terribly expensive.

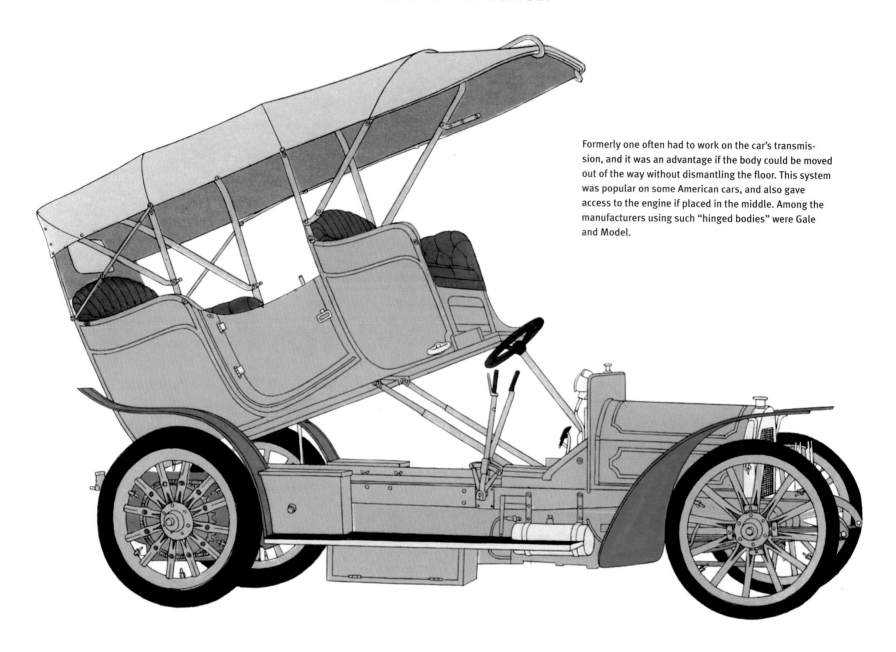

Formerly one often had to work on the car's transmission, and it was an advantage if the body could be moved out of the way without dismantling the floor. This system was popular on some American cars, and also gave access to the engine if placed in the middle. Among the manufacturers using such "hinged bodies" were Gale and Model.

and especially attractive to the young men among them. But development in Germany is not standing still, and Daimler Motoren Gesellschaft builds a four-cylinder engine. Also in the 1890s, Rudolf Diesel invents the diesel engine. Initially used as marine and stationary power sources, these engines are adopted in time by heavy vehicles such as lorries.

The vision of soaring through the air like birds has been entertained by many people in the past. Leonardo da Vinci designed a helicopter in about 1500, and countless contraptions have come to light since then, ranging from kites and balloons

to flapping wings. A French tailor sews an airtight gas-filled suit, jumps off the Eiffel Tower and is killed. Experiments are done in France with a soft, gas-filled airship driven by an electric motor. A German count, Ferdinand von Zeppelin, sees the advantages of the new internal combustion engine for a rigid, gas-filled, dirigible airship to serve military purposes. When Kaiser Wilhelm II ignores his idea, he develops his own "Zeppelins" and they prove to be practicable, though slow and clumsy. During the next decades, such airships make scheduled flights in various parts of the world. In North Carolina, the

The Cadillac Model B, with 9 horsepower (shown here from 1905), was similar to the Oldsmobile in many respects, but its "false" front hood – added in 1904 – gave a more modern look. Both cars had a horizontal one-cylinder engine in the middle of the frame, a two-speed planetary transmission, and single-chain drive. The rear part of the Cadillac's body was removable, and cost 100 dollars extra.

American brothers Wilbur and Orville Wright finally manage to construct and fly an airplane.

The Great Western Railway, in England and Wales, has been doing its best to maintain a very broad track gauge of 7 feet (2.134 metres), but ultimately has to accept the gauge of most other railway companies, which is 4 feet 8.5 inches (1.435 metres). This gauge derives from the famous train pioneer George Stephenson, who chose it for his first steam locomotive. As a transitional technique, the Great Western uses three-railed tracks to move wide and narrow wagons of both gauge systems in the same train set, and even makes switch points work with the double-width track. Equal ingenuity is shown by Guglielmo Marconi, who develops the applications of sending and receiving radio waves – a breakthrough of enormous value. In New Orleans, what comes to be regarded as the first jazz orchestra is founded by Buddy Bolden. His music, a mixture of collective improvisation and ragtime rhythm, becomes extremely popular and leads to further jazz bands.

Alexander III of Russia dies. His successor, Nicholas II, is also an autocrat, but does attempt some modernization of the country along West European lines. Due to his weak personality and reactionary advisers, including his wife Alexandra, the reforms bear little fruit. Japan fights a war against China and takes Formosa, the Pescadores Islands and the Liaotung Peninsula. Russia, France and Germany, fearing competition, force the Japanese to give back much of this territory. Japan wants revenge and allies herself with Great Britain. A few years later, she attacks the east end of Russia, whose defeat is an embarrassing blow to the Tsar's prestige. The oppressed Russian masses strike and the peasants revolt. Nicholas,

promising a liberal constitution, convenes an elective council, the *Duma*. These events sow the seeds for the October Revolution and the fall of his empire.

One of the most beloved French plays, *Cyrano de Bergerac* by Edmond Rostand, has its premiere in Paris at the Théâtre de la Porte Saint-Martin. A real-life drama, the so-called Dreyfus Affair, is taken up by the author Emile Zola. His open letter to the President of France, entitled "I accuse" in the newspaper *Aurore*, condemns the corrupt military establishment and the government for judicial murder and manipulations to hide the guilt of army officers. This article results in the complete vindication of Captain Alfred Dreyfus, who had been demoted and sentenced to ten years' imprisonment for espionage.

At Nice in southern France, the Austro-Hungarian consul, Emil Jellinek, is fascinated by the sporting potential of automobiles. Good at business, he sells German Daimlers to whoever has enough money and interest. His 24-horsepower Daimler is the last to reach the goal in a race between Nice and Marseilles, but he learns what the German car needs in order to compete with the more advanced French makes. In the Cannstatt factory, Wilhelm Maybach and Paul Daimler (whose father Gottlieb has died) heed his advice and start to build a better car. Named "Mercedes" after Jellinek's daughter, it is not entirely new. Rather, it combines well-known and mostly well-tested designs in a single chassis, yielding easier driving and smoother steering than any other contemporary car.

Among the most beneficial components of the Mercedes are its four-cylinder engine's mechanically controlled inlet valves. They enable the fuel supply to regulate the engine

A beautiful example of a Roi-des-Belges body, of the type designed by Henri Binder. This car is a 25-horsepower C.G.V. from 1904.

speed, which normally in cars of this period can only be adjusted marginally by the ignition timing. In addition, the engine's flexibility makes the gearbox much simpler to handle. The new chassis is lower, the radiator is in front of the engine, and the front wheels are as big as the rear ones. As a whole, the car gives quite a modernistic impression.

In 1901, the 35-horsepower Mercedes begins to race, but loses at first. Next year, with higher power and cylinder volume raised to 6.8 litres, things go better. When 1903 brings overhead valves, 60 horsepower and 9.2 litres, Mercedes proves unbeatable.

The Nobel Prize awards also commence in 1901, that in physics going to Wilhelm Röntgen of Germany for his discovery of X-rays. Simultaneous awards are made in chemistry to the Dutchman Jacobus van't Hoff, for explaining the temperature dependence of processes such as freezing and boiling; in medicine to Emil von Behring of Germany, for introducing serum therapy and treatments against diphtheria and tetanus; and in literature to the French poet René Sully-Prudhomme, who writes sad lyrics in the neoclassical Parnassian style.

Destiny smiles, too, in Bohemia – later part of the Czech republic – where Václav Laurin and Václav Klement become partners in a firm making bicycles and motorcycles. Laurin & Klement unveils its first car at an automobile exhibition in Vienna. Their company will subsequently turn into Škoda, a large manufacturer of cars and machine tools. Aluminium, a fairly soft and very light metal, is attracting attention, and in 1909 a suitable method of hardening is accidentally discovered in Germany. This creates huge opportunities for building strong structures with low weight. Hardened aluminium, called Duralumin, is used immediately in airships and, before long, in airplanes. ∎

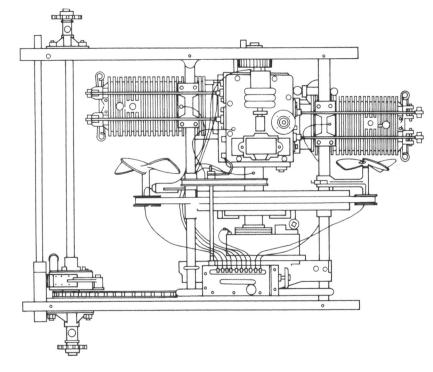

The Holsman Automobile Company, based in Chicago, was a pioneer of "high-wheelers". Its success during 1902–06 inspired numerous other firms to enter the field. As some of them were in St. Louis, and most in Chicago, this type of car had a "Midwestern" image. Not many examples reached the east coast of America, and few were exported to Europe, although they were not unknown in India, Australia and South Africa. Shown here are a 1908 Kiblinger (*opposite*) and the inside of a 1911 I.H.C. (*above*). The latter had a horizontal two-cylinder boxer engine, planetary gearbox, and single-chain drive. It was made as the Auto Buggy – with two lengthwise seats for passengers – or as the Auto Wagon, a light truck. The Holsman car's transmission was very peculiar, with forward drive via ropes that ran from a middle axle to big discs which were bolted on the rear wheels. Reverse drive was engaged by moving the middle axle backward, so that the rollers on the axle ends could act directly on the rear tyres. On later models, these ropes were replaced by wires, and the rollers were grooved more deeply in order to make contact with the wheel rims rather than the tyres.

(*Above*) This 1901 Lanchester, a double landaulet, characterizes the eccentric designs of "Doctor Fred" Lanchester in the years before World War I. Almost no front bonnet exists, but the car runs quite comfortably due to the engine's location – between the driver and front passenger – as well as the long wheelbase. All Lanchesters had a steering wheel in 1910, yet theoretically a control stick could be obtained as late as 1911. The engine is described on page 9.

(*Opposite*) A French way of approaching the sports-car era. In 1908, Maurice Sizaire and Louis Naudin put a horizontal one-cylinder engine into a light chassis. This had a very early example of independent front suspension, with transverse leaf springs. Sizaire & Naudin was highly successful in competitions, such as the Coupe de Sicile. The car was also somewhat cheap at 178 pounds (equivalent to about 40 times as much today).

Rolls-Royce Silver Ghost

A MEETING BETWEEN HENRY FREDERICK ROYCE and Charles Stewart Rolls in 1904 was the starting point for what would be one of the most distinguished, long-lived models in automobile history. The Rolls-Royce Silver Ghost enjoyed a run of eighteen years.

Henry Royce was born on 27 March 1863 and grew up in northern England. The poverty of his origins had a lasting influence and – like many other great men – he was characteristically serious, industrious, responsible and purposeful.

At the age of 19 Royce became chief electrician for a company in Liverpool, but after only a few years he started his own firm in Manchester. It was called F.H. Royce & Co. and produced, among other things, electric cranes and generators.

England did not have a wide range of cars to buy at the beginning of the 20th century. The nation's auto industry was in its infancy and many cars were imported, especially from France. So when Henry Royce wanted to purchase his first car, the choice fell on a Decauville. But the premiere tour was a disappointment: his engine refused to start.

Chagrined but not conquered, Royce accepted the challenge and resolved to build himself a vehicle. As he grew familiar with the "new technology", he was disturbed to see how bad the existing cars were. His aim became something that would be, and stay, much better.

The initial result appeared in 1904 and was named after Royce. Only three examples were made, and none of them survive today.

ENTER AND EXIT CHARLES ROLLS

In 1904, Rolls saw one of Royce's cars at a competition and was so enraptured that he got in touch with the designer. Soon they had established a name that was to be the world's most prestigious in automobiles, Rolls-Royce. Their cooperation proved to be rather short, for Rolls crashed in his Wright airplane at a flying exhibition on 10 July 1910. Yet during that time the company created the model that brought it the greatest fame: the 40/50-hp or, as it was later called, the Silver Ghost.

This car emerged from a new realization that the 30-hp model, which was the first to have a six-cylinder engine, did not perform as well as expected. Its crankshaft suffered from strong torsional vibrations, and often broke off.

QUALITY AT ANY PRICE

The Silver Ghost was not a revolutionary design, but it had such an edge over all contemporaries that it quickly earned the reputation of being "the world's best car". Main reasons were the enormous precision with which it was built, and the outstanding ways in which the materials for it were used. Thus, forged items were constructed so that the crystalline structure in the finished parts would be as advantageous as possible. A brake drum that weighed 48 kilograms before preparation had a weight of only 14.5 kg afterward.

Similarly, all drilled holes were reworked in order to cause no stresses that might give rise to cracks. Efforts were made to ensure that every detail was perfect, whether or not it was

This is the first Silver Ghost built in 1907. It was at Malwood Castle for 40 years, but is now owned by Rolls-Royce Ltd and often takes part in veteran car rallies and public-relations events. It has gone over 575,000 miles.

visible – and the list of measures taken could fill a whole book. Henry Royce's philosophy was that "quality would be there long after one forgot what price one had to pay".

And one paid indeed. The Silver Ghost was a pocket-puncher. At £1,400 it eclipsed the price of £200 for a contemporary Rover or De Dion.

The six-cylinder 7-litre engine had two separate blocks made of cast iron, on a long crankcase of aluminium alloy. The unusually strong crankshaft carried seven main bearings, and the cylinder blocks had fixed tops and side-valves. This meant avoiding the mechanical noise caused by pushrods.

Both the engine and transmission were extremely quiet and vibration-free.

While the engine was fairly simple in design, it was also very well equipped. The electrical system and components held to high standards. These were manufactured by Rolls-Royce, of course, and the Silver Ghost had a combined battery and magnetic ignition. Vibrator coils were used to start, and then the magnet was switched in to prevent discharging the batteries. Not until 1919 was the model given a generator that could charge the batteries and provide current for the lights and starter motor. Each cylinder had two spark plugs, and it was

Rolls-Royce Silver Ghost Alpine Eagle

possible to drive on both ignition systems at the same time.

At first the Silver Ghost had a four-step gearbox, but in 1909 it was replaced with three steps, the third being direct. The earlier fourth gear was an overdrive, too high to take the car over steep hills. Most drivers in those days did not like to shift gears, and preferred keeping the highest gear as long as they could. During that same year, the cylinder volume was raised to 7428 cc. But the four-step gearbox came back in 1913.

From the outset, Rolls-Royce adopted a policy of not revealing any performance figures for its cars. Still, we know that the 7-litre engine had a power of 48 hp at 1,500 rpm, which allowed a theoretical top speed of about 55 mph (90 km/h). Everything depended on what type of body the customer could obtain. And few cars have been endowed with bodies as fine as the Silver Ghost's.

A CAR A DAY, LESS OR MORE

The company's original production rate was four chassis per week. After a move in 1908 to larger premises in Derby, it grew to nine per week. During the eighteen years devoted to this model, a total of 6,173 were made. Throughout the period, few changes were made since the company took no interest in fashions. Rolls-Royce never wavered from this standpoint, so the Silver Ghost eventually became an "un-modern" car and was outdone by many other luxury manufacturers.

In May 1925 the war against time could no longer be waged, and Rolls-Royce unveiled the New Phantom with an overhead-valve engine. ∎

Oldsmobile Model R "Curved Dash"

IT IS WIDELY BELIEVED THAT HENRY FORD introduced mass production for cars with his assembly-line principle. Yet already in 1902, Curved Dash Runabouts were being built at a rate of 2,500 in one year by Ransom Eli Olds (1864–1950).

Olds – whose middle name recalled Eli Whitney, the inventor of mass production – was the originator of two American car makes that have gone into automobile history, Oldsmobile and Reo (his initials). In 1897 he founded the Olds Motor Vehicle Company in the small town of Lansing, Michigan, and built four cars. Each had four seats and a 5-hp one-cylinder engine.

In 1899 Olds moved to Detroit, where workers and customers were more numerous. He invested $400 and a timber millionaire, Samuel L. Smith, put up the remaining $199,600 which he needed. A fire in March 1901 destroyed all but one of the Olds prototypes. This was presented during the summer as an Oldsmobile Model R "Curved Dash". Its name meant that the front splash-plate was rounded instead of straight.

SIMPLE BUT STRONG

Olds had realized that a cheap runabout must be simple, and his slogan was "Nothing to Watch but the Road". Simplicity was the essence of a Curved Dash. It amounted to little more than a wagon minus the horse and shackles. The engine lay below in the elementary, metal-reinforced wooden frame, which rested on semielliptic springs between the front and rear axles. In front, the frame was strengthened with a fully elliptic spring structure.

The one-cylinder overhead-valve engine, reclining under the seat, gave 4.5 hp at just 500 rpm – or as somebody expressed it, "a puff for every telegraph pole you passed". Transmission was via a two-step planetary gearbox and a chain to the rear axle. In the right conditions, a Curved Dash could approach 20 mph (35 km/h). It was slowed only by a simple brake on the transmission, though in 1902 an "emergency brake" on the rear axle was added.

We might think that the car was intended for city use alone, but the contrary was proved in 1903 by L.L. Whitman and Eugene Hammond. They drove it all the way from San Francisco to New York in 73 days.

During the model's six years of production, its price stayed at $650, while many changes were made in the design. The

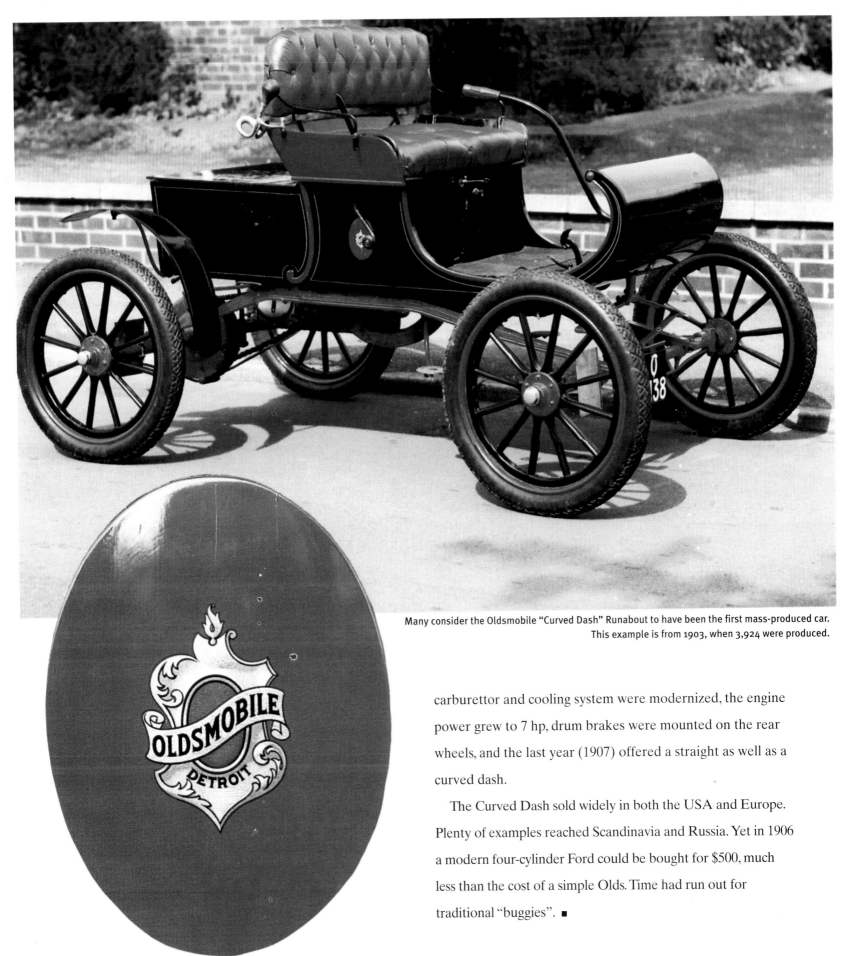

Many consider the Oldsmobile "Curved Dash" Runabout to have been the first mass-produced car. This example is from 1903, when 3,924 were produced.

carburettor and cooling system were modernized, the engine power grew to 7 hp, drum brakes were mounted on the rear wheels, and the last year (1907) offered a straight as well as a curved dash.

The Curved Dash sold widely in both the USA and Europe. Plenty of examples reached Scandinavia and Russia. Yet in 1906 a modern four-cylinder Ford could be bought for $500, much less than the cost of a simple Olds. Time had run out for traditional "buggies". ■

De Dion Bouton Quadricycle

A voiturette with tiller steering and a tricycle from circa 1900.

ONE RENOWNED CAR MAKE GOES BACK TO 1882 when a rich count met two men who specialized in building steam-driven toys. Georges Bouton and his brother-in-law, Charles Trépardoux, had started a workshop in 1869 to manufacture such gadgets. Thirteen years later, Count Albert de Dion de Malfiance bought one of their toy cars. Mightily impressed with it, he went to see the pair.

They were planning to produce a steam-powered tricycle,

and de Dion offered to sponsor the project. The first examples appeared in 1883, but did not go on public sale until 1888. Next year, de Dion and an engineer named Delalande began to experiment with radial combustion engines. But Trépardoux and Bouton were still more interested in steam power.

Another idea was to develop a special drive shaft, later known as the De Dion shaft, which would become very important. It worked by means of floating drive axles with

The famous De Dion back axle.

universal joints on both ends. The rear axle held up the vehicle, but did not take part in transmitting power to the wheels. This arrangement gave excellent road-holding, which has been appreciated by many sports-car and racing-car designers through the years. Bouton and Trépardoux also supported Michelin's development of tyres.

In 1894, however, Trépardoux left the company since he disliked petrol engines. De Dion Bouton was officially founded in 1898, half of its capital coming from a Baron van Zuylen.

A PROMINENT MOTORCAR MAKER

From 1895 onward, De Dion established itself as one of France's leading manufacturers of tricycles and engines. The latter were sold to many other auto companies, and were produced by licence in several countries including the USA. By 1902, no fewer than 33,000 engines had emerged – a fantastic record for that time.

The first tricycle, presented in 1895, had a simple design but was distinguished by the whiz of its little engine. The usual speed was then 500–600 rpm, yet De Dion's device

worked at 1,500 rpm and had been tested up to 3,000 rpm without flying to pieces – a rate that was regarded as science fiction. The tricycle engine's size increased from 137 to 269 cc, and its power from 1/2 to 2 1/4 hp.

For family use, the tricycle was also available with a small trailer, containing a seat and baggage space. The combination soon became fashionable. De Dion and Bouton, though, realized that a bigger car had to be built. In 1895 they announced a four-wheel four-seater, called *vis-à-vis* because the passengers sat turned toward each other. This model, too, was a rapid sales success.

De Dion Bouton Quadricycle was a conveyance that appealed to young people: fun to drive, simple but very well built, and professional in all details. The famous motoring journalist Griffith Borgeson once expressed a conviction that, if replicas were made today, they would definitely be worth the trouble.

Whereas the tricycle was built only until 1901, the car production lasted until 1932 when the firm went into eternal bankruptcy. ■

The tricycle could be equipped with a "drag hook" and coupled to a trailer with room for one person.

Baker Electric

IN THE EARLY DAYS OF CARS, COMBUSTION ENGINES WERE generally unreliable, noisy and smelly. Even then, inventors consequently looked for alternative sources of power. Many people at the turn of the century claimed that combustion would give way to both electricity and steam in automobiles, which had only existed for some fifteen years.

One man who believed it was Walter C. Baker in Cleveland, Ohio. After graduating from the Case School of Applied Science, he did many kinds of work, including construction of the Electrobat – an electric car – and organizing operations at the American Ball Bearing Company.

In 1898 he started the Baker Motor Vehicle Company in Cleveland, helped by the brothers Fred and Rollin White. This factory was to make electric cars, the initial sales argument being their reliability in comparison with steam- and petrol-driven vehicles.

The first Baker was presented in 1900 at what was also the first National Automobile Show, in New York's Madison Square Garden. There was only one model – a simple runabout that could, in addition, be obtained with a folding top on a Stanhope body. Among the customers was Thomas Edison, and his choice of a Baker gave the company good publicity.

Its electric motor provided a mere 3/4 horsepower and a maximum speed of about 20 mph (30 km/h). With fully charged batteries, the driving distance was some 50 miles (80 km).

Such performance earned no applause, but in 1902 Walter Baker decided to show the public that an electric car, too, could go fast.

He built a submarine-like contraption, the Baker Torpedo, with a 12-hp Elwell-Parker motor. In June 1902 he set an unofficial speed record on Staten Island, covering a mile in 47 seconds. This meant a final speed of 78 mph (125.5 km/h), around 60 percent faster than the record of Serpollet in France. Sadly, the achievement was marred when, just after the run, Baker crashed into the audience and two people were killed.

Electric cars grew ever more popular, reaching their peak between 1910 and 1913. Primarily they were praised for urban driving. They also greatly attracted women, as an electric car needed no starter motor. Petrol cars had to be cranked up, a task that was demanding even for a man.

Owning an electric car brought social status, and many models were extravagantly furnished. Thus, the 1910 Baker had a high covered body in black lacquer with six windows, red velvet upholstery, silk curtains, Venetian blinds, and flower-vases. Its price was $2,600 whereas a contemporary Ford Model T sedan cost $1,200.

What argued against electric cars, and ultimately defeated them, were the batteries' capacity and weight. Depending on speed, one could drive only 30–75 miles (50–120 km) before recharging. And to charge the batteries, one needed access to

1901 Baker Electric stanhope

a garage with expensive, advanced equipment. It was also possible to carry a special device for "tanking" from the overhead cables of tramways, but this procedure involved a certain risk.

Battery weight and lifetime were further problems that remind us of today's electric cars. Each set was expensive, could weigh 1,000 lbs (450 kg) and lasted three years on average. Not surprisingly, most buyers and drivers of electric cars were rich folk.

In June 1915, Baker merged with another electric-car maker, Rauch & Lang. That December, the firm bought out R.M. Owen & Co., which manufactured the Owen Magnetic. Baker's production of electric passenger cars stopped in 1916. ∎

Stanley Steamer

WHEN THE STANLEY STEAMER APPEARED IN 1897, it was 126 years since Nicholas-Joseph Cugnot in France had built the first steam-driven vehicle – a kind of tractor for towing a cannon. The first and only test-drive is said to have ended against a wall, but the vehicle happens to survive at the Conservatoire Nationale des Arts et Métiers in Paris.

Between the years 1770 and 1850, Englishmen completely dominated the development of steam-driven conveyances, and during 1825–35 there were several carriage-lines in traffic with more or less fantastic "steam coaches". But the fear of accidents, and the protests from British railroads and horse-riders, stopped all this activity in the 1840s.

The United States, an isolationist country, set its own course and learned the hard way, unaware of what happened in Europe. Most of its automotive progress occurred in New England and, surprisingly, by the 1890s Americans were much farther advanced in some respects than the Europeans.

Taking part in this trend were the twin brothers Francis E.

Long before the introduction of combustion-engined auto-mobiles, Europe and the USA saw a lot of vehicles equipped with steam engines. But the Stanley brothers were the first to mass-produce such cars.

and Freeland O. Stanley from Kingsfield, Maine. In 1896 they saw a failed demonstration of a Whitney steam car, and decided to build one of their own. They were not engineers, but generally curious, and had a solid grip on common sense when it came to mechanical matters. The next year, their car was ready, with a two-cylinder standing steam engine made by Penny & Sons. Most of its other parts also came from external suppliers.

The first Stanley had a simple two-seat runabout body. Driven by chain, it could do about 25 mph (40 km/h). By July 1898, the brothers were 200 cars richer, and established as the first to manufacture cars on a large scale.

An offer arrived for the operation in 1898, which the Stanleys could not resist. John Brisbane Walker, who owned the Automobile Company of America, promised them $250,000 and jobs as designers in his new firm, called the Locomobile Company of America. Francis and Freeland accepted and signed a contract that, for one year, they would not make any cars with their own name.

About a year later, Locomobile moved from Newton to Bridgeport, Connecticut, and the Stanley brothers bought back the old factory, as well as their patents. In 1902 they finished a totally new, refined model. It was so superior to Locomobile's products that the latter, in 1904, gave up steam cars altogether.

With this Stanley Steamer "Wogglebug", Fred Marriott set a world record of nearly 128 mph (205.5 km/h), fantastic for that time. A replica of the car is now in the USA.

THE BOILING-WATER BRUTE

In the new machine, a reclining steam engine drove the rear axle directly through a large cog-wheel, which engaged one on the crankshaft. No gearbox was needed, and Stanley kept this type of direct drive until 1925.

The first Stanley models were simple designs and, to hold down prices, rapid steam boilers were never used. Not before 1915 was a condenser added to the system. All Stanleys had a two-cylinder engine, its power being 6.5 hp until 1903, when a completely new 8-hp engine was introduced.

In 1906 came the most famous of all Stanleys, the Model H or "Gentleman's Speedy Roadster". It had a 20-hp engine and can justly be called America's first true sports car, with a top speed around 70 mph (115 km/h). A kind of half-racer with 25 hp, the Model K, appeared in 1907 – and next year

Stanley presented a first sedan, the Model J.

Publicity was dear to the Stanley brothers, who realized that competitions and record runs were important for their image. The most famous record-taker was the "Wogglebug", a cigar-like construction. At Daytona Beach in 1906, driven by Fred Marriott, it set a phenomenal pace of 128 mph (205 km/h). Marriott tried for a new record in 1907 and was clocked at 150 mph (240 km/h) before the bug flipped over and disintegrated. As if hard-boiled himself, the driver survived.

The decade 1900–1910 is regarded as the heyday of steam-car history, and during the whole "age of steam" about 150 manufacturers can be counted coming and going. Stanley's best years were 1904–05, when a thousand cars sold annually. In 1919 the twins retired, and the last Stanleys were made in 1925. ■

1910
–1920

The 1911 Regal had a 3.2-litre engine and a conventional three-speed gearbox, but its unusual chassis was "underslung" so that the main frame members lay underneath the axles.

The Italian auto industry had a quite limited home market, and tended to focus on large expensive cars for export sale – especially to France, Great Britain and the USA. As late as 1911, the Züst company in Brescia built a chain-driven monster with 50–60 horsepower, called Tipo America and costing 5,000 dollars in New York. But there were also more modern designs, such as the 4.7-litre 25/35-hp Tipo S305 (*above*). It used a four-cylinder side-valve (L-top) engine in a single block, rear brakes with compensation and pull-rod control, and one of the first examples of the pear-shaped radiator which, after World War I, was to become so typical of Italian cars.

WOMEN'S LIBERATION IS BECOMING MORE OF A REALITY. Finland leads Europe in having granted them the political right to vote. The most daring ladies cut their hair short and take up smoking. Flowery aromas from the past century give way to mysterious scents. François Coty creates a perfume of the Chypre variety – evoking fresh bergamot and warm moss – while Jacques Guerlain boasts the unforgettable L'Heure Bleue and Mitsouko. Eau de Cologne 4711 earns world fame and is here to stay. For many people, this is an age of carefree affluence and material progress; cities glow with electrical lighting,

The 1913 Lancia Theta was in many ways like the Züst: it had the same type of engine, joined to a four-speed gearbox. Together with Hispano-Suiza, Lancia could boast of being the first in Europe to have an electric starter motor as standard equipment. A pedal-controlled Rushmore starter motor came with the Theta model from 1914 onward. The manufacturer was so certain of this motor's function that the old starting crank was placed in the toolbox. Theta cars could be obtained with wire-spoked or artillery wheels, and were made from late 1913 until 1918.

(*Above*) The 1915 Pierce-Arrow "48" tourer. Partly recessed headlamps were a hallmark of most Pierce cars from 1912 until manufacture ceased in 1938. The designer, Herbert M. Dawley, was chief of the body department; he later became a famous Broadway actor and director. A type "48" cost between 4,900 and 6,250 dollars (equivalent to 15–20 times as much today).

(*Opposite page*) Cycle cars were driven on both sides of the Atlantic. The 1914 G.N. (*top*) was the most successful example in England, with sporty performance, good economy and fair reliability. The McIntyre Imp (*below left*) was built by a high-wheeler maker in Auburn, Indiana. It had a large V2 engine, and friction drive via a flat belt that was more than half as long as the car. The 1919 A.V. Monocar (*below right*) took simplicity to an extreme. Developed from a pre-World War I design by John Carden, it used a rear-mounted J.A.P. V2 engine in a very thin body of plywood, mahogany or cardboard.

The 1914 Morris Oxford was a typical English "small car" of the years just before the war. Its parts came from various suppliers: the engine from White & Poppe, axles and steering from E.G. Wrigley, wheels from Sankey, lamps from Powell & Hammer, and body from Raworth. At 175 pounds it was an excellent buy, and Morris sold 393 examples the first year – growing to 909 in 1914 with a choice of other, more expensive bodies. The company's factory, which also made most of the parts for Humber cars, was among the best-established in England and one of the twelve largest in Europe.

By 1918, Buick belonged to the respected makes and had built solid medium-class cars for 14 years. Its production statistics had been in third or fourth place for several years – but while more expensive than their rivals from Ford, Willys, Dodge and Chevrolet, Buicks also gave the customers more. This two-seat roadster of Model E-44, with a six-cylinder 4.1-litre engine of 60 hp, cost 1,265 dollars, and 10,666 such cars were manufactured in 1918, when Buick's total output reached 77,691.

and so-called Victrola horn gramophones play jazzy music for the new popular one-step dance. Then the *Titanic* goes under, taking with it the faith in unfailing technology.

A revolution in Turkey causes disintegration into small states of the Ottoman Empire's possessions in the Balkans and Eastern Europe. Serbia – allied with Russia, France and England – benefits most, but is denied access to the Adriatic coast. In North Africa, Italy conquers Libya. The bitter Balkan political conflict revives in June 1914, when a Serbian nationalist in Sarajevo murders the Austrian Crown Prince, Archduke Franz Ferdinand. Disturbances spread, and the Austrian government, backed by Germany, puts demands on the pan-

Slavic Serbians. These are supported by the Russian giant, which is first to mobilize its forces, despite a bad railway network and infrastructure. Germany declares war on Russia and France. She marches toward Paris through Belgium, whose old neutrality since 1839 is thereby violated. Consequently, England declares war on Germany, and World War I erupts.

The United States does not enter the fray until April 1917. At about the same time, Germany launches an all-out submarine attack on merchant ships going to the British Isles. Early that year, lack of food and necessities in Russia is catastrophic, and in March a great strike is held by dissatisfied workers, especially in St. Petersburg. The following "March

Station-wagons, or estate cars, were unusual before the 1930s. The 1913 Napier 16-horsepower model gave its passengers no protection. It was presumably used to shuttle hunting teams, who – in bad weather – would have been heavily clothed anyway. With its lengthwise benches and rear door, it was closely related to the first cars of this type, which were made by the English Daimler company in the 1890s.

Revolution" makes the Tsar abdicate, and the Mensheviks led by Alexander Kerensky establish a provisional democratic government. After an initial failure in July, the Bolsheviks seize power in November (the "October Revolution" according to the Russian calendar). Their leaders – Vladimir Ilyich Lenin and Leon Trotsky – promise peace, land and reforms, but push aside the *Duma* parliament and found the Union of Soviet Socialist Republics. Russia's short experience of a Western-type government thus ends as suddenly as it began. In Germany, a revolt overthrows the Kaiser.

With American help, the war stops in late 1918. It has fractured four empires: those of Russia, Germany, Austria-Hungary, and Turkey. The League of Nations is born, Poland regains independence, and Finland declares herself to be an autonomous democratic republic. New states arise – Czechoslovakia and Yugoslavia. In all of the war's participating countries except Russia, fully democratic political systems are established.

Two cars that taught the American public to appreciate a closed carriage were Dodge's 1917 centre-door sedan (*above*) and the 1922 Essex Coach (*below*). Wire-spoked wheels were standard on Dodge sedans and relieved their bodies' boring lines. Not until 1919 did Dodge offer bodies covered entirely in steel, namely the more practical four-door version. Essex, both good and cheap at 1,295 dollars, sold 36,222 of the Coach in 1922, despite its funereal looks.

A sporty car for the countryside could be built from a racer, like the 1911 Delage Coupe de l'Auto. Driven by Louis Bablot, this very car won the race it was named after (also known as the Coupe des Voitures Légères), with the same touring equipment shown here. Today it is one of the few old competition cars that take part in "touring races" – another being an Itala Grand Prix car from 1908. Curiously, it had a five-speed gearbox with fourth as high gear and fifth as overdrive.

A long-distance sporting version of the Hillman Ten from 1919. This two-seater car was quite like the pre-war design, naturally for a model that was released only months before the Armistice. Its side-valve engine of 1593 cc lacked a removable cylinder head, but had aluminium pistons, and 1919 brought electric lamps and a starter motor as standard equipment.

The Belgian auto industry was important before World War I, and built some fine cars just after the war. But signs of decline appeared in the early 1920s. This 1912 Linon came from a small factory at Ensival-Verviers, which made conventional cars between 1900 and 1914, using both its own engines and those of other manufacturers (De Dion Bouton, followed by Balot, Fafnir, Fondu and Vatour). Annual production seldom exceeded 200–300 cars, enough for bare survival at the beginning of the century, but not in the 1920s. Wisely, the Linon brothers decided not to re-enter the auto market after the war.

As technological change proceeds, European workers – notably in harbours and in the glass and steam boiler industries – adopt militant methods to prevent machines from doing simple manual labour. The development of high-quality steel, lubricants, rubber and other materials, as well as improved methods of manufacture by welding, forging and pressing, result in increasingly reliable automobiles. Henry Ford, with his pioneering assembly-line production, brings forth the Model T in growing numbers. Just 34,528 of these cars are sold in 1910, but the figure is up to 785,432 seven years later. The United States is then turning out several thousand makes of car, although some of them are put together with parts from other suppliers.

The engineer Ferdinand Porsche, technical chief at Austro-Daimler in Wiener-Neustadt, wins the Prinz Heinrich Fahrt competition in 1910 with an open four-seater Austro-Daimler. This type becomes a success, and gets its type name from the race. Ordinary car engines at this time have a top speed of 1,000-1,200 rpm, while competition engines run at least twice as fast.

Many Grand Prix racing cars still have simple four-cylinder engines, but huge ones with over 13 litres of volume. In 1911-12, Peugeot builds the version that will be ancestral to all efficient motorcar engines of the future. It has double overhead cam-shafts, four inclined valves per cylinder, central spark plugs in the combustion chambers, and a well-designed lubrication

By 1913, the softly rounded curves of Roi-des-Belges bodies had been replaced by straight lines, here on a 30/35-horsepower Napier. The bonnet line was soon raised in order to line up with the body's upper edge. This body type continued throughout the 1920s.

system. This initial 7.6-litre engine yields 140 horsepower at 3,000 rpm, equalling the output of contemporary engines twice as large. For the next five years, the Peugeot is the world's foremost racing car.

In Los Angeles, a little mechanical workshop is owned by Harry Arminius Miller. Concentrating at first on vehicle fuel systems and special carburettors, he obtains some patents on carburettor designs, and makes carburettors for racing cars. One of the famous Peugeot Grand Prix cars is left with Miller for repairs. Its design inspires him to start producing his own engines and cars for competition. The Miller engines are destined to rank among the world's finest in racing. Their power, beauty and precision of manufacture are light-years ahead of what Detroit then offers – and naturally much more

expensive. Steam automobiles are still being made in America by the Doble company, but will be given up during the next decade.

To coordinate and lead interrelated technical and economic activities, big companies are managed with ever greater professionalism. Factories, railways and similar companies expand, calling for better organization – which, in turn, is found to promote bureaucracy that can keep the firms from accepting changes. It is the small, flexible firms that contribute most to progress in, for example, the techniques of vehicles, aircraft, radio, chemistry, telephony and agriculture. Now, too, awareness of the effects of industrial production and steam-driven trains on the environment is increasing.

Even after the advent of electricity, paraffin (kerosene) for

Fiat Tipo 55 from 1914. The cylinder volume was 9 litres and the power 75 hp at 1,500 rpm. This is actually an American-built example, and the Italian version was called Tipo 5. Fiat's factory in Poughkeepsie, New York, was open from 1910 until 1918 and manufactured the larger models.

lighting continues to be used in vast amounts, compared with the need of fuels and oils for other purposes – particularly to run motorcars. In 1914, American refineries produce hydrocarbons in these proportions: kerosene 61.2%, petrol (gasoline) 13.8%, lubricant oil 9.9%, heating oil 15.0%.

As yet, electricity serves mainly for illumination, and numerous companies supply it. Their standardization is poor: London has 50 different systems in 1917, delivering 10 different AC frequencies at 20 different voltages! In countries with large rivers and waterfalls, the power starts to flow from hydroelectric plants. So does a stream of visitors from Japan, armed with cameras and sketch-pads, to exhibitions and businesses in both Europe and the United States. ■

Cadillac Thirty and 51

FOR MANY PEOPLE THE CADILLAC NAME IS synonymous with luxury, and with the giant fins that graced its cars during the late Fifties. But the make's renown goes far back in time, and two models that contributed to it were the Thirty and 51.

The Cadillac Automobile Company was founded on 22 August 1902 by Henry M. Leland. Its name derives from a French explorer, Antoine de la Moth Cadillac (1656–1730).

That same year witnessed the company's first car, Cadillac Model A. It was a runabout, with a reclining one-cylinder engine of 1609 cc. The price was $750, or $100 more with a tonneau body.

Equally memorable for Cadillac was the year 1909. All previous models were then replaced with a single one, the four-cylinder Thirty. It offered three different bodies: roadster, demi-tonneau and touring. No fewer than 5,903 examples were sold in the initial twelve months. Another significant event was the purchase of the Cadillac company by William C. Durant, the founder of General Motors.

The Thirty's engine had four individual cylinder blocks made of cast iron, an L-top, five main bearings, and a cylinder volume of 3702 cc. In 1909 the simplest version, a five-seat touring, cost $1,400. The model was produced without much change until 1912, when it acquired a Delco electrical system.

Very soon, Cadillac established a quality standard that was unique for the period. Henry Leland was obsessed with precision, and he even imported gauge blocks from the firm of Carl-Edward Johansson in Sweden. These "Jo Blocks" made it possible to manufacture parts that were fully interchangeable.

To prove this for the European public, a demonstration was held in 1908 by the British importer of Cadillacs, on the Brooklands race track. Three of the one-cylinder runabouts were dismantled, and the 2,163 parts were mixed in three piles. Then the cars were reassembled, and they worked perfectly. This feat (which had been done with rifles by Eli Whitney in the USA as early as 1801) earned Leland the "Sir Thomas Deware Trophy" for the year's most important contribution to automobile technology.

Cadillac Thirty

This was a big improvement, as the system included electric lighting – but best of all, an electric starter motor, which was a Cadillac first. The new system was one reason why Cadillac established itself firmly as a manufacturer of advanced cars. For these innovations, Leland again received the Deware Trophy.

In 1912 the name Thirty was dropped, and the model became known as the Four. Cadillac did not rest on its laurels but, in 1915, introduced the Model 51. The most striking thing about this model was that it had a V8 engine. Here the company had been preceded in 1910 by De Dion Bouton, who built a small number of cars with V8 engines. Yet Cadillac led the field with this type of engine as standard.

The engine had a 90-degree angle between the cylinder blocks, as well as side-valves, 5145 cc of cylinder volume, 70 horsepower at 2,400 rpm, and a top speed of 65 mph (105 km/h). In other respects, the Model 51 was traditionally built according to contemporary patterns. The concept of a V8 engine was soon copied by most of its competitors.

There were nine body variants and the cheapest one, a seven-seat touring, cost $1,975. As many as 13,002 examples were produced during 1915 – a high figure for such an untested design. The Model 51 was made for just a single year, but it should be considered a milestone in automobile history. ■

America led the world in developing commercial uses of V8 and V12 engines. Since the home market was so big, prices for these complicated engines could be kept at a moderate level. Wilfred Leland's 1915 Cadillac Model 51 had an overhead-valve V8 at 90 degrees, and was the first Cadillac with steering at the left. Six bodies were available, and it cost from $2,700 to $3,350.

Mercer T35 Raceabout

F EW JUGGERNAUTS IN AUTOMOBILE HISTORY ARE AS famous and sought-after as the Mercer T35 Raceabout. Some even say that it is one of the best sports cars yet made.

It resembles a specimen of the true trophy-takers at the beginning of the century, with no body at all and a couple of tiny bucket seats bolted directly to the floor. Behind these is a big round "bolster tank", and in front of the driver is a sloping instrument panel with a few gauges. There is no windscreen, and the only thing between him (or her?) and the breeze (or whatever) is a monocle-like pane mounted on the steering column. Probably this monocle is what most people think of when a Mercer is mentioned.

Already before World War I, it was widely realized that a car's performance could be raised dramatically by stripping down the body. Everything unnecessary came off. Whether the brakes and road-holding became worse as a result was ignored. Ideally the vehicle had to look as though it came straight from the Vanderbilt Cup.

Among the first efforts in this style was the Gentleman's Speedy Roadster built by Stanley, and around 1909 a number of manufacturers offered raceabouts or speedsters. Some of the better-known were the Pierce Arrow 24-hp Runabout, Studebaker Speedcar, Peerless 19 Roadster and Simplex Speed Car.

A raceabout's main aim was to attract maximum attention and, despite its sporty appearance, the owner usually had no intention of racing. What counted was to show that one could afford a car so useless that one could not even pack golf clubs into it. They were thrown nonchalantly onto the passenger seat beside the driver.

Just before the war, raceabout hysteria culminated in two spectacular cars, the Stutz Bearcat and the Mercer T35-C. Today they belong to the hottest relics in America, at least for sports-car enthusiasts.

These machines divided the country into two camps, regardless of whether you were an owner or an onlooker. Everyone dreamed of either a Mercer or a Stutz. Both sides hurled epithets and immortal puns such as "*You must be nuts to drive a Stutz*" or "*There's nothing worser than a Mercer*". Judging by all the contemporary newspaper articles, Mercer was one of the leading car makers in the USA. Facts, however, would soon prove differently.

It began with the Brooklyn Bridge

The Mercer Automobile Company (after Mercer County, New Jersey) was founded in May 1909 by two wealthy New Jersey families, Roebling and Kuser, who had become well-known for building the Brooklyn Bridge. The first model that left their factory was a little speedster called the Mercer 30-C. It had a four-cylinder Beaver engine with L-top, giving around 30 horsepower.

In late 1910 came the model that would make the Mercer

This was the dream car for a playboy in the 1910s. No body, no place for baggage, and no protection from weather and wind. In other words, an impractical vehicle whose sole purpose was to draw maximum attention.

name unforgettable, the T35-C. Its designer was a self-taught but clever engineer, Finley Robertson Porter. After only a year or two, it turned into a living legend, largely because of racing successes by great drivers of the day – Barney Oldfield, Ralph DePalma and Caleb Bragg.

The engine in the T35-C was a four-cylinder T-top. Each pair of cylinders was mounted in separate cooling mantles, since the techniques of casting and cooling had not yet been fully mastered. The cylinders lacked head gaskets, again due to the insuperable sealing problems. It would be another few years before the copper-asbestos sealing caught on.

On each side of the crankcase was a camshaft, and the cylinder volume of 4916 cc yielded 58 hp at 1,500 rpm. The gearbox was three-speed at first, and unusually smooth for

that period, as long as you learned how to double-clutch. The brakes were awful, as on all cars then: the footbrake acted on the rear part of the transmission, and the handbrake – which worked best – on the rear wheels. A Mercer in good condition could do about 75 mph (120 km/h).

Mercer, like Ford, used vanadium steel in the frame. It was a smart decision, for otherwise we would probably have no Mercers left. The wheel suspension was traditional with live axles, semielliptic springs, and adjustable Hartford friction dampers.

During 1911–14 about 150 of these fantastic cars were built, costing approximately $2,500 (equivalent to 15–20 times as much today). Some 20 survive today and are worth millions. ∎

Ford Model T

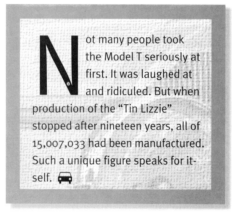

HENRY FORD PUT THE WORLD on wheels, and no other car has influenced the American lifestyle as much as the Model T. During the 1940s John Steinbeck wrote in his book *Cannery Row* that "two generations of Americans knew more about the Ford's ignition coils than about the clitoris, more about the planetary gear system than about the solar system...most children who were born during this time had been conceived in T-Fords and many were even born in them."

For his part, Henry Ford was not born in a Model T, but on a farm outside the small town of Dearborn, Michigan, in 1863. Much has been written about his childhood and it can be noted that, while he was no good at books, his father reportedly said that young Henry "had a head full of wheels".

He took a job at 16 in the James Flowers & Brothers Machine Shop in Detroit, and eventually moved to the Edison Illumination Company. There he got to know Thomas Alva Edison, who would remain a close friend until Edison's death in 1931. It was also during his time with Edison that Ford built his first car.

Not many people took the Model T seriously at first. It was laughed at and ridiculed. But when production of the "Tin Lizzie" stopped after nineteen years, all of 15,007,033 had been manufactured. Such a unique figure speaks for itself.

This appeared in 1896 and had a two-cylinder reclining engine. The rest consisted of various bicycle parts. Ford gradually improved the design, but in the end he sold the car for $200, which he used to make a new car that was ready in 1898.

At about the same time, Ford established his first firm, the Detroit Automobile Company, but it went bankrupt in 1901. Then he began to build racing cars with a new firm, the Henry Ford Company. It, too, went on the rocks and was reorganized in 1902 as the Cadillac Automobile Company. In October that year, a fresh start was made as Ford & Malcolmson, including the name of the firm's financier. But already in 1903 a reorganization led to the Ford Motor Company.

A LEGEND IS BORN

After producing several models – the A, AC, B, C, F, K, N, R and S – Ford in 1908 came up with the famous Model T, which was to change the lives of all who rolled on four wheels.

In those days, nobody had yet tried to manufacture a four-seat, four-cylinder car that cost under $1000. Moreover, the

engine had a removable top – and this aroused great suspicion, for contemporary cylinder-head gaskets were not well sealed.

The car's two-step planetary gearbox was the same as on earlier Ford models. A common feature of American cars then, it derived from the fact that ordinary Americans did not like to shift gears, since this caused a lot of trouble and noise when the cogs in the box scraped together. A planetary gearbox was easy to handle. Instead of cogs, it contained three textile-clad bands that could be tightened around rotating drums with different functions.

The chassis was very simple and light, with transverse semielliptic springs in front and back. Many people were sceptical about its durability, but the frame was made of vanadium steel and proved to be incredibly tough, coping

1925 Ford Model T Runabout

with every sort of road. Not even a road was needed – old "Lizzie" could go anywhere.

The four-cylinder engine was of monobloc design, meaning that all the cylinders were cast in one piece, including the cooling-water channels. Likewise, the upper half of the crankcase was united with the rest of the block. The cylinder volume of 2895 cc gave 20 horsepower at 1,800 rpm, allowing a top speed of about 45 mph (70 km/h).

DRIVING A MODEL T

Whether one drove an example of 1909 or 1927 made no difference, as the model was always the same in mechanical terms, although the car's appearance changed. I once owned a 1926 Model T and can describe a tour in it as follows.

The first task before starting the engine is to open the right half of the bonnet, then open the petrol tap on the firewall. If the car has not been driven for a while, there is also good reason to loosen the distributor cap on the front of the engine block and dry it out. The distributor is mounted on the camshaft, so a little oil will have oozed out and may make the engine hard to start. A further guarantee of starting the engine is to polish the breaker tips on the four ignition coils.

Cranking life into the engine can be a back-breaking procedure, and is nearly impossible in cold weather. Things became a bit easier when the Model T was provided with a starter motor. You just sat in the driver's seat, turned the ignition key to its battery start position, pulled down the petrol/ignition lever on the steering column, and drew the choke control all the way out. Next, your right heel pressed down a contact on the floor to engage the starter motor. If and when the engine woke up, you released the contact, quickly turned the key to magnetic ignition, and adjusted the lever until the engine purred like a cat – though a pretty loud one.

At last it is time to drive away, but a newcomer to the Model T will wonder what to do: there is no gear-shift! And since the petrol lever is on the steering column, why are three pedals on the floor?

To begin with, the left pedal is for the clutch and gears. If pushed down fully, it engages the low-speed band. Halfway up, it disengages the engine – and once let go, it engages the high-speed band. The handbrake also has a freewheeling function and must be pulled before you start.

The middle pedal is for reversing. When pushed to the bottom, it engages the reverse band. But then you must simultaneously push the left pedal to the disengaging position, so that the two bands do not counteract each other. Finally, the right pedal is for braking and works on the brake band in the gearbox.

To sum up: put your weight on the gear pedal, gas a little, relax the handbrake carefully, and off she goes. As the speed increases and the engine begins to sound strained, reduce the gas and instantly let up the gear pedal to the high-speed position, give her more gas and feel yourself flying forward. Well, maybe flapping – but the fact is that gears can be shifted much faster with a planetary box than an ordinary box.

LIZZIE'S AMAZING SUCCESS

As soon as September 1909, Ford had managed to make 11,000 cars and was among the leading American manufacturers. His cheapest model then cost $825. However, he was not satisfied with that. In August 1913 the new factory at Highland Park opened, raising the year's output from 170,211 to 202,667. In 1914, the first year with mass

1915 Model T Tourer

production, Ford built 308,162 cars. Two years later the figure was 734,811, about five times that of its rival Willys-Overland.

This was only the beginning. Fords spewed off the line and the rate reached 224,289 in one month, January 1924 – amounting to 7,235 per day – when the lowest current price was $260.

By that point, the Model T was definitely an old-fashioned design and could not be helped by cosmetic alterations. Henry Ford long ignored all advice about developing a new model, but the decision was taken on 25 May 1927. Next day, production of the "Tin Lizzie" was officially stopped.

Thus a legend went to the grave and, according to its sequel, many enthusiasts were so dismayed that they bought enough T-Fords to last all their lives, in order to avoid learning how to shift with a conventional gearbox. ■

Vauxhall Prince Henry

I
T IS DIFFICULT TO BELIEVE, AT THE SIGHT OF A
Vauxhall Prince Henry, that the model came into being by
sheer chance – but such is the case. This was also the first
series-produced British sports car.

Vauxhall Motors, today a part of General Motors, began
operations in 1903, yet originated at Alex. Wilson & Co. of
Wandsworth Road in southwest London. There a Scot named
Alexander Wilson began in 1857 to make steam engines for
marine use. In 1897 the company changed its name to
Vauxhall Iron Works. Soon it experimented with petrol engines,
and in 1903 a one-cylinder version was put into Vauxhall's
first car.

By 1905 the production ran out of room at Vauxhall Iron
Works, and moved to a brand-new factory in Luton. The same
year, Vauxhall presented its first four-cylinder model, with
3336 cc and 18 hp. This was replaced in 1906 by a smaller four,
having 2354 cc and 12/16 hp. About 100 examples were built.

FAME WAITS AROUND THE CORNER

The move to Luton was a turning point. At the same time a
young engineer was employed, who would acquire great
influence. His name was Laurence Pomeroy Sr (1884–1941).

Theoretical knowledge is one thing, but to put it in practice
is another. Through a coincidence, however, Pomeroy got the
opportunity. In the winter of 1907/08 the chief designer, F.W.

Pomeroy had deep theoretical knowledge
of how motorcars were designed. His
main source of inspiration was a
pioneering work by the Frenchman
Heirman, "L'Automobile à l'Essence: Principes de
Construction et Calcul". Heirman's principles made
such a strong impact on Pomeroy that they were to
be reflected in most of his designs. Simply to read
Heirman's book was a feat, since Pomeroy was at
first very bad at French.

Hodges, decided to take a long holiday in Egypt. Meanwhile
Pomeroy, his assistant, was to run the design work. This was
not in itself abnormal, but the result was unexpected.

During Hodges' stay in Egypt, Vauxhall's directors resolved
to enter three cars for the RAC 2000 Mile Trial in 1909. The
choice fell upon their 3.3-litre 20-hp model, which was fine
except that its side-valve engine gave only 23 hp at 1,800 rpm.
Pomeroy saw his opening and promised the board to get 40 hp
from an engine with the same cylinder volume. Surprisingly
enough, they believed in the young engineer's abilities, and
they were not to be disappointed.

Pomeroy totally redesigned the existing engine, using an
L-top and a single block. The new version had less volume
(3054 cc) but still gave 40 hp at 2,400 rpm. As to the race, it

Vauxhall Prince Henry, 1914

was a huge triumph for Vauxhall. Percy Kidner won with 77 penalty points. In second place came a Rolls-Royce Silver Ghost with 115 points.

Next year, two cars were committed to the German endurance competition "Prinz-Heinrich-Fahrt". Pomeroy raised the cylinder volume to 3964 cc, yielding 60 hp at 2,800 rpm. Now, too, the car bodies were more slender four-seaters with pointed-nose radiators. Ferdinand Porsche won in a much larger Austro-Daimler, but two of the Vauxhall cars completed the race nonstop, one of them clocking 116 km/h (72 mph).

After that, the model was renamed the Prince Henry. In November 1911, it went on public sale – and its racing success continued. For instance, Percy Kidner entered the Swedish

Royal Automobile Club's winter competition in 1912, as did a local driver named Kjellgren. They took 13th and 2nd places respectively, and respectably for the former in view of Englishmen's unfamiliarity with winter driving.

In 1913 the engine's final version appeared. Still with 3964 cc, it delivered 75 hp at 2,500 rpm. The chassis remained an "archaic" construction with longitudinal beams and semielliptic leaf springs front and back. Power was transmitted via a four-step gearbox and open cardan shaft to a rear axle with straight-cut pinions. The engine lay in an auxiliary frame, which did not help to stiffen the chassis, but there was a torque brace for the rear axle. Top speed was about 75 mph (120 km/h), and 140 examples were made. ∎

Packard Twin Six

JAMES WARREN PACKARD WAS BORN IN 1863 AND, TOGETHER with his brother William, founded a factory to manufacture electric doorbells, generators and lamps. Here, too, he had something in common with Henry Royce.

After arguing with Alexander Winton over the latter's cars, Packard unveiled his first automobile in November 1896. Ironically, the brothers were helped by two engineers whom they attracted to leave Winton and work with them.

The Packard Model A had an engine with a single big reclining cylinder, its volume being 2337 cc, and its output 9 horsepower at 800 rpm. Contemporary habits were followed in equipping the car with a two-speed planetary gearbox, lever steering and chain drive.

Further versions were built, and 1902 greeted the Model F, which was to make Packard's name. His first real car that no longer looked like a buggy, it had wire-spoked wheels and a proper steering wheel.

In 1903 Packard entered the "Hall of Fame" when a Model F, called the Old Pacific, was driven by Tom Fetch and Marius Krarup in 61 days from San Francisco to New York. This was two days under the preceding record set by a Winton!

Packard's slogan was "Ask One Who Owns One", and among the first such owners was the millionaire William D. Rockefeller, whose garages had previously held a couple of Wintons. Another blow was thus dealt to Alexander Winton's prestige, and Packard established itself as a favourite with the

Innumerable innovations and new products have begun with somebody's disappointment by existing ones. The same is true in the car world. Henry Royce sighed at the Decauville he bought. Feruccio Lamborghini shed tears over his Ferrari. When James Warren Packard complained about his Winton, the arrogant answer was: "If you're so smart, build a better car yourself!" Which is just what he did.

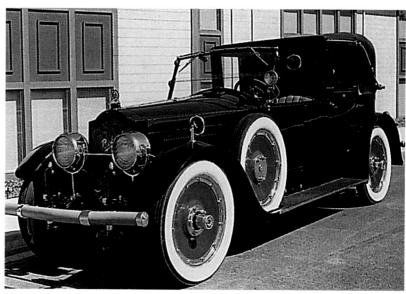
1920 Packard Twin Six town car

1915 Packard Twin Six

wealthy people on wheels along the East Coast.

A four-cylinder variant had emerged in November 1902, the Model K with 4116 cc and 24 hp. Next came a number of models that secured Packard's reputation for quality manufacture. In 1911 there was a six-cylinder engine with 8603 cc and 74 hp. A smaller model arrived in 1913, the Series 38 with 6800 cc, which also had a starter motor.

In May 1915 it was time for a completely new vehicle to confirm the company's leadership. The Twin Six, with a V12 engine, was planned by Alvin Macauley and designed by Jesse G. Vincent. At last the world witnessed a series-produced twelve-cylinder automobile. This engine had an L-top, 60 degrees between the cylinder banks, aluminium pistons, and a

volume of 6950 cc, yielding 88 hp at 2,600 rpm. Removable heads were adopted in 1915, and the power eventually rose to 90 hp.

Most of the bodies were from Packard's own workshop, and quite high in quality. In 1916, no fewer than 19 different body types were on the programme. The cheapest, a seven-seat "torpedo", cost $2,950 while the most expensive, a four-door brougham, stood at $4,050 (equivalent to around 15 times as much today). In total 30,941 examples were built by 1923.

The Twin Six was a mighty fine monster and, when the motoring journalist Ralph Stein got to try one during the 1960s, he said: "Every time I sit in it, I wonder how far we've really come during these fifty years." ■

1920
–1930

THE DECADE OF WORLD WAR I HAS CLOSED UNEASILY, YET optimistically. Industrial production accelerates. Automobiles are becoming serious rivals of the train. Whoever has the chance and wealth acquires a car, not only for the status it conveys, but also because he or she discovers how independent a driver is. To meet the challenge from motorcars, the railway lines in Great Britain now merge into four big companies.

Awareness that alcohol endangers the young is beginning to affect political life: Lady Astor, in the House of Commons, proposes a ban on selling liquor to those under 18. Her voice is heard, breaking another sort of barrier – this is the first time any woman gets a motion passed in Parliament.

Public affairs are restless in Central Europe. Germany sees dramatic inflation, a dollar in August 1923 costing 45 billion marks. The Bulgarians stage a revolution. Three of the renowned palaces in the Forbidden City of Peking are burned

Among the more distinguished and truly expensive American cars made in small numbers, the Cunningham was unusual for having a V8 engine in all models from 1915 onward. The big 7.2-litre 90-hp side-valve engine was designed by Volney Les in Rochester, New York. It sold to a few exclusive, demanding customers mainly on the east coast. These cars cost between 5,500 and 7,000 dollars, right at the top of the market. Annual production seldom exceeded 400 cars during the 1920s, and more than half were hearses – a specialty for James Cunningham & Sons ever since they had made horse carriages. Shown here is a sport tourer from 1926.

down. Telephone conversations start across the Atlantic. Iceland frees itself from Denmark and becomes an autonomous state.

Ever better automobiles are being developed. Some people consider four-wheel brakes a problem, but designers maintain that braking all round has left the experimental stage. This is proved by makes such as Hispano-Suiza, Lancia, Isotta-Fraschini and Peugeot.

The speeds in car competitions during the first half of the new decade run as high as 100 mph (160 km/h), with the engines turning at up to 5,000-6,000 rpm. The official motor car world speed record is raised progressively in these years. Major H.O.D. Segrave sets one record at 203 mph (326.7 km/h) in his 1,000-horsepower Sunbeam, which has two 12-cylinder Matabele engines. Just a year later, Malcolm Campbell reaches 207 mph (333 km/h) with his "Bluebird". A motorcycle record of 122 mph (197 km/h) is established by Temple on a British Anzani.

In contrast, the top speed of ordinary four- or five-seat

W.O. Bentley offered a 4.5-litre model in 1929. This example has a Vanden Plas body, with extra-wide footboards at the request of its first owner – an Indian Maharajah whose bodyguards stood on the footboards. Bentleys always used a single overhead camshaft. Many experts, however, consider that the Vauxhall 30/98 had better road qualities.

passenger cars at this time is 35–40 mph (60 km/h). Even so, their fuel consumption is at least 25 miles per gallon (10 litres per 100 km), and they need plenty of service – at maximum intervals of 5,000 kilometres for full greasing and engine oil change.

The design departments realize that streamlining is desirable, and experiments with it are done in several countries. Both Bugatti and Voisin present, during the first half of the 1920s, racing cars with rounded, almost tank-like shapes. The syn-chronization ring for the normal manual gearbox has not yet been invented, and various methods are tried to simplify the work of changing gears – mainly using automatic gearboxes, but without much success.

Daimler builds the world's most expensive automobile, thus outdoing Rolls-Royce temporarily. Volvo has made some experimental cars that are now on the roads. Henry Ford locates an assembly plant in Berlin to avoid Germany's

Austin's Twelve Four was among the most successful English designs of the 1920s – even though its fuel tank cap was under the front seat! It appeared in 1921 with a four-cylinder (72 x 102 mm) side-valve engine of 1661 cc. In 1927 this grew to 1861 cc (72 x 114 mm). Magneto ignition was used until the end in 1935. The above 1928 tourer cost only 255 pounds, but a saloon version brought 325.

The Riley was a solid, but not remarkable, car until 1926 when the Nine model arrived with 1067 cc. Its engine – designed by Percy and Stanley Riley – had two cam-shafts, each placed high on one side of the block, and inclined overhead valves. This became the basis of all Riley engines until 1957. Shown here is the Monaco saloon, one of the Nine's main variants, with a body covered in patent leather. Made from 1927 onward, it had good brakes and road-holding, a top speed around 60 mph (95 km/h), and a price of no more than 285 pounds (equivalent to 25-30 times as much today).

protective tariffs, and another Ford factory is inaugurated in Copenhagen. The straight-eight engine becomes a "must" in the luxury and competition car fields.

Electrification is brought to the railways. Coal, so important for the steam power in industry and the locomotive, is the focus of a strike in England. This develops into an industrial general strike. B. von Platen and C. Munters invent a "cooling machine" – subsequently known as the refrigerator. Marconi's "short waves" are harnessed for communication between the corners of the British Empire. In New York, a congress is held for international standardization, of great practical and indus-trial significance.

Steam technology is still ahead, especially at power plants. In fact, the latest technique for generating electrical current is the steam turbine. A "curious" new pastime, gliding through the sky, gains popularity. Travel by airship continues, in spite of certain risks; the French airship *Dixmude* is lost on a flight over the Mediterranean. The Zeppelin Z.R.3 makes a trip across the Pacific Ocean. Meanwhile, scientists announce that the planet Mars probably has a temperature suitable for humans to live there.

Flying airplanes around the world is attempted. In 1927, Charles Lindbergh performs his famous solo crossing of the Atlantic. An American Air Force lieutenant, Maughan, wins a

Minerva had an impressive image because it manufactured utility vehicles as well as its high-quality cars with Knight sleeve-valve engines. In 1927 it sold 2,500 cars. The most expensive model was the 6-litre type AK, which had four-wheel brakes with the Dewandre servo system. This two-seater body was made by Erdmann & Rossi in Berlin. The leading coachbuilders in Belgium, France, England and Sweden also created bodies for Minerva chassis.

The Belgian FN factory produced cars at popular prices. It had the advantage of belonging to a flourishing concern that also manufactured weapons and motorcycles. Its conventional small four-cylinder cars had overhead-valve engines and, from 1924, four-wheel brakes. In 1900 it began maufacturing a light two-cylinder voiturette, and in 1910 it was turning out normal four-cylinder cars at a rate of 4–5 per day. This 1300 tourer, from 1925, illustrates the best-known F.N. model, made between 1924 and 1933. In 1928 the engine was enlarged from 1327 to 1455 cc, and battery ignition was substituted for magneto. A further increase to 1628 cc came in 1930. During its nine-year lifetime, 7,302 of the little four-cylinder F.N. were sold.

bet by racing against the sun from New York to California. He takes off from Long Island just after dawn, and lands 17 minutes before sunset in San Francisco, having flown some 3,000 miles (5,000 km) in 18 hours and 26 minutes, with five stops enroute. Ever more air routes for passenger planes are being established.

Flights to the North Pole are made by other Americans, Byrd and Bennett – as well as by Roald Amundsen of Norway, who is later killed on a rescue mission. Cobham flies from England to Australia and back, and the American Doolittle

sets a speed record of 239 mph (385 km/h) in a hydroplane with a 625-hp Curtiss engine. Landry and Drouhin, from France, achieve the longest nonstop flight of 2,750 miles (4,400 km). A flying machine of "autogiro" type, developed by Juan de la Cierva in Spain, is a decisive step toward the goal of manoeuvering vertically in the air.

Winston Churchill returns to the British Government, as Minister of Finance under Stanley Baldwin. Giacomo Puccini, composer of immortal operas, dies in Brussels. The League of Nations – a forerunner of the United Nations – gets involved

Bugatti made sports cars for most price classes, except the very lowest. This Brescia model is a descendant of the original type 13 from 1910. Its four-cylinder engine had an overhead camshaft, the volume growing from 1453 cc in 1921 to 1496 cc in 1923. The postwar models had four valves per cylinder – and four-wheel brakes came in 1925, when the above car was made, although individual owners had already had them installed earlier. A Brescia with a touring body could do about 120 km/h (75 mph), which was a remarkable speed for a 1.5-litre car in the early 1920s – but neither was it cheap. A chassis cost 735 pounds in 1920 (equivalent to about 15 times as much today), sinking to 385 five years later.

In 1930 the Alfa Romeo company was well-established as the leading Italian sports-car make, a position it kept until Ferrari emerged after World War II. The 6C 1750 appeared in 1929, an enlarged variant of Vittorio Jano's successful 6C 1500, and was built in three different models: Turismo, with an overhead camshaft and 3.1-metre wheelbase; Gran Turismo, with two overhead camshafts and 2.75- or 2.9-metre wheelbase; and Super Sport, a supercharged Gran Sport with 85 horsepower and a top speed of 155 km/h (95 mph). Shown here is a 1930 Gran Turismo with a Zagato body.

in many international political issues and military conflicts. They also fascinate George Bernard Shaw, who wins the Nobel Prize for Literature. Sea water floods the Netherlands, and Belgium's Crown Prince Leopold marries the Swedish Princess Astrid in 1926.

The Soviet Union refuses to join the League's disarmament conference. Revolution arises in Poland, and the anti-Russian Marshal Pilsudski takes over its government. Inter-city telephone lines are laid everywhere. Joseph Stalin proceeds to persecute real or imagined counterrevolutionaries. In Rumania, a power struggle leads to the enthronement of Prince Michael, only five years old.

Nonetheless, the world's economies seem increasingly stable – apart from the effects of economic mismanagement in the Soviet Union and civil war in China. As the general strike in England fades away, trade and industry grow rapidly. But the Mississippi River overflows, threatening New Orleans and other cities; these are evacuated, and more than half a million people lose their homes. Lurking behind the scenes, too, is sudden financial disaster. A few months before the turn of the decade, the New York stock market collapses, starting a global wave of worry and woe. ∎

Citroën Type A and 5CV

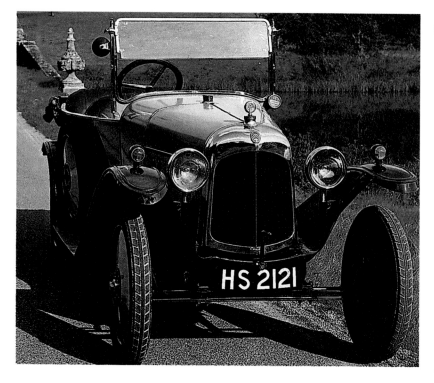

1921 Citroën Type A

ANDRÉ CITROËN WENT TO THE FORD FACTORY IN 1911 and stayed for two years, studying mass production. Like so many others, he was impressed by the process – but it would take until 1919 for his own cars to begin production.

André Citroën was born on 5 January 1878, the son of a rich diamond merchant, and studied at the École Polytechnique. On a visit to relatives in Warsaw, he met an uncle who had invented a spiral gear wheel, made of wood with reversed herringbone teeth. This device was to lay the foundation for Citroën's fortune, and it even became the symbol of the Citroën.

Citroën returned from Ford on the eve of World War II,

and he convinced the French minister of defense that he could provide 10,000 grenades per day. Five times this rate was eventually reached in his new factory, which he built on the Quai de Javel with money borrowed from his father-in-law.

A CAR FOR THE MASSES

As the war drew to a close, Citroën decided to use his factory capacity for manufacturing automobiles. In 1919 the Model A was presented, a simple and robust design by Jules Salomon. Inspired by Ford's vision, Citroën wanted it to be a car with wide popularity.

The first model had dish wheels, left-hand steering, and an engine of 1327 cc giving 18 horsepower. It weighed only 449 kg (990 lbs) and could thus attain a speed of about 65 km/h (40 mph). The only available body was an open tourer, and 28,400 were produced in all.

Then followed the B2, with a slightly larger engine of 1452 cc, and several more body types were added: a sedan, landaulette, and fixed-head coupé. The Citroën factory was equipped with an assembly line, and the model was made

Citroën 5 V from 1921 with an English body

from 1921 to 1925 in 106,800 examples. During the last year, 500 per day rolled out – and these included a great number of two- and three-seat 5CV cars.

The 5CV had an engine of only 856 cc and 11 hp. It was Citroën's last model with brakes on the rear wheels alone, and people joked that a 5CV was as hard to stop as it was to get moving. Yet it soon outcompeted the cyclecars on the French market. During five years, 80,232 of the 5CV were sold – and it later served as the basis for the Opel Laubfroch, which was a German mass-produced 5CV copy in the middle of the 1920s.

Worth recalling, too, is André Citroën's advanced talent

for advertising. In 1922 his name was written in smoke by an airplane over Paris. In 1923, Citroën cars became the first to cross the Sahara. And the most spectacular promotion occurred in 1925, when thousands of bulbs were lit up to display Citroën's name on all four sides of the Eiffel Tower. He also built up an elaborate retail network, service programme, and automotive infrastructure ranging from road maps and signs to gramophone advertising.

However, Citroën's grasp of economy was correspondingly weak, and in December 1934 he was forced into bankruptcy by more than 200,000 creditors. This affected him deeply and, already in July 1935, he died of cancer, only 57 years old. ■

Fiat 501

FIAT PRODUCTION BEGAN SLUGGISHLY, AS ITALIANS cared little about cars. The annual output did not exceed 10,000 until the year 1922, when Ford churned out 1,314,997 vehicles!

In 1901 the company's first designer – Aristide Faccioli – resigned, protesting at being forced to copy foreign cars. The replacement was Giovanni Enrico, who had no objections to such a procedure. On the contrary, he thought that the best on the market was represented by cars like those of Mercedes. As a result, many of FIAT's models came to resemble the latter.

Production rose slowly and passed the thousand-mark in 1906. At the same time, the cars increased in size, their engines reaching from 1082 all the way up to 11,044 cc. That year, too, the name was changed to Fiat.

TRIUMPHS ON THE RACE TRACKS

Fiat laid the basis of its fame with a long series of victories in competitions. The leading drivers were Vincenzo Lancia and Felice Nazzaro.

A good number of the race cars in this period were veritable monsters. For instance, the model S.B.4 had a cylinder volume of 18,146 cc and a power of 175 hp at 1,200 rpm. Worst, however, was the record juggernaut S.76 with 28,353 cc, delivering 290 hp at 1,600 rpm.

There was a time when rumour had it that Germany owned Volkswagen, but that the Italians were different – Fiat owned Italy. This was perhaps an exaggeration, but certainly no automobile make has so clearly dominated its country's economic life as Fiat has done for decades.

During the summer of 1899 four young men met over cappuccino at a café in Turin to discuss matters of interest. One of these was a plan to start building cars. The men concerned were Emanuele di Bricherasio, Giovanni Agnelli, Cesare Goria-Gatti, and Count Roberto Biscaretti di Ruffia. Their only decision that day was to call the prospective factory Fabrica Italiana Automobili Torino (FIAT). Any ideas about how the new cars would look were beyond them.

Shortly afterward, Giovanni-Battista Ceirano's work-shop was bought and his prototype car, with slight changes, became FIAT's first model. It had a two-cylinder reclining rear engine of 679 cc, giving just 4.2 horsepower at 800 rpm.

For several years, Fiat survived by manufacturing big, expensive cars. But the world's economic climate was changing, and cars became smaller. In 1912 Giovanni Agnelli visited Detroit, and is said to have been both impressed and terrified. Yet he learned from what he saw, and brought in capital which he earned during World War I by making staff cars, ambulances, lorries, airplane engines and whole aircraft. After the war, he built the Lingotto factory. It was ready in 1922 and

Fiat's Tipo 501 was manufactured between 1919 and 1926. During the mid-1920s, Fiat accounted for 87% of all Italian car production. This one has a body from Shorts in England.

produced, among other cars, the Tipo 501 – of which 69,478 examples were made between 1919 and 1926. This robust model proved to be one of Fiat's mainstays in the interwar years.

The Fiat 501 was designed by Carlo Cavalli and had a four-cylinder side-valve engine of 1460 cc, generating 23 hp at 2,600 rpm, with a removable top. Four speeds were in the gearbox and its top speed was around 70 km/h (45 mph). Though nothing to boast about in performance, it offered extreme reliability and soon grew popular – not only in Italy but in the rest of Europe, notably Great Britain.

The first bodies were quite simple and did not match the rest of the car. Hence, many 501s were exported in chassis form and locally built bodies were added. In England, Shorts at Rochester made several open bodies, as illustrated above.

Three different body types could initially be bought: the Torpedo, Limousine and Spider. They were also available in numerous colours. In 1923 came the 501 Colonial, used mostly as a taxi.

Between 1921 and 1926, the 501 had sportier variants as well, designated 501S and 501SS. The former had 26.5 horsepower and could do 100 km/h (60 mph), while the 501SS with overhead camshafts was capable of 130 km/h (80 mph). ■

Bugatti Type 35

MANY ECCENTRIC PERSONALITIES IN AUTOMOBILE history have fallen into obscurity, yet the name of Ettore Bugatti lives on. He created a number of unusual car models that were more like mechanical art works.

Bugatti was not, as might be guessed, an Italian make but a thoroughly French one. Its founder, however, came from Milan where his father was a furniture designer, silversmith and painter. Born in 1881, Ettore also intended to become an artist until, for various reasons, he went into engineering.

Around the turn of the century, Bugatti worked for local nobles who were crazy about cars and wanted to build their own. Family fortunes were frequently squandered on such projects, without getting the hopeful drivers far beyond their front gates.

In 1909, Ettore Bugatti started a company at Molsheim, which was then in the province of Alsace, Germany. His first vehicles were rather small and had little in common with the fantastic ones he would build later. Still, they quickly became known for running well and being easy to handle.

These qualities, together with excellent craftsmanship, were eventually to earn Bugatti's cars a legendary status. Neverthe-

less, historians have often wondered whether the man himself was really a good designer or only imitated other people's work. The latter view has much to be said for it. He did, though, possess plenty of charm, determination, and luck.

After World War I, the Treaty of Versailles forced Germany to give up Alsace, so Molsheim was suddenly in France. Bugatti revived his factory and assembled three cars with 16-valve engines, which he had hidden during the war. In 1920, three of his cars raced in the Coupe des Voiturettes at Le Mans, winning first and fifth places. Next year came an unprecedented Bugatti victory: 1–2–3–4 in the Italian Grand Prix at Brescia. This event made the Type 13 famous as the "Bugatti Brescia".

IT HAD TO BE A STRAIGHT-EIGHT

In 1922 Bugatti began to produce the kind of power plant that turned into a hallmark of the company. A straight eight-cylinder engine, with 1991 cc of volume, went into a model called the Type 30, of which some 600 were built. Another feature, shared by nearly all Bugatti's engines, was that they did not have a removable cylinder head.

Four years later the Type 35 emerged. Widely regarded as

The Bugatti Type 35 was the most successful racing car of the 1920s. This is a supercharged Type 35C from 1926.

Ettore's masterpiece, it is credited with most of the myths about him. Soon it was to make a clean sweep of Europe's race tracks.

The Type 35's engine differed from the Type 30's in having five, not four, bearings on its crankshaft. Its gearbox was the same as in both the Brescia and the 30. Definitely innovative in the Type 35 were its wheels, molded in one piece together with the brake drums. The body was pure and simple, with Bugatti's classic horseshoe-shaped radiator in front. Horses were a great passion for Ettore, besides cars.

This model was used chiefly in competition, but some examples had wings and lamps for touring. It offered a bewildering range of engine versions, including the plain Type 35 with 1991 cc, Type 35T with 2262 cc, Type 35B with 2262 cc and a supercharger, and Type 35C as a 1991-cc variant of the 35B.

The output was around 80 horsepower for a Type 35, and 120–160 for a Type 35B depending on the fuel. These two cars had respective top speeds of 160 and 215 km/h (100 and 135 mph). In 1927, an Englishman could get a Type 35 for £1,100 and the factory made 340 of them. Bugatti's total production is estimated to have been 7,833 and about 1,800 have survived – an amazingly high proportion.

During World War II, when the Molsheim factory was occupied, its cars and machinery were largely moved out of the combat zone, to Bordeaux. After the war, and tough negotiations, Ettore Bugatti managed to regain the factory. But he died in 1947 and, after fading for years, the glorious company closed down on 22 July 1963. ∎

Austin Seven

BUILDING SMALL, CHEAP CARS HAS NEVER BEEN a problem, but the same is not true of getting them accepted as genuine automobiles. A maker who certainly succeeded was Sir Herbert Austin.

Many people who first glimpse an Austin Seven are inclined to rub their eyes with glee and buy one immediately. Almost nobody would turn one down – especially families with children, who say something like "Dad, why not sell your E-Jag? It won't even hold but two."

A drawback in the beginning was that nearly all small cars were overdressed three- and four-wheel motorcycles. For a time, during the late 1950s, there was a flood of such products with noisy one- and two-cylinder engines, disappearing as soon as they reached the market.

Similarly, countless ingenious designs overwhelmed the public in the 1920s. A common option was to buy a carriage-like construction with two wheels in front and one at the rear. Then an old motorcycle, minus its rear wheel, was attached to the carriage's side, and presto – you had a motorcar.

WHY DID SIR HERBERT AUSTIN SUCCEED?

The secret of Austin's success is not easy to tell, for a host of factors played their roles, as often happens in history. Among them, at any event, were the following. People had grown tired of cyclecars with only a pair of seats. In 1921, new tax laws began to penalize powerful vehicles. Sir Herbert Austin was inspired by the achievements of Henry Ford, and he hit on a good idea that he exploited very well. In addition, he was lucky and found a superb designer. Last but not least, the Austin factory found itself in financial straits – and the only way out was to succeed.

A FAMILIAR OLD NAME

When Herbert Austin founded the Austin Motor Company, he was not a newcomer to the auto industry, but had been a designer at Wolseley. The first Austin car was given a four-cylinder engine with a T-top and chain drive. Though not a remarkable creation, it sold nicely with the help of Austin's good reputation.

Between 1910 and 1912, the firm expanded rapidly to a production level of 1,100 cars per year and a workforce of 1,800. During the war, operations swelled from employing 2,638 to over 22,000. In 1917 Austin was knighted for his wartime efforts and could be considered a rich man.

Austin had been deeply impressed by American mass manufacture, and he decided to focus on a single model.

A four-seat Austin Seven tourer known as the "Chummy"

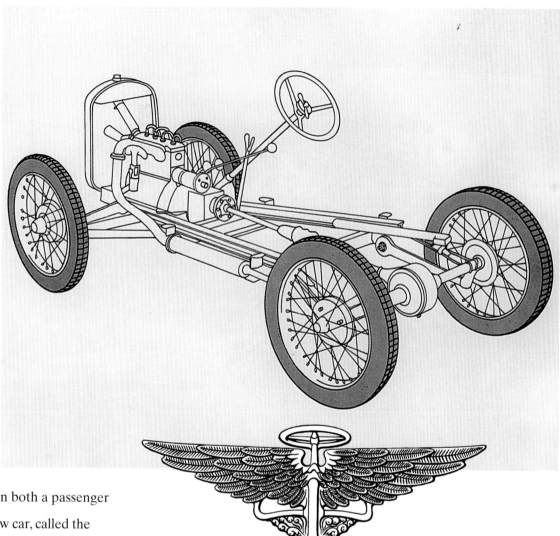

(*Above*) The Austin Seven's A-shaped chassis was derived from the design of the T-Ford. (*Below*) Austin displayed clear influence by the Jugendstil with its symbols of speed and freedom. Note the cloud of dust around the wheel.

Moreover, the engine was to be usable in both a passenger car, a utility vehicle and a tractor. The new car, called the Twenty, was built until as late as 1936. After 1935, its engine was also used in more than 7,000 London taxis.

DESIGNED ON THE BILLIARD TABLE

When it comes to identifying the designer of the Austin Seven, our sources are shadowy indeed. Some books give the credit to Herbert Austin and Stanley Edge, but others say nothing about Edge. The truth is apparently that Edge did most of the labour and Austin claimed all of the honour.

Due to the economic crisis, Austin thought his board of directors would take no chances, so all the development work took place at Sir Herbert's home. In September 1921, Edge took up the job. Drawings were ready just after Easter 1922, and Austin presented them to his suspicious bosses, who reluctantly agreed to invest in the new car. Three prototypes were built by early summer.

Normally Austin, like his competitors, announced new models at the London Motor Show – but this time he did so at a press lunch at Claridge's. The Seven was warmly received and drew many nice comments, despite Sir Herbert's poor relations with the media after some mean remarks about the motorcycle industry.

For all the enthusiasm, things started slowly and a mere 1,936 cars were built during 1923. A few technical changes were made, but the real boost came when the price was plunged from 225 to 175 pounds. This, of course, owed to Henry Ford's inspiration, and by 1934 the car would cost only £100. Production grew to 4,700 in 1924, and to 7,043 in 1925. Next year the figure hit 14,000 – Austin was back in business!

1928 Austin Seven

SMALL BUT SINCERE

What strikes us at the sight of an Austin Seven is its size. How can it be so small and still carry four people or, to be more exact, two adults and two children? A tourer from 1925 was only 106 inches (269 cm) long and weighed 725 lbs (330 kg). Under the bonnet lay a candidate for the tiniest four-cylinder engine ever made. Its block was 11.5 inches (29.2 cm) long and could easily be lifted together with the gearbox. As a former owner, I know.

The engine was originally of 696 cc, but already in March 1923 it was bored out to 748 cc and yielded 10.5 hp at 2,400 rpm. It had water-cooling, side-valves, a cast-iron block and head, and an aluminium-cast crankcase. Highly reliable, it brought the car to around 45 mph (70 km/h) depending on the body. Curiously, in 1936 a little one-seat racing car was given a trimmed Seven engine with double overhead camshafts, generating as much as 116 hp at 8,500 rpm. On the very first test, this car did 120 mph (195 km/h).

In the Seven's simple A-frame, the engine sat bolted directly to the beams. In front was a live axle with a transverse semielliptic leaf spring, and in back a live axle suspended in quarter-elliptic springs. At both ends were friction dampers as well. Rather unusually for the Twenties, the car had four-wheel brakes. They were not the best, and a panic stop was out of the question, but a good Seven driver soon learned to think ahead.

The initial Sevens were all open. Yet from 1926 to 1939, as many as 24 different body types left the factory – not to mention other variants that were built on the Seven chassis. Few British cars have led to such a wealth of special designs.

Several other countries produced the Austin Seven on licence: in Germany as the BMW Dixi, in France as the Rosengart, in America as the Bantam, and in Japan from the predecessor of Nissan. After 17 years and more than 290,000 cars, the model was put to rest in March 1939. ■

CARS OF THE CENTURY

Lancia Lambda

1925 Lancia Lambda

Thinking up model names for its products has preoccupied the auto industry ever since it began. The results have normally been just combinations of letters or numbers. But Lancia has a long tradition of naming many a car after a letter of the Greek alphabet.

Vincenzo Lancia was born in 1881, the son of a rich canned-food manufacturer in Turin. He took an early interest in machines, yet his father wanted him to study business. They compromised, and Vincenzo went to work as a bookkeeper for the bicycle-maker Giovanni Ceirano.

When the new F.I.A.T. company bought Ceirano's factory, it got Lancia in the bargain. He proved to be a talented racing driver, and brought home several victories for Fiat.

In 1906, however, he started his own firm, Lancia & Cie Fabbrica Italiana.

The first Lancia car was ready for a test run in February 1907. Then a fire destroyed it, including the drawings and tools. Lancia had to start all over, but he presented a new car only seven months later. A conventional design with a four-cylinder engine of 2543 cc and 24 hp, it was called the Tipo 51.

His next model, a little bigger, received the name Beta – possibly to suggest *beata*, as if it had been blessed by the Pope. Thus arose the tradition which still continues. One after the other, Lancia announced the Dialfa, Gamma, Epsilon, Zeta, Theta, Kappa, Dikappa, Trikappa... What could possibly follow?

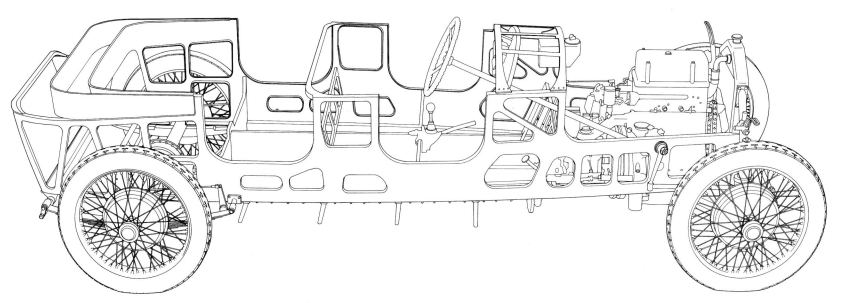

Vincenzo Lancia's patented chassis of 1918 was far ahead of its time, and can rightly be called a sensation that pushed the development of cars ahead by decades. The combined frame and body shell consisted of many sheet-metal parts welded together. Unique in the Lancia Lambda, too, was its V4 engine with only a 13° angle between the cylinder banks.

So far, Lancia's models had been ordinary designs, with modest technical refinement. But in 1922, the Trikappa introduced a V8 engine of 4594 cc, with an angle of just 22 degrees between its cylinder banks, generating 98 horsepower. This type of V8, albeit in smaller form, was to stay with Lancia through the years.

At the same time, Lancia created his perhaps best-known model. While the Trikappa disappeared in 1925, the Lambda went on to become one of the most important designs during the interwar period. The Lambda's engine was a V4, but had a bank angle of only 13 degrees, compared with 90 degrees for the standard type of V-engine. Seen from above, the cylinders seemed to lie in a zigzag, rather than in two rows. The block was made of light metal, and the cylinder volume of 2570 cc gave 69 hp at 3,500 rpm, for a top speed around 120 km/h (75 mph).

More was spectacular about it than the engine. The self-supporting body's base plate and lower section were a skeleton of 2-mm pressed sheet metal. This structure was extremely rigid, and its weight was minimized by openings in the sheet metal.

The Lancia Lambda had a very odd front end, indeed sensational for its time. The front wheels were independently sprung, with kingbolts extending upward into a sheath that also contained a telescopic shock absorber – probably one of the first ever built. The damping medium was a lubricating oil which, through a system of valves, smoothed the car's movements.

At the rear, though, was a customary suspension: live axle, semielliptic leaf springs, and friction dampers. Despite its relatively low engine power, the Lambda was seen in its day as unusually fast on curves. It never had much success in races, but provided an ideal touring car, and was made in 13,501 examples until November 1931. ■

Bentley 3-litre

AUTOMOBILE HISTORY IS FULL OF ADVENTURERS, cranks and geniuses. Walter Owen Bentley was perhaps not a genius, but he created a series of cars that would never be forgotten – if only because they won the Le Mans 24-hour race five times.

Bentley was born in London in 1888, and at 16 he went to work as an apprentice on the Great Northern Railway. This experience had a clear influence on him, as the robust chassis he later designed bore many resemblances to railroad wagons. Ettore Bugatti reputedly said that Bentley made "the world's fastest lorries".

W.O. was a passionate motorcycle driver, and competed eagerly in the Brooklands and Isle of Man races. Starting in 1912, together with his brother, he also sold the French D.F.P. car, making continuous improvements in its construction.

During World War I, Bentley joined the Royal Naval Service and refined the Clerget airplane engine from France. Gradually he developed the nine-cylinder radial engine to perfection. The BR1 and BR2 (Bentley Rotary) were regarded as masterpieces and second to none in reliability.

In 1919, Bentley Motors was founded. But W.O. had less talent for business (see the article on Citroën Type A) and the company's finances suffered, until it was saved by the diamond millionaire Woolf Barnato. Thus, at an early stage, Bentley lost control of his own firm.

The first model was the 3-litre, presented in 1919 by the May issue of *The Autocar* magazine, long before even a prototype was built. Not until September 1921 did deliveries begin. A chassis then cost £1,050, making the Bentley one of the most expensive cars on the English market. Yet its sales rose exponentially: 122 in 1922, 204 in 1923, and 402 in 1924. Total production of the 3-litre model was 1,619 during 1921–29.

This car was a well-planned design without being in any way radical. It had a four-cylinder 2996-cc engine with

It is said that W.O. Bentley was a very strict boss. As he walked around in the factory, if he thought that someone had made a mistake, he stopped and gave a piercing glare that made the culprit cringe. If the error was really bad, he took his pipe from his mouth, and his icy eyes shrank the poor fellow into eternal dwarfdom.

one overhead camshaft, which operated four standing valves per cylinder. The block, with a fixed head, was of cast iron while the crankcase and sump were of aluminium. Double magnets fed current to two spark plugs per cylinder.

The standard model's engine gave 70 horsepower, but the Speed Model and Super Sports (1923–29) had 80–85 hp at around 3,200 rpm. Top speed varied between 120 and 160 km/h (75–100 mph). The gearbox was separately mounted behind the engine and had four forward speeds. Transmission was via a cardan shaft to a live rear axle with helical bevel gears.

A traditional frame was used, with longitudinal beams and

four pressed cross-bars. The suspension consisted of semielliptic leaf springs and friction dampers. Until 1923, the 3-litre model had brakes only on the rear wheels. Bentley did not build its own bodies, and most were made by Vanden Plas, a firm near its Cricklewood factory. The commonest type of body was a four-seat tourer.

Already in May 1921, the car enabled Frank Clement to win at Brooklands. In 1922, Bentleys placed second, fourth and fifth in the Tourist Trophy. At Le Mans, Clement and John Duff won in 1924, as did Dudley Benjafield and Sammy Davis in 1927. But that was the end of the 3-litre's prowess at great events.

Meanwhile, one of the most famous teams in racing history was formed – the Bentley Boys. Its members were Barnato, Benjafield, Davis, the brothers Clive and Jack Dunfee, Glen Kidston, Bernard Rubin, Jean Chassagne and Sir Henry Birkin. They completely dominated Le Mans between 1928 and 1930.

In July 1931, Bentley's capital ran out and Woolf Barnato, who had economic trouble due to the Depression, refused to help further. An offer for Bentley Motors was made by a consortium, the British Central Equitable Trust Ltd – behind which, as it turned out, lay Rolls-Royce.

W.O. Bentley would doubtless spin in his grave if he knew that both BMW and Volkswagen struggled during the spring of 1998 to take over Rolls-Royce/Bentley. The upshot was that Volkswagen bought the venerable British company while BMW bought the rights to the names Rolls-Royce and Bentley. How such a tangled deal will work out, the future must tell... ∎

M.G. Midget

As can be seen in many chapters of automobile evolution, single-minded men with unusual ideas about car production have done much to move the industry forward. An English example was Cecil Kimber (1888–1945), who created one of the world's best-known sports-car makes.

In 1921, Kimber became the sales chief at Morris Garages, owned by William Morris. After only a year, he was managing director. By this time, Morris had grown into one of the biggest car manufacturers in Great Britain. Cars were rapidly being accepted by both high and low society, and Kimber had an idea. Some customers felt a need to set themselves apart from the rest, though not at any price.

Among his first steps, therefore, was to put special bodies on the company's Morris Cowley. At that moment, the M.G. was born – its name being, of course, an abbreviation of Morris Garages. The name was officially introduced in March 1924, by the initial issue of *The Morris Owner* magazine. To begin with, the product was simply a modified Morris with an M.G. emblem.

But 1924 also brought the first series-manufactured M.G., called the 14/28 tourer. A catalogue from 1925 presented it as the M.G. Super Sports Model. In September 1926, Morris's bullnose radiator was replaced with a flat radiator. Other changes accumulated, giving the cars a refined M.G. character.

"The most remarkable thing about the castle was its purified architecture. An octagonal shape distinguished both the main building and its inner courtyard. At each of the outer corners stood, only slightly higher, an octagonal tower.

M.G. enthusiasts today might well be thrilled to behold this repetitive residence. Cecil Kimber was already obsessed with octagons when he started the M.G. factory. Besides an eight-edged grille emblem, the cars sometimes had octagonal instruments, and further little octagons in the most surprising places. People said that if Cecil had been able, he would have given the cars octagonal wheels."

From Bengt Ason Holm, *The Seventh Elephant*.

Morris Garages registered as a corporation in July 1927, and moved two months later to its first factory, in Oxford. The M.G. Car Company was formed during the next spring. Now it stood on a solid foundation, though William Morris was still the owner.

A model that would really secure M.G.'s future was announced in October 1928: the M-type Midget. This little two-seat sports car used components from the new Morris Minor. Its unusual feature was that the engine had an overhead camshaft, something extraordinary in those days for a mass-produced small car.

The Minor's engine derived from a Wolseley design, acquired by William Morris when he bought Wolseley in 1927. Originally, however, it had been an aircraft engine from Hispano-Suiza, which Wolseley made under licence during World War I. With four cylinders and 847 cc, its M.G. version generated 20 hp (later 27 hp) at 4,000 rpm.

An M.G. M-type Midget Double Twelve Replica. In 1930 it cost £245, compared with £175 for the standard model. Only 30 were sold.

Almost the same chassis was used as in the Minor. The coachwork, by Carbodies, was a two-seater with a tapering tail, made of ashwood and dressed in plywood and artificial leather. The price of a body was only six and a half pounds, and the whole car cost a mere £175 when introduced.

While a Midget could hardly reach 60 mph (95 km/h), it was "sporty" and soon became popular. Long afterward, a M.G. devotee, Rivers Fletcher, wrote: "The M-type is a car whose significance is nearly impossible to overestimate. Many motorists who had believed that a sports car lay beyond their economic means, or their ability to drive a car, became enthusiastic M-type owners."

The model boosted sales dramatically, and in 1929 the M-type accounted for 58 percent of the total production. That year, a move was made to Abingdon, seven miles outside Oxford. There the company stayed until 23 October 1980, when the assembly line stopped for good. One can still buy an M.G., but today from the Austin-Rover Group. ■

Mercedes-Benz K

I T IS ALWAYS HARD TO SELECT A PARTICULAR MERCEDES AS representing the company's glorious past. A make that goes back to the 19th century and has become permanently allied to high quality offers many such choices. But the K model, a fine example from the 1920s, is as good a reason as any to recall how Mercedes-Benz grew up.

When Benz and Daimler combined forces in 1926, their own companies had been active for more than 40 years. Carl Benz's first car, ready in 1885, had three wheels and a one-cylinder reclining engine of 954 cc, delivering 0.75 horsepower at 400 rpm. Benz found it difficult to begin manufacture, but in 1899 he contacted a French bicycle-maker, Emile Roger, who became his general agent. By 1893 a total of 69 Benz cars were produced, 42 selling in France, where the new invention was wholeheartedly embraced.

Daimler, for his part, soon got in touch with Wilhelm Maybach, and they concentrated on designing a stationary engine for diverse uses. Building cars was far from Daimler's intention, and he satisfied himself with testing the engine in a motorcycle that he completed in 1885. It had a cylinder volume of 264 cc and gave 0.5 hp at 700 rpm. Next year, a larger version of the engine was installed in a horse-wagon, and not until 1889 did another car appear.

Besides his business in Germany, Daimler established relations in 1888 with Frederick Simms of Great Britain. The

In the mid-1880s two men, Carl Benz and Gottlieb Daimler, quite unaware of each other, designed the first petrol-powered vehicles in history. The amazing thing is that they were both German and lived only a dozen miles apart.

The resultant pair of companies merged in 1926 to form Daimler-Benz AG. The name Mercedes derived from the daughter of a banker, Emil Jellinek, who had competed with a Daimler under the pseudonym "Herr Mercedes" in the early 1900s. The three-pronged star was an emblem of success belonging to the Daimlers.

latter, in 1890, gained control of all Daimler's engine patents throughout the British Empire. The first entirely English Daimler appeared in 1897, but by then the British and German companies had separated.

During the first quarter of the 20th century, Benz and Daimler built numerous superb cars, and the Mercedes – as Daimler's cars were called on the market – celebrated plenty of triumphs in racing. A merger between Daimler and Benz had been discussed since 1919, but in 1925 Benz faced serious economic problems, which led directly to the combined company.

At that time, Daimler-Benz AG included several talented designers – such as Hans Nibel and Friedrich Nallinger from Benz, and Ferdinand Porsche from Daimler. Porsche had helped to design Daimler's large six-cylinder cars, which now received the model names Mercedes-Benz Typ 400 (3.9 litres) and 630 (6.2 litres) as well as Typ K 24/110/140 PS (and, starting in 1928, the 160 PS for both the Typ 630 and the K).

The K-model from 1926-1928 was a predecessor of the S-type. Not quite as sporty, it still had a supercharger. The body came from Erdmann & Rossi.

All models used aluminium for the block and crankcase, and cast iron for the cylinder head. They had an overhead camshaft and a supercharger. The car illustrated here is a K 24/110/140 PS, its "K" standing for *Kurz* (short) – the wheelbase is only 3.4 metres, compared to 3.75 for the Typ 630. Its compressor boosted the engine from 100 hp at 2,800 rpm to 140 hp at 3,100 rpm.

The top speed was about 145 km/h (90 mph) with an open car weighing some 2,600 kg (1,180 lbs). Actually, the K model was planned as a fast, comfortable tourer. Yet only a month after the merger, three K cars finished 1-2-3 in an overland race at San Sebastiano, Spain.

Typ K was available only with open two- or four-seat bodies, and cost between 20,750 and 26,000 Reichsmarks. In all, 150 were made during 1926-28, before giving way to the famous S-series which was based upon the K. ∎

Ford Model A

The Ford A station-wagon's seats were turned forward as in a normal passenger car, but there was a back flap that could be lowered as on a truck. This example has an Australian body on a chassis made in Canada, though very like the cars made by the factory in America.

WHEN IT BECAME CLEAR THAT FORD WOULD BRING out a successor to the Model T, the parts suppliers celebrated, the stock market set a record, and riots broke out at the car's presentation.

As we have seen in the tale of the Model T, it took a long time before Henry Ford decided to replace his beloved Tin Lizzie with a new model. The T-Ford was the foundation of his industrial empire. Whoever criticized or tried to persuade him was forced to leave the factory.

But on 25 May 1927 came the announcement, and next day the last T-Ford rolled off the line. Then the factory closed for five months, and it has been said that Henry Ford was so rich that he could afford to pay the workers during this period. Still, he did nothing for them and thousands lost their jobs, causing great social problems. The only concerned voice from

Ford was that of Henry's son Edsel, who donated to various welfare projects.

A leading topic of debate leading up to the presentation was what type of engine the new model would have. Many believed in a six-cylinder engine, and there were even rumours of an X-8. The latter proved too complicated for mass production, and Henry Ford rejected all thought of a straight-six due to the failure of the T-Ford's predecessor, the Model K. So it had to be a four.

The chosen engine was a side-valve of 3286 cc, generating 40 hp at 2,200 rpm, which was twice as powerful as the T-Ford's. Like the T-Ford, the Model A had transverse leaf springs. In addition, however, it boasted hydraulic shock absorbers, a conventional three-speed gearbox with sliding cogs, four-wheel brakes, and a top of speed of about 60 mph (100 km/h).

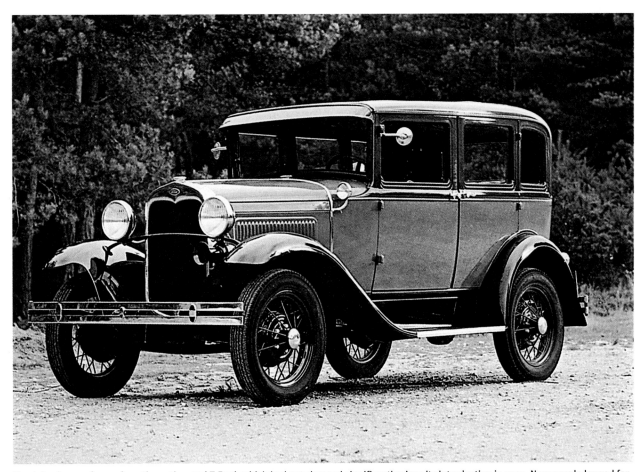

The A-Ford was a far cry from the antiquated T-Ford, which had not changed significantly since its introduction in 1907. Now people longed for a simple, tough, reliable car and the Model A was the answer.

The first engine emerged on 20 October 1927. A day later, it was mounted in the first Model A. On 2 December, the result was shown to the public, and by month's end the retailers had orders for 727,000 cars. This incredible figure is something a manufacturer hardly can dream of today.

One factor responsible for the car's happy welcome was the handsome body, designed by Edsel Ford and Joe Galamb. As so often at that time, favourite cars were praised in musical compositions which became popular hits. To the A-Ford's honour was written the song *"Henry's Made a Lady out of Lizzie"*. Other Ford-inspired tunes were *"You Can't Afford to Marry If You Can't Afford a Ford"*, *"The Little Ford Rambled Right Along"* and *"The Scandal of Little Lizzie Ford"*.

During the model's initial year, no fewer than nine body types were available. The cheapest, a four-seat open phaeton, cost $460 (equivalent to about 10 times as much today). Triumph was so total that production of the Model A amounted to 3,572,610 between 1929 and 1931. Plenty were also built by licence in other countries, including the Soviet Union.

On 31 March 1932, Henry Ford again created motoring history when he introduced the Ford V8. ■

Duesenberg Model J

Frederick Samuel Duesenberg was born in December 1876, and his brother August Samuel a couple of years later. Growing up on their uncle's farm, they learned about diverse machines that were then being adopted in agriculture. When Fred turned 20, he and Augie opened a workshop to build and repair bicycles. The technical genius of the pair, Fred soon also won recognition as a racing cyclist.

In 1902, Fred sold the shop and went to work for Thomas B. Jeffery, who manufactured Rambler cars. But he grew dissatisfied, eager to make his own cars and run them fast. Some years later, he met a wealthy lawyer and was given the means to design a car, which appeared in 1905.

Named the Mason after its financier, this two-cylinder car fulfilled Fred's dreams of driving to victory in competitions. Its advertisements stated immodestly that "Mason is the fastest, strongest two-cylinder automobile in America".

Success spurred the brothers onward, and in 1913 a small factory arose in St. Paul, Minnesota, producing racer engines. In 1917, the United States entered World War I and new, interesting work began for the Duesenbergs. They moved to Elizabeth, New Jersey, where they built boat and airplane engines. Among the latter was a 16-cylinder V-engine with 900 horsepower. Furthermore, they contributed to designing the famous Liberty engine for aircraft, which was later built by Packard.

History is a gold-mine for speculation about "what might have happened otherwise". The automobile's past is no exception, and it has often been wondered what would have happened if the widow Duesenberg had not emigrated from Lippe, Germany to Rockford, Iowa with her two sons. For we know what happened because she did – the birth of some very fine vehicles.

With the war behind them, Fred and Augie moved again – to Indianapolis, a city that would earn renown for its 500-mile race. In 1920, the first car bearing the Duesenberg name emerged, under the designation Model A. This was a luxury conveyance with a straight-eight engine. From the very start, Duesenberg was one of the ten most expensive makes on the American market. Depending on the type of body selected, a Model A in 1922 cost at least $6,500.

In spite of performing far better than average, the Duesenberg had to fight hard for its sales. But triumphs on the race track kept the marketing alive. For example, Jimmy Murphy won the 1921 French Grand Prix in a Duesenberg – the first time an American car or driver won a major European competition. In 1924 and 1925, Duesenbergs won the Indy 500.

Yet the company was not managed well and by 1926 its finances were in bad shape. The cars' prices rose and, more seriously, the rest of the industry was catching up. Now almost every make offered a straight eight, and hydraulic brakes were no longer a novelty.

But for a single person, Duesenberg would thus have vanished into obscurity. This was Erret Lobban Cord, a dynamic promoter who had rescued the problematic Auburn and tripled its sales in three years. Cord – like Ettore Bugatti – had a vision of building a luxury car that would outclass everything else. Duesenberg's crisis had not diminished its excellent reputation, so Cord bought it for a million dollars: it became a wholly owned subsidiary.

THE MODEL J ARRIVES

Fred Duesenberg's hands were left free, and in December 1928 he presented the Model J. It had a straight-eight with 6882 cc, two overhead camshafts, and four valves per cylinder. The engine, all of four feet long (122 cm), was said to deliver 265 hp, which beat the closest American rival – Pierce Arrow – by 140 hp. With a light body, the top speed was 110 mph (175 km/h).

One paid $8,500 for a J chassis, and $11–14,000 for a complete car. The best-known bodies included a convertible-sedan from Murphy, a tourer from Derham, and a torpedo phaeton from Brunn.

Rapid fame awaited the Model J in Hollywood. It was owned by Gary Cooper, Clark Gable, Cary Grant and Mae West, to mention a few. Other illustrious Duesenbergers were the queen of cosmetics, Elizabeth Arden, the oil millionaire

John Paul Getty and the newspaper king, William Randolph Hearst. Fifty-odd examples came to Europe, their owners ranging from Spain's King Alfonso XIII and Rumania's Prince Nicholas to the financier Clarence Hatry.

It was soon clear to Fred Duesenberg that some customers

Duesenberg Model J from 1929 with dual phaeton body by Murphy

wanted even more powerful cars. In 1932 he began to develop 36 of the Model SJ, with a centrifugal supercharger. This gave 320 (later 400) hp and a top speed of about 130 mph (210 km/h).

That year, however, Fred died in an automobile accident. His brother Augie lived until 1955, the Cord empire going bankrupt in 1937. Today, the magnificent cars they created are as sought-after as any. ∎

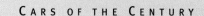

1930–1940

THE GREAT DEPRESSION MARKS THESE YEARS FROM their outset. Raging unemployment helps the National Socialist (Nazi) party in Germany to win elections. At a conference in Geneva, countries continue the effort to disarm after World War I. Stalin begins his reign of terror, and Soviet soldiers plunder churches. The Russian landscape is collectivized into *kolkhoz* farms by confiscating all property. In India, Mahatma Gandhi defies the English salt monopoly with passive resistance, and is imprisoned when Lord Irwin calls him a danger to world peace.

Nicaragua's capital, Managua, is destroyed by an earthquake at the cost of 5,000 lives. Sport programs are broadcast for the first time on television, in Japan. A new building-block of matter, the neutron, is discovered in England by James

Franco Fessia's masterpiece was the 1936 Fiat 500 – called the Topolino ("Mickey Mouse") in Italy, the "Mouse" in England, and Mariehønen ("Ladybug") in Denmark. This is the French-built Simca version, as only the grille emblem reveals. Note, that one could remove the front bonnet part and that the little hatch in the firewall gave access to the fuel tank. Also noteworthy are the sliding windows, which allowed thin doors and more interior space, and the recessed door handles. Even tall people could sit comfortably in the front seats, but the rear area was meant only for baggage – or, at best, small children. Adults might easily bump the battery compartment and get a shock or a squirt of acid. However, the car's oddities were far outweighed by its superb road-handling and monk-like drinking habits – about 5.5 litres per 100 km (45 miles per gallon)!

Chadwick. Benito Mussolini rises toward power in Italy, while Adolf Hitler is made Chancellor and next President of Germany, which leaves the League of Nations.

Two petroleum companies, Shell and Standard Oil (Esso), want nothing more to do with oil from Russia, and this makes it harder for the Soviets to obtain Western credit. In Cuba, the military revolts against the government. Women's fashions begin to agree on the same skirt-length, replacing the old

range of variable, short or sweeping creations, and their hats expose the forehead.

The awful effects of the decade's early economic crisis are extended by a drought in the United States; crops wither and millions of people migrate. Mussolini declares that "Asia and Africa are Italy's aim, now as in ancient times". The police in Bucharest jail 18 conspirators against the Rumanian royal family. Latvia's government is shaken by revolutionary

Here is a magnificent 1931 Bentley 8-litre in original condition. This ghost from the past had a six-cylinder engine with overhead camshaft and 7,983 cc of volume. The block and (unremovable) head were in one piece, and both magneto and battery ignition were provided. A combination of 230 horsepower and high gear ratio yielded a top speed of 100 mph (160 km/h), even with a heavy enclosed body work and a weight over 2.5 tons. Nothing limited the body weight; these 8-litre giants carried whatever a coachbuilder could think of.

Communist plots. In Tokyo, 30 Russians are arrested for conspiring to overthrow the Japanese regime in Manchuria.

An international exhibition is held in Brussels for industry, trade and culture. Wind comes into use for power generation, with an electricity plant in Crimea delivering 6,000 volts. A German engineer, Kruckenberg, constructs a propeller-driven railway wagon that reaches 143 mph (230 km/h) on a test run. The tyre mogul André Michelin dies.

At the beginning of the 1930s, every fifth person in America owns an automobile. Despite the severe depression, many companies persist in producing luxurious super-cars, and often go bankrupt as a result. More fortunate are the firms that merge with each other, design simpler and cheaper models and rationalize their manufacturing methods.

Car makers start to understand that the vehicle must be rigid in order to achieve good driving qualities. However, cars built in the traditional manner, with a body mounted onto a separate chassis, lack enough rigidity. Different kinds of stiffening

Singer Nine Le Mans, 1934

are added to the frame, such as cross-stays. But passenger cars are being made in ever larger series, and investment in pressing machinery becomes more profitable. This leads to the fully welded, self-supporting, very rigid steel body – a *monocoque* with no frame members at all. The technique's most famous illustration is probably the front-wheel-drive Citroën B7, later developed into the classic type B11.

European motorcars are increasingly provided with independent front-wheel suspension. Double, parallel, transverse leaf-springs, or a system of link-arms and helical springs or torsion bars, are preferred. Detroit goes its own way with independent suspension, using the Frenchman

Dubonnet's "knee-joint" system on its more expensive models. Lancia had invented an advanced telescopic front-wheel suspension system already during the 1920s, which works perfectly on all the company's models in the 1930s.

Some makes in Central Europe also have the rear wheels sprung independently. Most rear-wheel systems are of the swing-axle type, which certainly lowers the unsprung weight. But this, at the same time, creates gyroscopic forces and track-width changes, giving a worse grip on the road. These effects are avoided by Lancia in the mid-1930s with a superb independent rear-wheel suspension. It achieves even lower unsprung weight by mounting the rear-wheel brakes

The 1936 Cadillac (*opposite*) was virtually mass-produced, though studded with Fleetwood emblems. That year alone, more than 3,000 were made of this eight-cylinder model 75 with long wheelbase. An American buyer could acquire five such cars for the price of a single Phantom III – and even an Englishman could obtain a couple, despite the import taxes. Besides, the Rolls-Royce used streamlining only in its wings and rear-wheel spats. The Cadillac represents the biggest variant of General Motors' "turret top" style from 1936. Indeed, the same body – without the Fleetwood details and changes – occurred on the Buick Limited, which cost over 2,000 dollars. Interestingly, the Cadillac shared some technical features with Rolls-Royce, such as front-wheel suspension by spiral springs, semielliptic rear springs, and a V-engine. Both cars weighed around 2,300 kilograms, and had synchronized gearboxes and servo brakes. Predictably, however, the American car had three forward speeds while the British used four. And Rolls-Royce preferred mechanical brakes to the modernity of hydraulic ones. Each car could do about 90 mph (145 km/h), but the Cadillac's 5.7-litre side-valve V8 was much easier and cheaper to maintain than the Rolls-Royce's 7.3-litre overhead-valve V12.

The 1939 Buick Special (*above*) also shows certain similarities to the Cadillac. General Motors did, of course, elaborate its designs during the three years that separated these models. Yet Buick's convertible was meant for the middle class, costing 1,077 dollars at home in the USA and 535 pounds in Great Britain. Production of the model (as distinct from the body variant) reached five figures in some years. Under the alligator hood was a well-tried 107-horsepower straight-eight engine, with overhead valves and 4.1 litres. The rear axle had spiral springs, and could act strangely on bends – not that it mattered much, since in America only the crooks and cops took corners fast. Outwardly, the car is a classic case of 1939 design, which was transitional: a rather shallow divided grille, pontoon fenders, semirecessed headlamps, and footboards on the way to extinction. The side-mounted spare tyres looked like an afterthought; they were no longer sinkable into the fenders because of the latter's new shape. But they were essential on some export markets, due to sheer snobbery – without them, the Buick might be mistaken by ignorant people for the considerably cheaper, more plebeian Oldsmobile.

The straight-eight La Salle was the leader in style for its time. When this example was built in 1935, its lines were a year old and their influence could be seen in makes such as Studebaker and Hudson and certain General Motors' makes. Perhaps most typical are the body's softly curved "turret top", pontoon fenders, and ever smaller grille. Signs of the growing effort to design a car as a unit are that the headlamps no longer sit entirely free, and that the radiator cap has disappeared under the hood. The hood's port holes would return as a hallmark of the 1949 Buick. In mechanical terms, the La Salle was the first General Motors car to have hydraulic brakes, and its independent front-wheel suspension with spiral springs also occurred on 1934 Cadillacs (as well as on the cheap GM makes in a somewhat different form). The mechanical parts were mostly shared by the Oldsmobile Eight. But the new car, as a sedan, cost only 1,650 dollars in 1934, when the straight-eight La Salle accounted for more than half of the 13,014 cars sold by the Cadillac Division.

Between 1928 and 1930, Opel produced the 7/34 PS and 7/40 PS models. They looked identical, but the four-cylinder side-valve engine under the hood was of 1.7 and 1.8 litres respectively. Both cars cost 4,900 Reichsmarks. Here we see a Packard-inspired radiator, which of course should be nickel-plated, not brass, and there is no bumper.

centrally at the differential housing. English manufacturers stick to the live rear axle until the early 1960s.

The fuel system is based almost entirely on the well-established carburettor. Forced feed by a supercharger – which had been reserved for competition cars – is introduced on some sporty Italian and French makes, besides luxurious German and American ones. Four-wheel brakes become generally available. There are still mechanical brake systems, a few of them quite good, others having a bad compensating device that causes unequal braking. This disadvantage is removed by the hydraulic brake system and, towards the end of the decade, even simple cars can slow and stop smoothly.

At Camden, New Jersey, the world's first drive-in cinema opens, with 4,000 parking places. Ernst Henne of Germany reaches 159 mph (256 km/h) on a motorcycle. Malcolm Campbell in his "Bluebird" sets a new land speed record of

301.5 mph (485.2 km/h). Soon, 12 mph (20 km/h) are added to the record by George Eyston's "Thunderbolt", which goes on to attain 357.5 mph (575.3 km/h). Finally in 1939, John Cobb's "Napier Railton" roars at a rate that will last beyond the next world war: 369.74 mph (595.04 km/h). Campbell takes the speed record on water at 141.7 mph (228.1 km/h).

The first submarine that can carry an airplane, the British M2, sinks and 60 men perish. Experiments are made with an autopilot for airplanes. Direct flights from Paris to New York are pioneered by two French aviators, Costes and Bellonte. The world's biggest airship until then, England's R.101, takes off for India but, after only a few hours, crashes in France and burns with 48 people aboard. Clydesdale and McIntyre, from Britain, fly over Mount Everest.

A balloon, bearing the Swiss physicist Auguste Piccard, soars into the stratosphere, setting an altitude record of 53,153 feet (16,201 metres). Wiley Post, an American racing aviator, climbs to 50,000 ft (15,240 m), unprecedented for an airplane. During 1937, more than forty flights break records for height, endurance, distance and speed. The age of airships ends when the *Hindenburg* crashes in New York. On the initiative of Howard Hughes, the longest flight in history is made – from New York around the globe to New York.

In Moscow, negotiations on debt repayment collapse, and the Communist International Congress meddles in the United States' internal affairs, so the American consulate closes. Britain strengthens its air force. The world's largest steam vessel, the *Queen Mary*, begins her transatlantic voyages in 1936.

The Volvo PV 36 Carioca was a Swedish copy of Chrysler's 1934 Airflow. From the sloping stern, rear-wheel spats, and divided windscreen to the high bonnet sides with recessed headlamps, everything was Chrysler-inspired. On the other hand, Volvo did not use the Chrysler grille (which looked most like a waterfall in 1934). Unfortunately, Swedes scarcely admired the design and only 500 Cariocas were sold.

Chiang Kai-Shek, the dictator of China, is captured by rebels who want to declare war on Japan. Traffic commences across the Golden Gate in San Francisco, the biggest of all suspension bridges. General Franco grabs power in Spain, while Japan invades China and Austria is swallowed by the German Reich.

After some good years in mid-decade, the business cycle falls again in the late 1930s. General Motors lays off 30,000 workers. But the armament industry is flourishing, and in Germany Hitler takes command of the German military forces and re-orients every economic activity to serve the state's purposes. The Jews' cultural life in Germany is squashed, their newspapers are banned, associations are dissolved, stores and synagogues are wrecked. The Soviet Union attacks Finland and prepares to engulf the three Baltic republics. ∎

Rosengart was the French licence-built Austin Seven (as Dixi was the German, and Bantam the American). What chiefly distinguished the variants was their appearance, since the bodies were built in the respective countries. Manufacture took place at Neuilly-sur-Seine, Paris, and continued from the late 1920s until the start of World War II. The above LR4 type's body reflects – despite its small size – the typical charm of French coachbuilding lines in the 1930s. While the Austin "original" had wire-spoked wheels, more characteristic of a British car, the Rosengart's perforated dish wheels and handsome hubcaps spoke of contemporary Gallic elegance.

The engine was a little side-valve 750-cc with low power, but the programme was expanded in the early 1930s by a six-cylinder engine of 1.1 litres and 20 hp. Later some front-wheel-drive models were presented with still larger engines, one being based on the Citroën type B11.

Cadillac V16

ALREADY AT THE BEGINNING OF THE 20TH CENTURY, prestige was measured by a car's number of cylinders. A straight-six was presented as early as 1902 by Spyker in Holland and, one year later, a V8 by Ader in France. The first V12 came from Packard, and in January 1930 a series-produced V16 was presented by Cadillac.

This sensation placed the company among the industry's leaders. Interestingly, the reason why a few American manu-facturers began to make 16-cylinder engines was not to obtain high power. They wanted their luxury cars to run as softly and quietly as possible.

Cadillac's engine – created by Ernest W. Seaholm, W. R. Strickland and Owen Nacker – was designed without any care for cost. Basically it consisted of two eight-cylinder blocks with overhead valves and a common crankshaft. Cadillac's choice of straight-eight blocks may seem strange, because

1930 Cadillac V16 Fleetwood Convertible Coupé. This car was called "Madam X"

they had never before built such an engine. The angle between the blocks was only 45 degrees. The cylinder volume was 7413 cc, and the output 165 hp at a modest 3,400 rpm. Later on, the power increased to 185 hp – but since the cars usually weighed well over two tons, the top speed remained 80–90 mph (125–145 km/h).

The refinements included hydraulic valve-lifters, which were said to be so silent that, when running in neutral, the engine could be heard only by the sparks in the distributors.

In 1930, a Cadillac V16 of Series 452 carried a price between $5,350 and $9,700 depending on the type of body. This was more expensive than the contemporary Packard Twin Six, but still cheap in comparison with a Duesenberg SJ, whose chassis alone was worth $9,500!

During the first year 2,887 examples were sold, which was not bad in view of the customers' confusion as they faced a choice of 54 different bodies. Next year, sales plummeted to 364 cars – and then only 1,152 were made annually until 1940, when production stopped. As late as 1938, Cadillac introduced a new V16 engine with a design that was considered a masterpiece.

Some other American makers using V16 engines were Marmon, which built 360 specimens of the Sixteen, and Peerless which assembled only three cars. But this was a doomed breed of dinosaurs, and no V16 engines have been series-manufactured since World War II. ∎

Bugatti Type 57

THE EXPRESSION THAT APPLES DO NOT FALL FAR from pear trees (or chips from old blocks) is certainly appropriate to Jean Bugatti, whose father was the famous Ettore Bugatti. Unfortunately, Jean did not live long, but he left a classic Bugatti model, the Type 57, which is now among the world's leading collection cars. It was also Jean who persuaded Ettore to begin building engines with two overhead camshafts. On the other hand, he never got far with his ideas of independent front suspension. They were beyond the limit for the conservative elder Bugatti.

On August 11, 1939, Jean Bugatti was about to test-drive a Type 57 that would race in the Baule Grand Prix. The factory mechanics had signposted a stretch of road near Molsheim. But a bicyclist ignored the warnings, and when Jean tried to avoid him by swerving at very high speed, tragedy followed.

The origins of the twin-overhead-cam engine can be traced back to 1929. In exchange for three of his Type 43, Ettore Bugatti acquired the Miller cars from America which had raced at Monza that year. The Miller engine was obviously

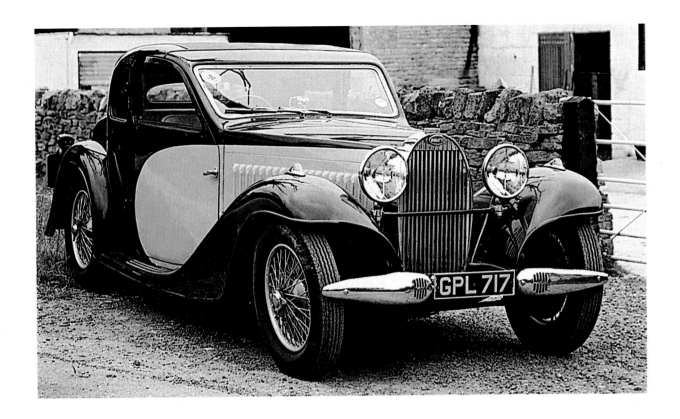

much stronger than what had powered the Bugatti Type 35B. Jean's suggestion prevailed, leading to one of the finest engines Bugatti ever built.

The first model to use this engine was the Type 50, a large and sporty luxury car. With 4972 cc, the straight-eight developed at least 200 hp at 4,000 rpm. Next came the Type 55, a top contender for being the company's loveliest creation. Of the 38 that were made, 28 or more survive today. In good condition, a Type 55 could do over 115 mph (180 km/h). Its body was designed by Jean Bugatti.

In 1934, Bugatti presented the most renowned of his touring models-Type 57. Of the approximately 7,833 Bugatti cars produced, it accounted for 683 between the years 1934 and 1940. There were four versions: Types 57 (the standard model), 57S (a sports variant with a lower and shorter frame), 57C (with a supercharger) and 57SC (a supercharged 57S).

The cylinders measured 72X100 mm and stroked a volume of 3257 cc, giving 175 hp at 5,500 rpm. Top speed exceeded 125 mph (200 km/h) for a 57SC, making it one of the fastest contemporary tourers. Despite this, the Type 57 did not get hydraulic brakes until the end of 1938.

Most of these cars had bodies named Ventoux, Galibier or Stelvio. Some were endowed with Atlantic bodies and just three had the bizarre Atlantic coupe form, with aluminium panels riveted together and doors that went up to the roof.

From 1936 onward, the factory produced no other models but the Type 57. While it was meant to be a speedy, comfy long-distance car, in 1939 a 57S "tank" driven by Jean-Pierre Wimille won Bugatti's only victory at Le Mans. ∎

Tatra

1937 Tatra T87

THE VERY MENTION OF TATRA IN MOTORING CIRCLES is an invitation to smiles. "Oh, yes! Those were the weird streamlined cars from Czechoslovakia."

Originally, the company was named Nesseldorfer Wagenbau Fabriks A.G. When the Republic of Czechoslovakia was founded in 1918, the factory changed its name to Tatra, after the famous mountain range in the northeast part of the country.

The first cars after World War I were old designs made by Hans Ledwinka, who had moved to the Austrian manufacturer Steyr. He now returned to Tatra, and in 1923 the Tatra 11 was introduced. It had a simple but very robust structure, with a two-cylinder boxer engine in a central-tube frame, transverse leaf springs and rear swing axles.

Its top speed was just 70 km/h (45 mph) but, in view of the poor road standards in Central Europe at that time, it was an excellent car. Indeed, a Tatra 11 won the Leningrad-Tiflis-Moscow race, over 5,310 kilometres of awful or nonexistent roads.

Tatra also made six- and twelve-cylinder cars, and the Tatra 80 had a V12 with 5976 cc giving 120 hp. This vehicle was quite expensive, and only some twenty were produced.

REAR-ENGINE CARS

Already in the early 1930s, Ledwinka began to experiment with rear-powered automobiles. His assumption was that a rear engine would be less disturbing to the passengers, especially if one used an air-cooled boxer engine.

In 1933, Ledwinka presented a small two-door car with a rounded front and streamlined tail. It was not unlike the prototypes for the Volkswagen. The Tatra V-570 had a two-cylinder engine of 854 cc and a top speed of around 80 km/h (50 mph).

The Tatra's bonnet (*a*) was used to hold the spare tyre, or normally two tyres, and the container of the chassis-lubrication system. But there was ample space for baggage above the petrol tank behind the rear seat (*b*). The central-tube frame (*c*) is visible behind the front seat. Farther back, the frame divided to create a place for the engine. The front suspension was independent, with transverse leaf springs; at the rear, longitudinal cantilever springs (*d*) were combined with swing-axles. The engine was an air-cooled V8 with 60 hp, and the transmission went forward via a single-disc clutch to a four-speed gearbox. The car was equipped with a starter crank (*e*), which sometimes made bystanders think that the driver tried to start it "at the wrong end". The whole engine and transmission unit could be removed for easier service.

With its appealing looks, this model could have replaced the Tatra 12, but Ledwinka went further in his development work. He designed a four-door car with a 2965-cc V8. The central-tube frame was of box-beam type, and divided in back to fit the engine between the shanks. There were also hydraulic brakes. The prototype had a mid-mounted steering wheel, recalling the Panhard Dynamic, but this placement was quickly abandoned.

The new model, named the Tatra 77, was unveiled at the Berlin auto show in 1934. Two years later came the Tatra 77a, with a 3380-cc engine. Tatra cars were very comfortable to drive, but like all rear-engine cars they tended to swing their tails when taking a curve fast. Consequently, Ledwinka shortened the car to 4.74 metres (187 inches) and changed the model's designation to Tatra 87.

The big Tatras proved popular among German officers during World War II. However, the military command reputedly banned their use, as several officers were injured or killed when the car's rear end slid off the road.

After the war, the Tatra 87 revived – and 1947 brought the Tatra 600, also known as the Tatraplan. This had an air-cooled four-cylinder boxer engine of 1952 cc. Of the 6,334 Tatraplans produced, not a few were exported. The Tatra 603 appeared in 1956, and more than 23,000 were made. ∎

Mercedes-Benz 500/540 K

Mercedes-Benz 540 K

To PRESENT A striking summary of the Mercedes-Benz 500/540K models is impossible, as they are surrounded by myths and prejudices. To some people, they stand for the ultimate in the art of building cars, while others see them as symbols of a political system that set the world on fire.

During the 1920s, most of Mercedes' luxury and super-charged models were designed by Ferdinand Porsche. But the 500K emerged under the leadership of Hans Nibel, who was chief designer from 1919 until 1934. It was to be a product that outshone the majority, and in 1934 the price of a 500K corresponded to at least $100,000 today. One can easily understand that the customers were restricted to film stars, bankers and heavyweight businessmen.

The 500K was introduced at the Berlin automobile show in 1934. It had a straight-eight engine of 5018 cc, with a normal output of 100 horsepower. This, however, could be boosted to 160 hp by coupling in the supercharger, to which the letter "K" for the German term *Kompressor* referred.

ENGINEERING AT ITS BEST

The Mercedes 500K was a very complicated machine, and must have contained twice as many parts as a contemporary American luxury car. This also had the consequence that a second-hand 500K did not cost much, since it was terribly expensive to service after a few years of age.

With a weight of more than 2.5 tons and a top speed of 160 km/h (100 mph), such a car demanded considerable courage to be driven fast, even on an *autobahn*. In this respect, things

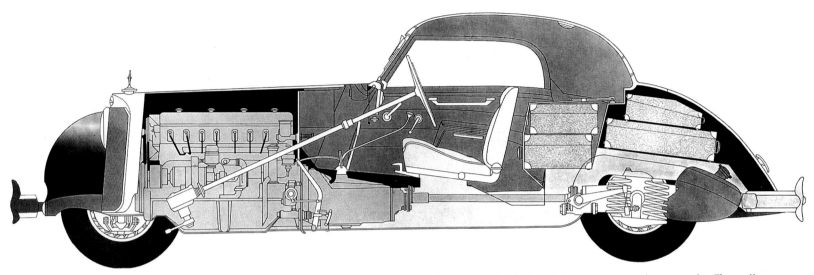

A view through this 540K shows what a huge engine was used to take two people on a very comfortable tour. Specially made bags were among the accessories. The 540K symbolized wealth, and in 1936 this Cabriolet B cost 22,000 Reichsmarks. If one did not need such a giant, ten Opel Kadetts could be bought for the same sum.

were not improved by the 500K's sporty appearance with low windows, amazingly long bonnet, and nearly nonexistent view to the rear. It was certainly a monster, and one of the last true giants in motoring.

Several types of bodies were available, the most popular being the open carriages. A few coupé models were also built, and the extreme end of the series was the streamlined *Autobahn Kurir* (Courier).

All of Mercedes' cars were superbly manufactured, but the 500K in particular. Its furnishings and instrumentation had no equal, and the folding top was a wonder of handicraft with many layers of sound-insulating material. Behind its two seats could be strapped a pair of specially made suitcases, and there was room for two more bags in the trunk.

Among the most conspicuous details of the 500K were the chromed exhaust pipes, protruding from the right side of the bonnet – a feature that also occurred on Duesenberg's SJ model, a mastodon of the same date.

In 1936 came the 540K, which had a somewhat bigger engine of 5401 cc. Its output was raised to 115 hp normally, and to all of 180 hp with the supercharger engaged, giving a maximum speed of 180 km/h (115 mph). Outwardly, the two models were quite similar.

Total production amounted to 354 of the 500K, and 444 of the 540K. Both models appealed greatly to high-ranking Nazis and were often used in parades. Hence they became hallmarks of a period which is far from worth glorifying today. ■

Citroën 7 CV and 11 CV

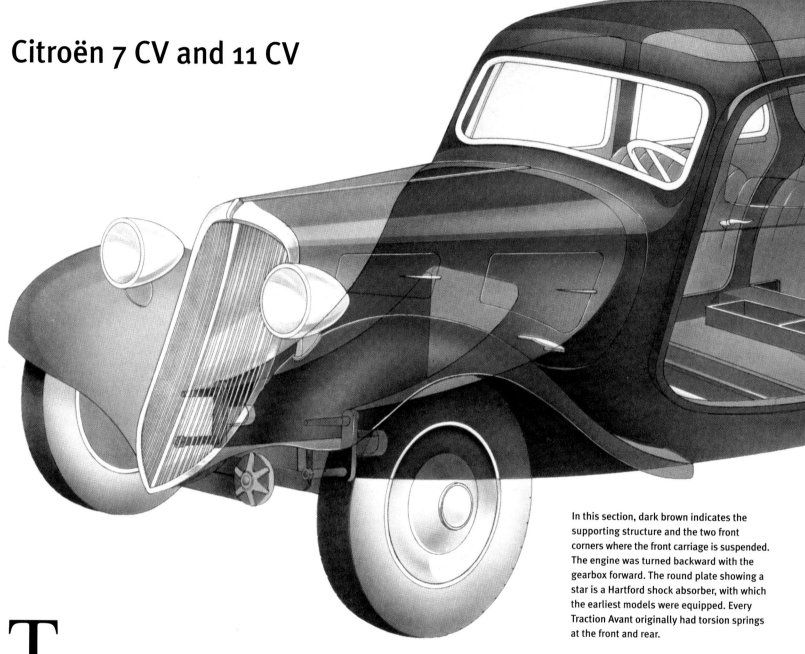

In this section, dark brown indicates the supporting structure and the two front corners where the front carriage is suspended. The engine was turned backward with the gearbox forward. The round plate showing a star is a Hartford shock absorber, with which the earliest models were equipped. Every Traction Avant originally had torsion springs at the front and rear.

THE ORDERS FROM ANDRÉ CITROËN WERE QUITE clear: design a car that was fundamentally revolutionary. It should weigh around 850 kilograms (1,870 lbs) so as to need no large engine, consume fuel moderately and perform well. To be classed 7CV (with seven French horsepower), it would have four seats, front-wheel drive, and a top speed of about 100 km/h (60 mph). If constructive solutions could also be found to make the car unique, that was excellent.

Thus, front-wheel drive was required at Citroën's express wish. It was nothing new, for several such cars had already emerged. But as a solution it was uncommon, and this appealed to Citroën. Moreover, he wanted the car to have an automatic gearbox. At the Paris Salon in the mid-1920s, an automatic gearbox had been presented in a Voisin, and he called for the same in his car. However, difficulties led to its abandonment and a three-gear manual box was quickly designed. The manual box was never very good, but it stayed with the car to the end.

The new car began to take shape. It was given a self-supporting chassis, rather unusual then. Most cars in the 1930s had a basic structure with a stout frame – normally two strong iron beams – which held together and held up the entire car, into which the front unit and rear axle were bolted along with the engine and transmission. But Citroën's independent chassis was a sheet-metal affair: to put it simply, the chassis was strong enough to "carry" the car. A frame of the old sort was unnecessary. As a result, the frame's weight was saved, and Citroën's new car proved to be lighter than corresponding models from other companies.

This project was termed PV, an abbreviation of *petite voiture* (small car). Volvo has also used these initials, but to mean a "personal vehicle" with no reference to the Citroën.

In March 1934, the PV project was demonstrated to a number of financiers, who instantly promised to back Citroën in making the new car. The press was first allowed to see the car in mid-April, and sales commenced at the beginning of May. It was a success in every way. *Traction avant* (front

drive) became a concept forever associated with this car. Its handling properties were superb for the period, combining front-wheel drive with a low centre of gravity, almost perfect balance between the front and rear axle loads, and ample space. Such balance was achieved by placing the gearbox in front of the engine, so that the engine's weight lay between the axles, as did the passengers and baggage.

The Citroën B11 won high appreciation through the years as a medium-class car with fine driving qualities. Its front-wheel drive made *traction avant* ("pulling in front") a term familiar to millions.

The 7CV *faux cabriolet*, manufactured during 1934–1938, featured a "mother-in-law" seat at the back. This example was made in England.

Soon, though, flies crept into the ointment. The car's quality was not up to its technology. Countless breakdowns occurred, chiefly in the drive shafts, which were remade several times before they started to work fairly well. The lower suspension arms broke, the torsion-rod shock absorbers snapped, the brakes were unreliable, overheating was common, the handbrake was poor, and the chassis cracked at diverse points. In addition, the design with its front-wheel drive, backward-facing engine, and self-supporting chassis was so peculiar that ordinary auto mechanics could not understand it. The car gained a reputation for being hard to fix, contributing to its bad image.

Neither was the engine a masterpiece. It had "wet linings",

meaning that the cylinders were loose and could be set directly down in the block's cooling mantle. From the viewpoint of renovation, it was ideal: when a cylinder and piston were worn out, both could be removed easily and the new ones stuck into the block. This arrangement has become rather frequent in French cars through the years.

The first engines were too weak. Their scanty 1300 cc and 32 hp rapidly gave way to 1500 cc and 35 hp, which did little better. Next came 1600 cc and 36 hp, until the "ultimate motor" B11 with 1911 cc and 46 hp, followed by one of 56 hp.

On the model programme were three different wheelbases: 291 cm, 309 cm, and 327 cm. The shortest axle separation was used in the four-door models 7 and 11, as well as the cabriolet and coupé. Intermediate models were built with more or less the same chassis variants, and were later called Normale. The longest were the Familiale, with up to nine seats, and the Commerciale with an adjustable rear seat and a two-part rear combi-compartment.

It can be challenging to keep track of all the versions of Traction Avant during past decades, but a few minor details reveal the year or period of a model. In 1938 came the "pilot rims" on wheels, with leaf spokes, which were abandoned in 1947. The big hatches on the engine bonnet's sides were replaced in 1947 with thin gills. The large rear hatch was added in 1952; previously one reached the baggage space by folding away the rear seat. Also in 1952, the wipers were moved from the windscreen's upper to its lower edge, and two other innovations were made: the gray instrument panel,

and flashers instead of turn signals.

The B11 gradually won great appreciation as a medium-class car with fine handling. It enjoyed many triumphs in competitions, despite the engine's feebleness. What it lacked in power was recaptured in road-holding, which allowed higher speed on curves. There was also a six-cylinder version of it, the 15 Six, and a V8 that basically had two 11 engines combined to provide eight cylinders. The latter engine was shown at the Paris Salon in the mid-1930s and delivered 100 hp, but never went into production.

The Traction Avant, 7 and 11, together with all variants, saw more than twenty years of production in just over 750,000 examples – an extraordinary record for a car that embraced so much novelty when it emerged. ■

Chrysler Airflow

THERE IS ALWAYS A TEMPER OF THE TIMES THAT auto makers are eager to capture and translate into their models, so as to offer a product that looks more modern and will appeal to customers.

One of the most typical examples of this attentiveness in automobile history is the Chrysler Airflow. What was to be a great success according to the manufacturers went nowhere. It took off fast and fell flat as a pancake.

At the end of the 1920s, flying was an inspiration to most designers. Aviation had become ever more popular, and all that had to do with it stood for modernity and the future.

In America, the Depression naturally also gave car companies a desperate urgency to find trends that would help to sell vehicles. Streamlining was a fine idea, as it played a key role in airplanes and would thus seem essential to cars.

Such was the reasoning, anyhow, at Chrysler where Carl Breer wanted to create a futuristic car. For many years Breer had been fascinated by flight, even studying birds and their forms in the air.

The vertical radiator, the separate headlamps and the upright windscreen – characteristic of cars in the early Thirties – were of course fatal to a streamlined shape. Instead, the whole front and the windscreen ought to lean backward, and the headlamps should be built into the body, if the car was to obey a fast flow of air past it.

Correct though the idea sounded, in practice everything turned out wrong. The worst that can happen to a car maker did happen – people refused to buy the product.

In 1934, the Airflow's first year, it was available with a straight-eight engine, as well as a six from the De Soto company. The eight-cylinder version had nearly 5 litres and gave 112 hp, enough for a top speed over 90 mph (150 km/h). There were also 5.3-litre and 6.3-litre eight-cylinder engines. None of these engines were especially modern, and they had been used for several years in other Chrysler cars.

Besides their appearance, which was widely regarded as peculiar, the Airflow cars acquired a reputation for careening

unsteadily – not exactly an attractive trait. Dubious behaviour on the road was bound to render their marketing situation still weaker.

The initial problem with the Airflow was that, despite being presented in January 1934, it could not be delivered until April. As a result, numerous impatient buyers cancelled their orders. Difficulties with delivery were exploited by competitors, who spread rumours about the new car and why it was delayed. The truth was that Chrysler did not dare to release such a bad product.

Many factors, therefore, contributed to the lack of a warm welcome when the Airflow at last could be delivered. It had simply lost respect before it was ready to be sold, and this is a cardinal mistake in the auto industry.

Nonetheless, the car possessed good features. One was a kind of self-supporting frame, consisting of steel profiles in a box form, on which the body panels were mounted. The engine had been moved forward and lay above the front axle – a position which was unusual in those days but became very common in the 1940s. The advantage was that neither the engine nor the gearbox encroached on the space for the passengers. All of the seats were between the axles, and there was plenty of room in both the front and back.

However, this did not help. Barely 11,000 Airflows were bought in 1934, while the conventionally built Chrysler models sold more than twice as well. Next year, the grille was changed in order to look more traditional, but it made no impact either. Customers continued to reject the car, and figures flaunted the fact. Sales declined annually by around a quarter – to 7,751 Airflows in 1935, and 5,911 in 1936, ending with only 4,391 in 1937.

Although the Airflow was an economic catastrophe for Chrysler, as a car model it was a pioneer that had several followers. Toyota's first own model, the AS, and Volvo's PV36 model Carioca are very similar to the Airflow – so similar that

chance can definitely be ruled out.

When one studies the "case" of the Airflow in retrospect, it is hard to understand that the body's relatively modest differences from other models could meet such resistance among buyers. Retracting the headlamps into the body and rounding them backward, sloping the grille and putting a little cover on the wheels: why were these measures so displeasing?

A possible explanation is that, at the time, it was mainly the richest Americans who bought cars. They tended to be older people and wanted nothing as shocking as a streamlined car. Theirs had to be a conformist conveyance, comprehensible to the crowd, not a novelty that nobody knew a thing about.

Ironically, the Chrysler Airflow is now a car with enormous collection value. The same is true of the Toyota and Volvo models that shared both its style and its lack of success. Occasionally, even a flop can hit the jackpot – all it needs is more time. ■

Cord 810/812

Cord 810

W HILE TASTE MAY BE A MATTER OF OPINION, one can well wonder whether Gordon Buehrig's creation from 1936 was not one of the most beautiful cars ever built. It was also a technical breakthrough.

The Model T Ford gave rise to an empire, and in its shadow countless companies appeared that, in one way or another, reflected "Tin Lizzie". Such a businessman was Erret Lobban Cord. He bought ailing T-Fords, repaired and polished them, sold them at high prices, and then turned to racing cars before starting a bus line between Arizona and Los Angeles. By the age of 21 he had made three fortunes and lost them just as fast.

Eventually Cord left Los Angeles and moved to Chicago, where he worked for an agency that sold Moon cars. After five years, earning $30,000 annually on commissions, he was named the best retailer in the state of Illinois.

Next, he took hold of the insolvent Auburn Automobile Company and, with experience from Ford days, soon managed to sell 700 cars that had been considered unsellable due to their ugliness. Now every Auburn was sold the moment it left the factory, and in 1925 Cord demanded ten percent of the company's shares. He was 30 years old and an auto manufacturer in his own right.

Cord's interest in the stock market had thus been awakened. In 1926 he bought the Duesenberg factory, which was technically quite advanced for the time. Further firms were absorbed into his realm, such as the Lycoming engine works and the Stinson Aircraft Corporation.

Once Cord decided to build a car with his name on it, he

120

1937 Cord 812

wanted it to be something special, so he opted for front-wheel drive. To cope with the design, he engaged the famous race-car designer Harry Miller.

What emerged was the Cord L29, presented in September 1929. Much lower than its competitors, it had lovely lines and won many Concours d'Elegance contests. But despite the enthusiastic reception, it immediately suffered hard from the crash on Wall Street. Nor was the public ready for front-wheel drive, and only 4,429 examples were sold by 1932.

Nothing daunted, Cord introduced a new front-wheel-drive car in 1934. The Cord 810 was extremely beautiful and drew the same ovations as its predecessor. While exhibiting it at fairs in Chicago and New York, Cord received 3,600 orders and had a queue of 7,640 buyers. But the company's economic problems delayed the production, and not until February

1936 did the first specimen take to the road.

Designed by Gordon Buehrig, the car was an aesthetic masterpiece from any angle. It had small window-panes, a streamlined coffin-like front, and retractable headlamps. The engine was a Lycoming V8 with 4729 cc and 125 hp at 3,500 rpm, bringing it to about 100 mph (165 km/h).

In 1936, only 1,174 were made. The company was in dire straits, and Cord's stock deals were coming apart at the seams. Desperately trying to resolve the situation, in 1937 he presented the Model 812, equipped with a centrifugal super-charger from Schwitzer & Cummings. This spun at a speed of 24,000 rpm and helped to boost the output to 195 hp. The car resembled the 810, but had an external exhaust pipe.

America, though, was still not prepared for such a pioneer-ing car, and Cord disappeared. ■

Fiat 500

Fiat 500, 1936

T HE MENTION OF FIAT DOUBTLESS MAKES MOST
people think of small cars. This is fair enough for the postwar
period – but before then, Fiat was definitely not a manufacturer of midgets. Its products were of normal size in the
"general" class of the time.

Nonetheless, Fiat was one of the automobile companies
quick to understand that the small car had a future, perhaps
due mainly to the economic problems of the Depression.

Fast profits could no longer be expected by a big-car
builder. To survive the crisis from the early 1930s onward,
cars needed modest dimensions with low price-tags. This
was the only chance for Fiat to hang on as a significant
manufacturer.

Instead of high profits on a few expensive cars, the aim
became a little profit on each of many cheap ones. Such a
philosophy led to the nickname *La Topolino* (Mickey Mouse)
for the Fiat 500.

Actually it was not much of a conveyance – only 326
centimetres long – but the 500 proved a huge success. Strictly
a two-seater, it had a flat-floored baggage-space at the rear,
where an optimist could squeeze in some half-grown
children. Sitting in back was, however, no ideal of comfort.

Moreover, the room meant for baggage could not be

reached from the outside through an ordinary hatch. As in
many contemporary cars, you had to get there by collapsing
the back of the front seats.

The engine delivered only 13 hp, an unimpressive feat. But
another trait of the tiny Fiat 500 was striking indeed. Rather
than making something between a car and a motorcycle, like
most of its competition, Fiat constructed what could only be
regarded – in spite of small size – as a real automobile. Consequently, you felt the right driving qualities on the road.

Due to its girder frame with weight-relieving holes, the 500
had a torsional stiffness that improved its handling. The chassis
did not twist when it bounced, so the work of providing a soft
ride was left to the wheel suspension.

Granted that the four-cylinder side-valve engine's volume
was a mere 569 cc, it played the same role as power plants in
big cars. The steering was a proper worm type, and the front
wheels were sprung individually with transverse leaves. The
live rear axle was hung in leaf springs, at first quarter-elliptic
and later semielliptic.

The Tipo 500, introduced in 1936, immediately appealed as much to housewives as to famous racing drivers. Among the latter were Prince Bira, Dick Seaman and Earl Howe. The model was constructed by Dante Giacosa, Fiat's chief designer for many years, and Franco Fessia.

The gearbox was four-speed at a time when most cars had just three gears. In fact, the four gears were essential to exploit the little engine's output well, so that the car could keep up with other traffic.

Fiat departed from a standard car design only by putting the radiator behind the engine, not in front. The reason was a desire to give the front body line a rounded shape. On this basis, a vertical radiator at the front took up too much space.

The Topolino soon became very popular. More than a practical money-saver, it also fired the enthusiasm of people who liked its compact form, as well as its manoeuvrability in tight spots. What better way to save the day in traffic-clogged cities such as Rome or Paris? And the fuel consumption was expressed in espresso-cups when other drivers spoke of decilitres.

Not that this could be a great racer. It hardly exceeded 70 km/h (45 mph), although its adequate structure made it fairly easy to trim. There were even conversion sets for transform-

ing the engine into an overhead-valve with excellent performance. A supercharger was used on some 500 models built for competition. In the 1937 Mille Miglia, all of thirty-two Fiat 500s met at the starting line.

Several versions of the 500 were produced. The two-seater's roof could originally be opened by rolling it back, but a full steel roof came later on. In addition, there was a genuine "Woodie" station-wagon, among the prettiest of its kind in the history of motoring – with solid wooden strips outside the plywood panels of its rear body. Yet on the estate model too, the whole body was turned into sheet metal when this became more available after World War II.

A bit over 120,000 of the original 500 had emerged by 1948, when the 500B arrived with an overhead-valve engine of 16 hp. From 1950 onward, the C model displayed a new grille, an external baggage-hatch, and a separate compartment for the spare tyre behind the rear number-plate.

Almost 400,000 of the B and C were to follow. ■

BMW 328

This 328 is renowned, as it was bought new by the prominent English racing driver Betty Haig.
To save money, she purchased it from a Hungarian BMW agent for £300. In England it would have cost £700.

NEW CAR MODELS ARE NORMALLY PRESENTED AT an automobile show somewhere in the world, but the BMW 328 made its début on a race course. It did so with emphasis, on 14 June 1936, enabling Ernst Henne to win in the 2-litre class of the Eifelrennen on Germany's Nürburgring.

BMW may not have as solid a reputation as the venerable Mercedes-Benz, but today its name stands for German quality and thoroughness. The company started in 1916 when two aircraft-engine makers merged into the Bayerischen Motoren Werke, which supplied the German and Austrian air forces with many a motor in World War I.

After the Versailles Peace Treaty, manufacture of such engines was impossible and BMW began in 1921 to produce others for cars, boats and motorcycles, as well as making pneumatic brakes. In 1923 the company introduced its first motorcycle, with a two-cylinder boxer engine of 500 cc and cardan drive. These features have ever since been characteristic of BMW's superb motorcycles.

At the end of 1928, BMW bought the Fahrzeugfabrik Eisenach, which licence-built a small English car, the Austin Seven, under the name Dixi 3/15PS. But in 1932 BMW broke the contract with Austin, wanting to make a more advanced car of its own. This initial all-BMW design was called the 3/20PS AM 1.

Several models followed, leading eventually to the 300 series. This range of numbers originally referred to design projects but, from 1934 onward, the last two figures indicated the engine's cylinder volume.

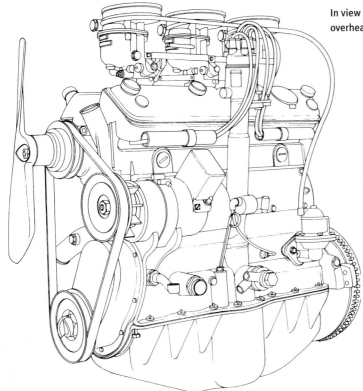

In view of the two valve covers, it is easy to believe that this is an engine with overhead camshafts (see the text for explanation).

The output of a 326 was at first 50 horsepower, increased to 80 hp by the new cylinder head. The top speed of a 328 was about 155 km/h (95 mph), but cars prepared with the help of the factor's trimming equipment could do over 190 km/h (120 mph) – which, in those days, was fantastic for a 2-litre sports car. Neither was the 328 awfully expensive. In 1937 it cost 7,400 Reichsmarks (equivalent to around £20,000 or $35,000 today), compared with three times as much for the cheapest Mercedes 500K.

The BMW 328 was a hugely successful race car and remained competitive as late as the 1950s. In 1952 it won a class victory in the Alpine Rally, and in 1958 it brought the Swedish driver Bosse Ljungfeld close to a sensation when he almost won the "Porsche class" in his country's *Kanonloppet*. Of the 462 examples built in all, several are still used in races for historical sports cars. ■

COMPETITIONS WERE CRUCIAL

From its very beginning, BMW took part officially in races. A team with 3/15 PS cars won a class victory in the 1929 Austrian Alpine race. The first BMW sports car, the 315/1, repeated the feat in 1934 – and in 1936 it was time for the BMW 328 to appear.

The design of this elegant little two-seater was due to Fritz Fiedler, who had previously worked for Horch. The frame was almost the same as on the BMW 319/1, and the engine block came from the BMW 326. But the 328's novelty was a cylinder head with a construction unique for its time.

In the head were hemispherical combustion chambers with oblique valves. The low-set camshaft controlled the intake valves as usual, via pushrods and rocker arms. But from the intake side's rocker-arm axle, horizontal pushrods worked transversely to move the exhaust valves through rocker arms. This system gave the same advantages as did double camshafts, yet was much cheaper to make.

The instrument panel is dominated by the speedometer and tachometer.

1940–1950

THE VERSAILLES PEACE TREATY OF 1919, so humiliating to Germany, had provoked thoughts of revenge, expressed in Adolf Hitler's aggressive politics and ominous rearmament, which led in turn to the German attack on Poland. Great Britain and France respond by declaring war on Germany, and a major European conflict begins. Life continues elsewhere: Initial treatments with penicillin on people prove beneficial. Nylon and Perlon hit the market. In New York, 18 members of the "Christian Front" are arrested for trying to cause a revolution, to replace the American government with

dictatorship; their large arsenal of weapons is confiscated. French police raid the Soviet trade office in Paris and arrest some of its "employees"; the Russians howl in protest. In Canada, too, the police crack down on Communist agitators. Molotov, the Soviet foreign minister, accuses the Western powers of hostile behaviour, saying that his country will stay neutral in a war involving them. He also objects to a suggested Scandinavian defensive alliance, which in his view would only yield plans for vengeance.

Winston Churchill becomes both Prime and Defence

The 1949 Alfa Romeo 6C-2500 Sport. Like the more normal models, it had a six-cylinder 2.5-litre engine with twin overhead camshafts, independent suspension all round, hydraulic brakes and (unfortunately) a steering-column gearshift. With 110 horsepower available, it could do 160 km/h (100 mph). It was also popular among body designers, and Pininfarina's cabriolet version is shown here. The standard Alfa grille was generally used, but this car's recalls that of Jaguar's in the late 1950s, and might have been either inspired by a vision of the future or borrowed from a subsequent model.

Minister of Great Britain. English troops arrive in Iceland to protect it from possible German invasion. Germany takes over Denmark and Norway – a loss of prestige for the Western powers, which were not entirely prepared for it. Belgium, the Netherlands and Luxembourg are also invaded by the Germans, who explain that they want to ensure these countries' neutrality in case the British and French attack from that direction. They proceed toward Paris, thwarting France's proud "Maginot Line" of defence. In June 1940 the French, once regarded as Europe's strongest military power, are crushed. Italy, an ally of Germany, declares war on Great Britain and France. The Germans bomb London. Finland surrenders to the Soviet power but is considered through her brave fight to have defended Western civilization. The Baltic states are left helpless and have to sign Soviet aid agreements, whereupon the Russians invade them and overthrow their democratic governments, setting up Communist puppets.

Refusing to negotiate peace with Hitler, the British carry on a solitary struggle. He tries to invade them, resulting in the "Battle of Britain" – but this requires Germany to achieve supremacy of the air, and it fails. Meanwhile, the United States supports Great Britain without going into combat. Italy invades Albania and is repulsed by the Greeks, then rescued by the Germans who conquer the whole Balkan peninsula. Drunk with success, Hitler thinks he can defeat the Soviet Union in a few weeks and occupy all of its European territory. Great Britain and the United States offer to help the Soviets against their common enemy. The Germans actually manage to get nearly as far as Moscow and Stalingrad, but the cold winters of 1941–42 and the stubborn Soviet resistance wear them down. At the same time, Britain's "desert rats" start to evict Rommel's from North Africa.

Despite setbacks, Hitler is planning a vast offensive toward the Middle East through Bulgaria, Libya and the Caucasus. One aim is to maintain supplies of oil, since military vehicles swallow plenty of fuel. Another is to link up with a fascist

Ferrari type 166

ally, Japan, and attack India as well as America. The United States is drawn into the war by a Japanese sneak attack on her bases in Hawaii (Pearl Harbor) and Guam in the Pacific Ocean. Great Britain also declares war on Japan, and the full scale of World War II is a fact.

Industrial production in Europe has almost entirely changed from civilian purposes to the manufacture of weapons, ammunition, and other tools for both defence and offence. Situations of crisis and conflict are often stimulating to ideas, and many clever inventions come to light now. An ingenious American example is the army jeep, advertised as able to do anything but make a bed. Germany has a similar terrain vehicle, the *Kübelwagen*, with an air-cooled engine. Designed by Ferdinand Porsche and based on the Volkswagen, it is followed by a four-wheel-drive amphibious car, the *Schwimmwagen*.

Ball-point pens commence their career, invented by a Hungarian, Ladislaus Biro. Synthetic materials, derived from silicon, are being made in variants such as lubricant oil and resin. Due to its excellent insulating properties, silicon paves the way for compact electrical devices and other products. The first atomic bomb is exploded in the desert of New Mexico. Suddenly even the moon can be seen on radar screens. A working computer is at last constructed, big as a house and

1 Bond 1949. **2** Citroën 2 CV. **3** Continental 1948. **4** Kaiser 1948. **5** Rovin 1948. **6** Lincoln V 12 1946.

Standard Vanguard

The Allard was lighter than pre-war "Anglo-American bastards", since it originated from trial competitions. Fairly simple in construction, it had a wheelbase of only 2.8 metres – and mediocre performance, as the engine was Ford's old faithful 3.6-litre side-valve V8.

containing 18,000 vacuum tubes. EP (Extended Play) and LP (Long Play) gramophone records are introduced in America. At the Mount Palomar Observatory in California, the world's largest reflecting telescope is inaugurated. The carbon-14 method for exactly dating ancient bones is presented.

The Japanese expand rapidly across the islands of the Pacific. They occupy much of Burma, Sumatra, Borneo, the Celebes, New Guinea and the Philippines. But in Europe the allies make great strides against Germany, thanks to the United States, and the Soviet Union is no longer threatened on the eastern front. Italy's dictator Benito Mussolini is toppled. The American, British and Soviet leaders – Franklin D. Roosevelt, Winston Churchill and Joseph Stalin – hold

The 1948 Cadillac typified an American private limousine in the late 1940s. Its arched windshield, large rear window and rudimentary tail-fins (these being inspired by the Lockheed P38, a twin-engine wartime fighter plane) pointed toward things to come. Most of the year's cars were equipped with the Hydramatic automatic transmission, first used by Oldsmobile in 1940. However, the engine was still the traditional side-valve V8 from 1936, with 150 horsepower and 5.71 litres. This was its last season, though it remained effective enough to give the heavy body a top speed over 95 mph (150 km/h). Costing 2,833 dollars (about 1,000 pounds sterling), the car seems cheap compared with later prices, but it could empty a bank account at the time.

conferences. When Italy surrenders, Germany is weakened and her other allies begin to disappear. An attempt is made to assassinate Hitler, partly by some of his own officers. A combined American and British invasion of Normandy and southern France foreshadows the end of the war. The Germans retreat from France and Belgium. Another top-level conference takes place at Yalta. Finally Germany surrenders, and Europe feels a deep debt to the United States. Roosevelt suffers a stroke and dies.

Since the Japanese prefer to negotiate rather than surrender, the Americans put pressure on them by dropping atomic bombs on Hiroshima and Nagasaki. The Soviet Union

1949 Oldsmobile

Peugeot 203

1949 Chrysler Town and Country

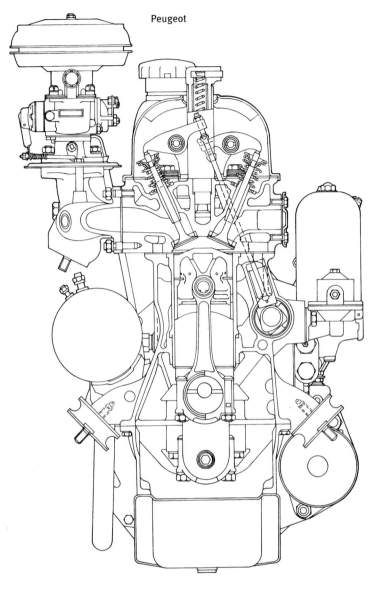

Peugeot

Both Oldsmobile and Peugeot 203 had engines with hemispherical combustion chambers. The Oldsmobile V8 engine generated 135 hp, while Peugeot was satisfied with 42 hp from its 1290-cc engine.

A very different convertible was Chrysler's Town and Country. Early examples had mahogany panels which, by 1949, gave way to a blend of real and imitation wood. The engine was the old straight-eight of 5.3 litres and 135 horsepower. Not until 1951 did the legendary V8 with hemispherical combustion chambers arrive.

declares war on Japan and occupies Manchuria. Only then does Japan surrender unconditionally. Churchill, who has successfully led Great Britain through the war, loses an election and the Labour party, under Clement Attlee, forms a socialist government. To guarantee world peace, the United Nations is founded. The British grant independence to their old colonies India, Ceylon and Burma, yet Churchill accuses Labour of "dismantling the Empire".

An American economic aid initiative – the European Recovery Program, popularly called the Marshall Plan – is presented by Secretary of State George Marshall to rebuild Europe after the war. None of the Communist countries accept it, but sixteen West European nations form the Organization for European Economic Cooperation (OEEC) to administer and distribute the aid. During the next four years, about 15 billion U.S. dollars are contributed. Germany divides into East and West, while the Soviet Union consolidates its power all over Eastern Europe. With the Marshall Plan and hard work, the West Germans quickly regain their industrial and economic strength.

In 1948, Mahatma Gandhi is murdered in India, and the British Mandate in Palestine is replaced by the State of Israel, which then goes to war with Arab countries. Berlin is divided administratively into eastern and western sectors, because the Soviets allow German Communists to oppose the city's democratic authorities. The "Cold War" takes on sharp outlines. A defensive alliance, the North Atlantic Treaty

Organization (NATO), is formed by the United States and Canada with several European countries. In China, the Communists triumph under Mao Tse-Tung, and Chiang Kai-Shek flees to Formosa (Taiwan). Another colonial bastion falls at decade's end, when the United States of Indonesia obtains full sovereignty from the Netherlands. ∎

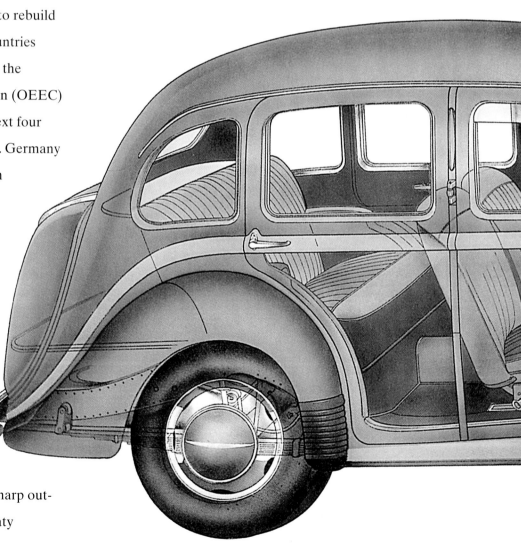

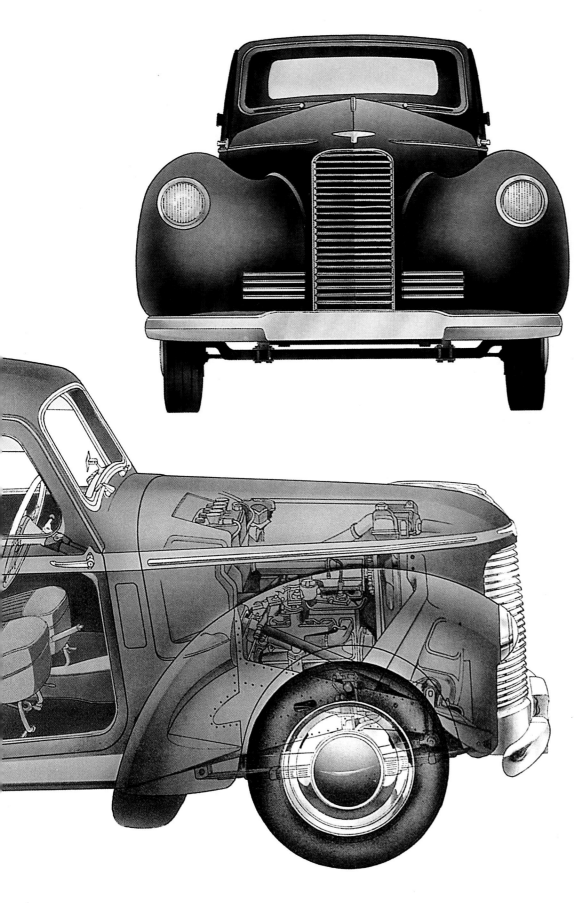

Hillman Minx

You thought you were buying a brand-new postwar model...but the improvisations could be extreme, as is illustrated by this 1948 Hillman Minx model, the Phase II. Its front end (*left*) looks entirely fresh, due to the built-in headlamps and the American-style three-part grille. The alligator bonnet, though, existed already on the Phase I, made between 1940 and 1947.

The elementary three-bearing side-valve engine (*below*) was to be kept until 1954. Its 1185 cc developed only 35 horsepower, since the Rootes company had not yet celebrated the abolition of the horse-power-tax system by boring up the engine. But the truth is revealed in the cutaway view (*below left*): the car's design was a survival from 1938-39, now with monocoque chassis/bodywork and some superficial changes to modernize its appearance. Also still present (in their final season) were the long, semielliptic front springs. Tiring, and rather unreliable, Bendix mechanical brakes were another relic.

Nonetheless, the Minx was a trusty little worker. It could run all day long at nearly its top speed, about 65 mph (105 km/h). This was not advisable, however, if one wanted to drive as far as possible on a moderate amount of fuel. The consumption, advertised as 8 litres per 100 kilometres (around 30 miles per gallon), easily became worse by 50% or more if the driver stamped on the gas pedal.

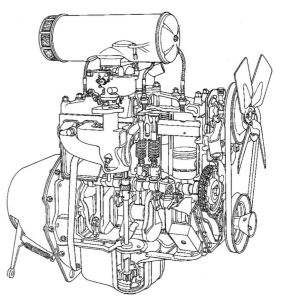

Willys Jeep

The Jeep in its proper surroundings. This picture was taken somewhere in France, just after the Allied invasion of Normandy in June 1944.

IT MAY WELL BE TRUE THAT THE MODEL T FORD PUT THE world on wheels, but there has never been a utility vehicle as widely used as the Jeep – first in military hands, and then among civilians..

After the rapid German advances in the beginning of World War II, it occurred to the American armed forces that a light terrain-going conveyance was needed. Thus, in June 1940, the U.S. Ordnance Technical Committee announced the requirements for such an automobile. It was to have low weight, a low silhouette, great mobility and speed, and four-wheel drive.

Of the 135 firms invited to submit offers, just three did so: the Bantam Car Company, the Ford Motor Company, and Willys-Overland. Only Bantam managed to deliver a prototype within the stated limit of 49 days. All three manufacturers proceeded to do intensive development work, but in the end it was Willys that got the first contract – for 16,000 Jeeps.

Subsequently, Ford also produced Jeeps on licence. From 1942 onward, the bodies were built by the American Manufacturing Corporation in Connersville, Indiana – an offshoot of Auburn and Cord, whose cars are described elsewhere in this book. The term "Jeep" was actually a nickname, derived from the designation "GP" (General Purpose), and was not used officially until after the war.

Originally the model was called the Willys MB. It had a four-cylinder engine of 2199 cc, giving 60 horsepower at 4,000 rpm. The three-speed gearbox was coupled to a two-step auxiliary box with gear ratios of 1.97:1 and 1.00:1. In third and high gears, the top speed was 65 mph (105 km/h). The front axle was full-floating and, with no trailer, the car could climb a grade of 60%.

Between December 1941 and the summer of 1945, a total of 639,245 Jeeps was produced. Many were also sent to Allied countries; some even had propellers and could move on water. Everyone loved the Jeep, and it was said to be capable of anything except making a bed. The American motoring journalist Michael Lamm once wrote: "For thousands of soldiers the Jeep was the closest thing to a sports car of all the automobiles they had driven: roadster body, separate cupped seats, collapsible windshield, fast and exact steering, steady suspension and good performance. Everybody wanted one."

After the war, there was indeed a huge demand for the Jeep, as it had proved its worth. And people were no longer doubtful about four-wheel drive, as in the days when Auburn and Cord presented such cars. Jeeps fitted into all sorts of activities in a world that was reviving and rebuilding in peacetime.

Today the techniques of four-wheel drive are entirely accepted, not only in terrain vehicles but in ordinary passenger cars. Every major automobile company has four-wheel-drive models in its range. The Jeep is still manufactured, but the make is now owned by DaimlerChrysler. ■

1998 Jeep Wrangler

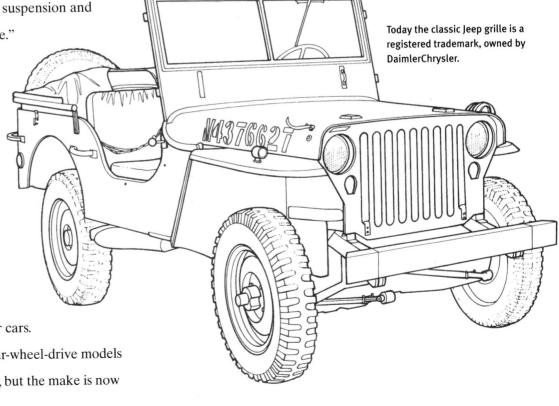

Today the classic Jeep grille is a registered trademark, owned by DaimlerChrysler.

M.G. Midget TC

THE M.G. TC IS INDEED A CLASSIC – THOUGH perhaps not remarkable as a car, for it was already old when it was new. Its proportions were extraordinarily harmonious, even when the soft top was up.

Origins of the TC can be found as far back as the M.G. M-Type, the first Midget model, which we describe in another chapter. The Midget cars were small two-seaters (with a few exceptions), had four-cylinder engines and were quite easy to drive. Their performance could not be bragged about, but their excellent handling got ahead of most other vehicles on the narrow roads in England.

Moreover, they were cheap and this enhanced their popularity. One paid £175 for an M-Type in 1929–30, and £222 for a PB in 1935, whereas in 1945 the economic situation forced the price of a TC up to £375 (equivalent to about £7,500 today) – not including the loathsome "purchase tax"

Not many cars have done as much to arouse Americans' interest in sports cars as the M.G. TC. Plenty of soldiers who were stationed in Great Britain during the Second World War drove it, and took it home afterward. An M.G. of one kind or another was also to be seen in numerous war films.

introduced by the postwar government.

At the same time, the British industry was urged to go all-out for export, since the country had nearly gone broke due to the war. Luck was with the M.G. factory in Abingdon, as no bombs had fallen on it. Orders streamed in for what was now called the TC – basically a TB Midget from 1939 with some modifications. The two models are hard for anyone but an expert to tell apart.

In view of the car industry's problems with steel supplies, it is phenomenal that M.G. built 81 cars by the end of 1945. The very next year saw a TC manufacturing run of 1,675.

SORRY, NO OVERHEAD CAM

The initial M.G. Midgets had an overhead camshaft on the four-cylinder engine. Yet in 1935, when Lord Nuffield sold the M.G. Car Company to Morris Motors, these firms began to coordinate their production. The new TA Midget, which emerged in 1936, received a "boring" pushrod engine from the Wolseley Ten.

M.G. enthusiasts were dismayed, having expected something much better. But in fact the TA was a great step for-

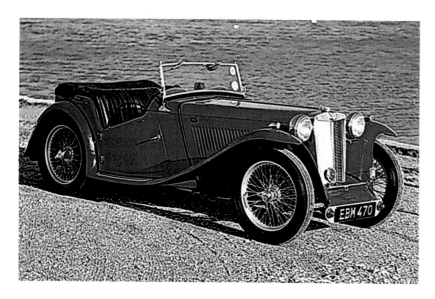

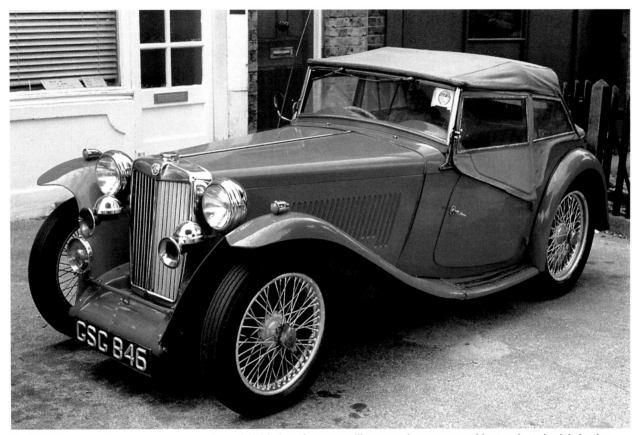

The M.G. TC was a car that became even more beautiful with the soft top up, unlike many other open cars with a top that ruined their otherwise fine lines. This TC was noticed on a walk in London during the early 1970s. Its horn and extra lamp are not original.

ward. It had more space, speed and flexibility. Built until 1939, it was replaced by the TB, which enjoyed only a few months of production. Such was the foundation that gave rise to the M.G. TC.

Like its predecessors, the TC used a simple beam frame, swinging up over the live front axle. Between the main beams stretched five crossbars, and at the height of the pedals stood a firewall holding, among other things, the tool and battery box. Both the front and rear ends had leaf springs and hydraulic shock absorbers.

The four-cylinder 1.2-litre Wolseley engine generated a modest 54.5 horsepower, but this could be boosted considerably with trimming accessories. The gearbox had four speeds, and a TC accelerated in 23 seconds to 60 mph (0–100 km/h). Its

maximum of 73 mph (117 km/h) sounds dull for a sports car – yet as every driver of an open car knows, one need not go fast to feel that one is flying.

Exactly ten thousand were built, of which 2,001 came to the USA. In our day, the TC is much-sought by collectors and can still be bought for a comfortable sum, relative to what is asked for a Ferrari, Aston Martin or Maserati. Furthermore, the TC is easy to tinker with, and many specialist firms live on renovating and delivering spare parts.

In 1949 the M.G. TC was succeeded by a completely new Midget, the TD. This was produced in 29,644 examples, no fewer than 23,488 being exported to America – which by then had acquired an appetite for sports cars that were cramped, impractical and noisy. ∎

Tucker Torpedo

Swindler or genius? This is the question posed by Preston Tucker, who made one of the most spectacular postwar automobiles in America. The likelihood is that he was neither, but an enthusiast who just did not have a businessman's gift of the gab.

A swindle is widely claimed to lie in the fact that Tucker collected over 20 million dollars, and then vanished, without literally selling a single vehicle. In all, 51 cars were reputedly made, and were used for public relations or test purposes. Of these, 22 survive today.

Tucker was clever at promising that his new product would be a breakthrough, offering what the country's car industry had been unable to manufacture. Whether or not this was the actual intention – a mystery which will remain unsolved – the outcome was that no genuine production took place, and the investors lost their money. For a few dozen four-wheelers, the cost was phenomenal.

Another rumour is that the American industry did its best to stop Tucker's car, and was helped by extremely corrupt

officials in the national bureaucracy. Here we would be wrong to believe much, if anything. The industry had little cause to be afraid of Tucker, and probably not a single dollar in bribes was needed to kill the car: it expired by itself.

Preston Tucker was seemingly so obsessed with the notion of creating a distinctive car that it gained an audience for that very reason. And he went far toward succeeding. The car had beautiful lines and a central spotlight at the front; it must have been generally admired. Not only that, but the technology was advanced. Streamlined bodies, derived from the shapes of aircraft, were all the rage after World War II, and gave rise to long rear sections on the most modern cars. Since the roof became low in back, the passengers had to be moved forward, so a rear location for the engine was ideal. However, this logical approach ruined the road-handling properties.

Nor was the engine exceptional. The postwar shortage of raw materials forced Tucker to take whatever he could get, and this turned out to be a 6-cylinder boxer engine from a helicopter. With good will, one might call it thrilling: such all-aluminium engines were not common, especially with a volume as large as 9.5 litres. It delivered a modest 150 hp, and its low speed of 1,800 rpm was supposedly so free of wear that the engine could be run for 300,000 kilometres with no renovation.

At first, instead of a gearbox, the car used only a torque converter between the engine and transmission; later a four-speed box was added. A 24-volt electrical system was standard – as were disc brakes on all wheels, which had independent suspension as well.

Safety concepts were extraordinarily advanced, at least in theory. Each seat had a belt, and the body was said to be built so that the windscreen would pop out during a collision, to

The design is typical of the period, with a drawn-out rear end, so it is hard to guess
that the Tucker Torpedo actually had the engine in back. The car was made in only one year – 1948.

avoid injuring the passengers. Still, the car's heavy tail made driving quite dangerous, notably on ice, and did not suit a real concern for safety.

It soon became obvious that the initial cars were monstrosities. The engine was replaced by a smaller 6-cylinder boxer, with an automatic gearbox as standard. The originally mid-mounted steering wheel was moved to the left side, and the three swinging headlamps merged into the central one, which followed the front wheels in the turns.

The best feature was the amazing speed provided by the new engine's 166 horsepower. In 1959, a car was clocked at 131 mph (211 km/h) in test runs on the Bonneville Salt Flats.

Tucker's plan was to begin production in the biggest factory hall of the time, in Chicago. This had previously been owned by Dodge and used for making airplane engines. To get enough starting capital, Tucker sold contracts to almost 1,000 retailers, promised fat future benefits, and issued shares to the public for about 20 million dollars. We should remember that the United States, like the rest of the world, was shouting for

new cars in the wake of the war. The ease of attracting money for an automobile project, therefore, was not as surprising as it may sound today.

But Tucker's way of gathering funds also aroused the interest of the stock-market supervisors, and he was accused of fraud. After a long trial, he found himself acquitted – and broke. His reputation was worse than tarnished, and the car project collapsed.

Preston Tucker was undoubtedly naive in thinking that he could invent a new, exclusive make of American automobile. Moreover, the problematic design with its rear engine, the unacceptably poor quality, and the much too low price advertised for the car, did not help matters a bit. Consequently, the Tucker Torpedo died before it was properly born.

Arguments continue in motoring circles as to whether Tucker did want to build cars, or whether he simply saw a chance to cheat people by using a car for bait. At all events, the car involved was hardly such a stroke of genius that it would have sold in great numbers. ■

The VW Story

MASSES OF BOOKS HAVE BEEN WRITTEN ON, AND under, the spell of the VW phenomenon. Technicians, economists, social scientists and, not least, politicians have tried to explain how such a car could become a world leader. For actually it was not qualified to play that role.

In the first place, we should keep in mind the relative rarity of small cars during the 1930s. England had succeeded with the Austin Seven, which spread to Germany as the BMW Dixie and to France as the Rosengart. Fiat had begun to think in tiny terms; so had Renault. But as a clear alternative to big cars, small ones scarcely existed. Cars in the Thirties were toys of the rich, and the little man in the street was not yet considered a strong market force.

Certainly, though, cheap automobiles were "on the way". Makers had mulled over Henry Ford's triumphs in America, with the Model T and next the A, which sold more or less universally. These achievements showed that the commoner's car consumption was not to be chuckled at.

Ferdinand Porsche, who had his own design office at Stuttgart in the 1930s, was hired by the German motorcycle company Zündapp to create a small car, with a radial engine at the rear. Three prototypes were constructed, but soon the design turned out to be too complex for mass production, and the idea of a Zündapp small car died out.

Another German maker of motorcycles, NSU, caught onto the idea and asked Porsche to come up with a small car on torsion springs, its rear engine being air-cooled. The four resultant prototypes bore obvious similarities to what would later be the Volkswagen. But NSU, too, had to put the plan aside, mainly because of an agreement with Fiat not to manufacture small cars. One might think that NSU should have remembered this agreement before the design work started, but there are many dark spots in the story.

HITLER WANTED A WORKERS' CAR

Like thunder and lightning, though, a new financier appeared. Only a month after becoming Chancellor of the Reich in 1933, Adolf Hitler said at the opening of the Berlin car exhibition: "Without cars, sound films and radio, there will be no victory for National Socialism."

A year later, when the next car show opened, he declared: "I see no reason why millions of honest, hard-working people should be prevented from owning a car."

By then, Porsche had begun to design a car that Hitler was very interested in. It had a rather round shape and looked like a beetle, so it quickly earned the nickname *Der Käfer* (beetle).

In June 1934, Porsche signed a detailed contract for developing an automobile with the name Volkswagen (people's car). It was to have a top speed of 100 km/h (62 mph), expend at most 8 litres per 100 km (around 30 miles per gallon), and cost no more than 1,000 Reichsmarks (roughly 4,000 U.S. dollars today).

The last requirement did not please Porsche. He knew it

would be difficult to hold that price. Opel's little 1.2-litre model cost 1,800 Reichsmarks and the small DKW cost 1,750. But when his car started to sell in 1938, it asked for just 995 Reichsmarks. At least 5 per month were to be deposited and, when paid off, the car would be delivered.

This payment scheme was called KdF (*Kraft durch Freude*, strength through joy), and initially the car was termed the *KdF-Wagen*. But the scheme vanished after the war, when deliveries to ordinary buyers began, so that term was dropped and the name Volkswagen remained.

It was meant to be a tough car with no need of a garage. Since air cannot freeze or boil, the engine was made air-cooled, thus avoiding a number of problems in contemporary cars. Only 25 horsepower were drawn from the original engine of 1000 cc, which did not strain it much even at top speed, thereby increasing its reliability and lifetime.

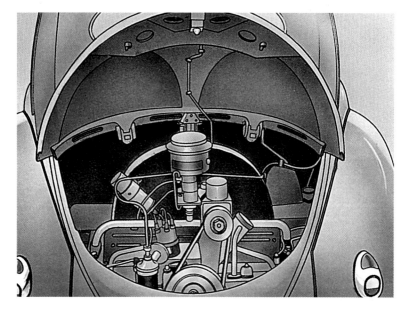

The suspension was of torsion type at both the front and rear, a system that very seldom breaks. Torsion springs also enabled the wheels to be hung independently, yielding greater comfort than on the normal live axle at each end.

In sum, the Volkswagen had quite a robust structure, contrasting with most other small cars in its dependability and durability. You had only to jump in and drive away; troubles were rare indeed. Driving it, however, was not the best of experiences.

As the engine and gearbox were in back, the heavy rear tended to cause skidding on slippery roads. This behaviour was not improved by the swing axles, which allowed the wheels to fold. Hence the car could be overturned by a strong side force, for example when the steering-wheel spun.

The heating was somewhat symbolic. Cold air passing the cylinders warmed up only slightly, and had to be fanned through ducts from behind the engine to the car's front floor and windscreen, losing most of its warmth on the way.

As for safety, it was not even thought of. The fuel tank lay

The "Beetle" was not a spacious car, as the suitcases behind the rear seat might suggest. They cannot have been very large. Certainly the front end also held baggage, but a family on holiday with two children could not take along much – unless a roof-rack was added, and this was a popular accessory.

above the front passengers' legs, so a head-on crash usually made the tank burst, starting a fire. The chassis had a central tube for longitudinal reinforcement and, with the transverse torsion springs in front, it collided like a metal stamp, absorbing no energy at all. This task was left to the passengers' bodies, which also got banged up because the interior was completely metallic.

But people did not worry about such things in those days. The point was to put together a car that would be cheap to buy, to run and – most importantly – to own. And the Volkswagen fit the recipe.

Few cars have managed to compete with the VW as a trustworthy, long-lasting vehicle. For a while, the company actually gave gold watches to drivers who reached 100,000 kilometres – an amazing distance even well into the 1950s.

CHEAP TO OWN

Another novel feature was that VW maintained an efficient sales and workshop organization which took good care of its customers. The cost of ownership was also lowered by using factory-renovated replacements instead of new components.

Many of the car's evident disadvantages could therefore be outweighed by its excellent economy, not to mention all else – and this was a guarantee of success. Throughout automotive history, we often find that technical refinements and clever designs are beaten by a solid appeal to simplicity and to the money in our pockets.

Nothing more is needed to solve the mystery of why a bug like the VW Type 1, whose chances should have been quite slim, became perhaps the most familiar machine ever to take the road.

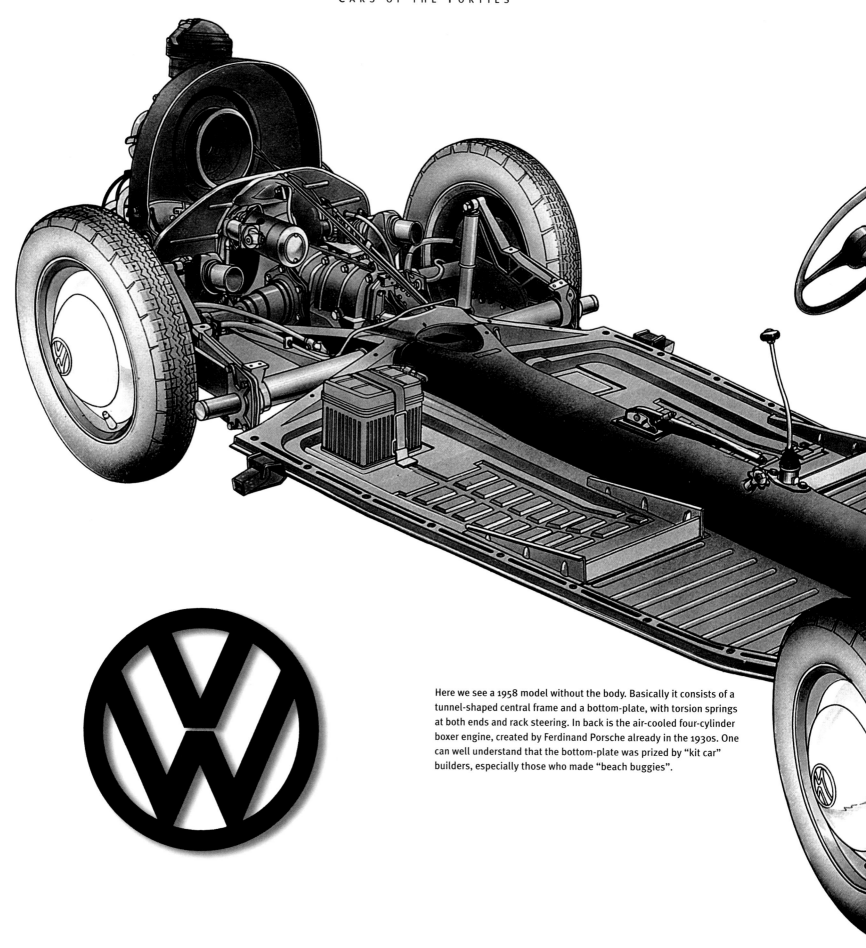

Here we see a 1958 model without the body. Basically it consists of a tunnel-shaped central frame and a bottom-plate, with torsion springs at both ends and rack steering. In back is the air-cooled four-cylinder boxer engine, created by Ferdinand Porsche already in the 1930s. One can well understand that the bottom-plate was prized by "kit car" builders, especially those who made "beach buggies".

When Volkswagen resumed manufacture after World War II, something close to an ultimate model could be found in a series of test cars, designated W 30 because of their number, which were built by Daimler Benz in 1937.

These cars had the so-called E-engine that was designed by Franz Reimspiess, an Austrian who also created the VW emblem. It was a boxer-type engine with four opposed cylinders, a volume of 984 cc, and a central camshaft that operated overhead valves via pushrods. The cylinder head was made of aluminium, with a long intake tube to the single

carburettor. Due to its air-cooling, the engine was rather noisy, especially since the exhaust system was short and included only one transverse sound-damper just behind the engine.

The next year saw Daimler Benz produce a further series of prototypes, known as VW 38. They emerged in May 1938 at about the same time as Hitler laid the cornerstone for a Volkswagen factory near Fallersleben, about 80 kilometres east of Hannover. Here grew a city, planned largely by his architect Albert Speer and named for the KdF-Wagen itself, to become Wolfsburg after the war.

The first Volkswagens did not leave the factory until May 1940, when the war had begun and civilian industry stopped. So the cars went to official administrations, and only 630 were made, as the production was turned into the Type 82. This vehicle, built essentially on the same bottom as the ordinary VW, was intended for military use.

Called the *Kübelwagen*, it had a jeep-like open body with four seats, higher road clearance and a bigger engine of 1131 cc, and differential braking for the powered rear wheels. There was also a special damper, with a hydraulic cylinder, to prevent the steering-wheel from twisting when the front wheels shook. Thus the car could travel fairly fast even on bad roads or moderate terrain. A simplified form of the steering damper became standard on the series-produced cars after the war.

More than 50,000 such jeeps were manufactured between 1940 and early 1945. Being cooled by air instead of water, their engines served as well in the hot deserts of North Africa under Rommel as in the icy winters on the Russian front.

Yet another military version of the VW was made during the war – the *Schwimmwagen*. As the name showed, it did not have to stay on land. Though basically still a VW, it had a

From an angle like this, the 1952 Beetle seemed bound to give a feeling of claustrophobia inside. Actually it did not: the VW 1200 was at least as roomy as the smallest cars today, although not as safe to drive. In 1952 a total of 114,348 were made, compared to 44,000 for the Opel Olympia.

boat-like bottom and could float. At the rear was a down-folding propeller that engaged an axle extending from the engine's crankshaft. This arrangement drove it forward in the water, crudely steered by turning the front wheels as usual.

The Schwimmwagen had four-wheel power and a five-speed manual gearbox. Because of its more advanced construction, however, only about 14,000 examples were produced for the war. Today, along with the Kübelwagen, it is a coveted collectors' object.

Even in the midst of the conflict, Porsche continued to develop his car models. For instance, experiments were done with turbocharged engines, diesel engines, and synchronized gearboxes. The Volkswagen factory also supplied items ranging from aircraft parts – such as engines and the shell of the V-1 flying bomb – to stoves for heating households.

The company's peacetime manufacture began already in June 1945, with 138 of the Kübelwagen. Its chassis was used for the next model, the "501", which had a four-door body. A few of the ordinary VW sedan cars were made, too, but this line did not really get under way until 1946.

Hopeless, said the British and American automobile experts, who were supposed to evaluate Volkswagen's possibilities in the future car business. Nobody wanted such a car, they claimed, expecting the whole effort to fail. They only approved of keeping the factory going in order to create jobs for the war-torn country.

As we know, fortune had more than relief work in store for VW at Wolfsburg. It was to be one of the century's star cars in the great drama of popular transport. ■

Morris Minor

WHILE MANY REMARKABLE MODELS HAVE emerged from Morris through the years, perhaps none has been more popular than the modern one which launched the postwar era: the Minor.

Immediately after the war, Morris produced the 8 and 10 models. These, however, were not novel designs but slightly modernized cars from the Thirties. Alec Issigonis, a brilliant automobile designer with Greek roots, joined Morris as a development engineer in 1936. During the later years of World War II, he laid plans for a modern car to follow it.

This construction, called the Mosquito, had a body that was regarded then as nicely streamlined, the front wings extending onto the doors. Several types of engine were tried, such as a "boxer" with opposed cylinders and, oddly enough, a three-cylinder two-stroke. Yet they failed to impress the directors, who settled for the old reliable side-valve engine of 918 cc and 27 horsepower. Its abilities were well known, as it had been in use since 1934.

At London's first car show after the war, in October 1948, the new Morris Minor created by Alec Issigonis was shown to the public. A two-door saloon, it looked a bit blunt – and its width was unusually great for the time, mainly so that the intended boxer engine would fit between the front wheels. With a wheelbase of 218 cm and a total length of only 374 cm, the width made its shape almost squarish. The head-

William Richard Morris, later to become Lord Nuffield, took a tangled track through life, to say the least. He began as a bicycle-maker and learned the craft from the bottom up. At that time, when the century was young, no prefabricated parts existed for the purpose and his knowledge as a smith came in very handy. Eventually he progressed to be a motorcycle manufacturer and a workshop owner of the Morris Garage.

As early as 1910 Morris started planning to make automobiles on a large scale, which meant a cheap car that people could afford. The first sketches for it were drawn up at the Morris Garage in Cowley, a suburb of Oxford. Worth mentioning is that the same workshop, led by Cecil Kimber, rebuilt the original Morris Oxford cars with more sporting performance, resulting in a new name – MG (Morris Garage). 🚗

1956 Morris Minor Series II

Morris Minor 1948

lamps, pulled down to the grille, added to its snub-nosed appearance.

Apart from independent front-wheel suspension with torsion bars, the car was conventionally built with a live rear axle and leaf springs. A floor lever shifted the four-speed gearbox. As for space, the interior seemed ample and the boot had an external hatch, which was somewhat uncommon in those days.

Despite the fairly sluggish side-valves under its bonnet, the Morris Minor was relatively good to drive. It stood up solidly against competitors, and became much better in 1952 when given the same engine as the Austin A30. This featured over-head valves, 803 cc and all of 30 hp. Most importantly, though, the A-engine, destined to be a classic, was easy to tune.

In 1953 came the Traveller, a station-wagon with wooden strips along its sides. As an estate car, the Morris Minor thus acquired a special look, and plenty of people fell for its charm rather than its performance and practicalities.

Austin's engine grew in 1956 to 948 cc and 37 hp, which naturally went into the Minor as well, besides modernization with a one-piece windscreen and a wider rear window. The instruments were also changed to a single large central panel. In 1962 the power was increased again to 1098 cc and 48 hp,

giving the Minor a top speed of no less than 80 mph (130 km/h). The model continued for many years, but modifications were ever fewer.

Production ceased for the saloon car in November 1970, and for the Traveller in April 1971. By then, over 1.5 million Minors had been made – one of England's favourite small cars was finished.

The Morris Minor's huge sales success paved the way for sound economy in the Nuffield concern, or British Motor Corporation (BMC), and enabled new models to be developed. While it, and the Austin A30, made money for the company, Alec Issigonis designed an entirely new car – the "Doghouse". But that is another story.

Even today, the Morris Minor is much appreciated not only by collectors, but also by individuals who really enjoy using it. In England, some firms specialize in fully renovating the Minor, and keep stocks of spare parts that would make any car manufacturer envious. ■

Studebaker Champion

In 1902, the famous inventor Thomas Alva Edison built the first electric car that bore Studebaker's name. For some years, the company proceeded to bring out simple electric cars with bicycle wheels and leather fenders.

Further products were on the way. The first Studebaker whose parts were wholly made within the company appeared in 1913. A wide range of models spanned the 1920s and 1930s, when Studebaker tended to mirror the rest of the industry and maintained average standards.

Not until Raymond Loewy and Virgil Exner presented their ideas of the "New Look" for cars after World War II did Studebaker attract serious attention. Earlier automobiles had fenders that were more or less visible in the body shape. The fenders might be rounded, extended onto the doors, detached, or of the plain jeep type – but you could see that the fenders were there. Studebaker's lines were novel in displaying no fenders at all.

This style was called the "torpedo", suggesting that the car was a projectile, looking much the same from either end. As a result, many people wondered whether its engine was at the front or rear. Indeed, discussions about where to put the engine had occurred during the planning process. Other American manufacturers, too, were taking up the idea of a rear engine. What ultimately became the Lincoln V12 was a rear-engine prototype in the Thirties – and Preston Tucker,

When Studebaker passed away in 1966, it was among America's oldest automobile companies. In 1852, the Studebaker brothers started to make horse-drawn wagons. Orders poured in during the Civil War, and production flourished so far that, in 1872, Studebaker was considered the world's largest manufacturer of wagons. According to legend, a new wagon left the factory every seven minutes, which was not bad in the nineteenth century.

Towards 1900, an electric car is said to have been built, but no details are known about it. What we do find is that Studebaker, around the turn of the century, was delivering carriages to other makers of electric cars. 🚗

1939 Studebaker Champion

also one of the eccentric car makers, used the same concept.

The new Studebaker was an instant hit. Its style excited buyers and in the first year, 1946, nearly 230,000 cars were sold, setting a record. Why it won such popularity is debatable, but there was certainly a great need for cars after the war. Automobile manufacture had been virtually stopped in the United States for some years, with all industry concentrated on military

Studebaker Champion, 1949

production. Probably almost any kind of new car could have been sold, and if it resembled a moon rocket – clearly inspired by flying – it was bound to prove appealing.

However, the vehicle itself was not very advanced. Two different 6-cylinder side-valve engines were available, with 2779 cc in the Champion model and 3706 cc in the Commander. At both front and rear, the axles were live with leaf springs, laid transversely in front. As time passed, the body lines changed little, only the front being given a new look each year. In 1950, an enormous central nose-cone was added, strongly resembling that of an airplane – and the front transverse spring was replaced by independent suspension with spiral springs. A year later, the V8 engine arrived.

In 1952, Studebaker celebrated its hundredth anniversary as a carriage-maker, having produced over seven million cars. The "New Look" was alone responsible for millions of them. Yet it disappeared in 1953 and led to a still more refined body form.

The enormous contemporary demand for cars was, of course, not the sole explanation for Studebaker's success with the Champion and Commander from 1946 onward. Their fresh shape was a real innovation, and pointed to better times for the world in the future. Such a style meant that the dark memories of the war could be left behind.

In any case, it must be admitted that these cars were handsome. Whoever drove a Studebaker during the late 1940s was conspicuous in traffic. And that was quite enough reason to buy one. ■

Citroën 2 CV

IT ALL BEGAN WITH A SIMPLE ORDER FROM CITROËN'S administrative director, Pierre-Jules Boulanger:

Build a car that can carry four passengers and a 50-kilogram sack of potatoes, with a minimum top speed of 60 km/h (37 mph), using at most 3 litres of fuel per 100 km (around 85 miles per gallon). And it should not cost more than a third the price of a Citroën 11CV Traction Avant.

Rising to this challenge already in 1936, Citroën's engineers built what was to be one of the world's best-known cult cars, the Citroën Deux Chevaux (two horses).

Quite early on, a large number of prototypes were constructed – 250 or 300 of them, according to various sources – so as to evaluate the planned vehicle properly.

It was not exactly a beauty. The nose looked like a waterfall of corrugated metal. At the front was a big crank, because the car had no starter motor. There was only one headlamp, as another would have added 6 kg and the craze was to save weight; besides, the law did not demand two.

The entire body was made of aluminium, magnesium being used for the wheel suspension. Although the gearbox lacked a reverse, the car was so light that it could easily be backed up by hand. Torsion springs provided the ride, and the roof consisted of cloth stretched over an aluminium frame. The same canvas was used to cover the steel seats.

In contrast to its status today, this contraption deserved no worship at the outset. For an ordinary person without mechanical training, even its basic service was almost impossible to do. Check the oil level in the gearbox? First unscrew five bolts on the right front wing and lift out the battery! Or remove the carburettor? Take away the whole engine – and it was so hard to reach that your hands had to be like snakes! Neither had anybody realized that the windscreen, made of plexiglass instead of glass to save weight, would become charged with static electricity, attracting plenty of dirt and dust.

However, several of the prototypes were equipped with BMW's 500-cc motorcycle engines. With this power plant, the Deux Chevaux was a true speed-devil. It could do over 100

Besides demanding a car for four people, fifty kilograms of potatoes, 60 km/h of speed, as well as comfort and cheapness, Boulanger had other requirements. It should be drivable on a narrow country road by a woman who had never driven a car before. And how it looked did not matter. Yet as history shows, the designers succeeded.

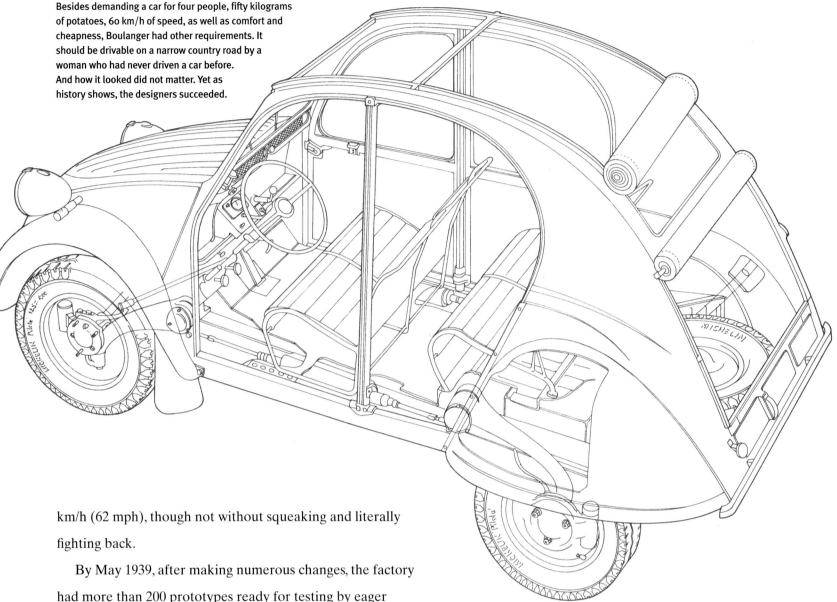

km/h (62 mph), though not without squeaking and literally fighting back.

By May 1939, after making numerous changes, the factory had more than 200 prototypes ready for testing by eager buyers. The car was to be presented at the year's Paris Salon, but none took place: a certain Mr. Hitler, who preferred vast vehicles, shook up Europe and a world war began.

The French, knowing that the Germans were also launching a "people's car", wanted to prevent them from learning about the 2CV. When France was occupied, Citroën's board issued an order to destroy all the prototypes so that none would fall into Hun hands.

This was generally obeyed, but the test chief, Henri Loridant, ignored it. One car was disassembled and packed into bags and boxes. The body was hung from the laboratory roof, with the official explanation of wanting to see how it rusted. Today, this car has been restored and is the only surviving example of the pre-war prototype series.

The car that went into production after the war differed in many ways. It was largely redesigned, for the main purpose of being easier to service. On October 7, 1948, the Citroën CVB 2 was presented at the Paris Salon and struck the public dumb. They had never seen anything so peculiar.

Citroën 2CV
1984

As soon as the practical uses of such an ugly duckling became clear, most people loved it. One reason may be that a good share of the French nation drove cars that were over two decades old. Against this background of the 1920s, the 2CV was a great technical advance.

When it was introduced, the wheel suspension had an enormous springing distance. Consequently, the car was widely found to be comfortable, and to behave rather like a terrain vehicle. Its wheels were kept from hopping by a kind of inertial damper, for which Citroën remains unique.

The body was hardly more than a shield around the simple seats. With the roof and rear seat removed, the car turned into a little lorry. The air-cooled engine needed no water or anti-freeze, but this also meant poor heating. In fact, the engine had only 375 cc and 9 horsepower, giving a top speed around 65 km/h (40 mph). On the other hand, it consumed just 4 litres per 100 km, and a thorough service was not required until 160,000 km.

As a result, two schools of opinion exist about the 2CV. Those who adore it have a special attitude toward car ownership, emphasizing practicality and disregarding the usual signs of high performance or status. Likewise, those who hate it overlook the car's comfort and adequate baggage-space, not to mention its economy.

In February 1988, manufacture of the 2CV stopped in France. But it started again in Portugal and now stands at 20,000 cars per year. The model is still modern, or at least has become modern once more. Our desire for ever smaller, less fuel-hungry cars – ideally also handy, roomy and comfy ones – was anticipated by the new 2CV already in 1948. While the engine gradually grew to 602 cc and all of 29 horsepower, the outcome has been very little exhaust pollution. So even there it can be called up-to-date.

Yet an undeniably primitive feature is, and will be, the car's safety. Its thin shell offers about as much protection as a tin can on present-day highways. ∎

Jaguar XK 120

AT THE AUTO EXHIBITION IN LONDON'S EARLS COURT on October 27, 1948, the sports car for the modern age was unveiled: Jaguar XK 120.

As for whether it was really intended to be series-produced, opinions differ a bit. William Lyons, the Jaguar chairman, had ordered only 200 cars of the model. So nothing suggested an expectation of success – yet that was what happened.

The initials XK referred to the completely redesigned engine, a straight six with double overhead camshafts, generating raw power both at top revolutions and during stepwise loading. This engine's torque made the car as muscular as a lorry.

Many people wondered, of course, if the figures 120 in the car's name meant that it could actually do 120 miles per hour. An ancestor of Jaguar, the SS 100, had done 100 mph in the late 1930s and been designated accordingly. But was the 120 a sign of such incredible speed? All too true – and in fact, an underestimate of the car's performance. About half a year afterward, a record drive on the Jabbeke-Aeltre motorway in Belgium showed that the XK 120 had an average speed in both directions of 132.596 mph, or 213.4 km/h. An astonishing pace in 1949, and even today a respectable merit for a sports car.

The mistake of planning for only 200 cars was soon corrected, and the first examples' hand-beaten aluminium bodies was followed by a steel bodies. Most of the aluminium cars were exported to the United States, and collectors now covet them.

So beautiful were the lines of the XK 120 that they did recall a jaguar, or a black cat leaping. The long bonnet told a tale of speed and power which certainly was confirmed. The rest contained two seats and a baggage space that was quite good for a contemporary sports car. It was a lot of car and a little leg-room, with more than enough velocity.

Soberly speaking, the XK 120 was not very advanced, using a live rear axle in semielliptic leaf springs, and independent

The XK 120 was a sensation when presented at Earls Court in the autumn of 1948. But the first car could not be delivered until next summer, and the English themselves had to wait until 1950. Export at any price was the name of the game after the war.

front-wheel suspension with torsion rods. But the lines and engine gave it an irresistible unity. Besides, it was balanced about equally between the front and rear axles, with the engine over the former and the passengers almost on top of the latter. This contributed greatly to its phenomenal road-handling, in spite of its somewhat conventional chassis structure.

William Lyons understood immediately after the war that a car made in England would have no future if it was labelled SS, which aroused memories of German terror troops. Consequently, the company changed its name from Standard Swallow (SS) to Jaguar in 1945.

The first postwar cars were, as a whole, just belatedly assembled pre-war cars. Then the time came to make an entirely new engine, which could be used in prestige and luxury vehicles as well as in a sports car. One member of the engine

FACTS ABOUT THE
JAGUAR XK 120
PRICE: 1,601 pounds.
ENGINE: Straight 6-cylinder with
double overhead camshafts.
Cylinder volume 3442 cc,
power 160 hp.
TRANSMISSION: Manual box
with four gears (unsynchronized
in first) and reverse.
DRIVE: Rear-wheel, via cardan
axle to stiff rear axle.
CHASSIS: Independent front
suspension with torsion rods.
Semielliptic rear springs. Box
frame with two-seat roadster
body. Hydraulic four-wheel
brakes.
DIMENSIONS: Wheelbase
259 cm, length 439 cm,
empty weight 1280 kg.
TOP SPEED: Over 125 mph
(200 km/h).
NUMBER MADE: 12,078.

NUB 120 was one of the most famous XK 120s ever. With this car, the Appleyard couple won the 1950 Coupe des Alpes. Ian Appleyard was the best driver individually, and won almost every leg of the race.

team was Harry Weslake, on his way to becoming a legend, who excelled at designing high-performance cylinder heads. Another was Wally Hassan, a veteran of the Bentley's heyday in the 1920s, who would eventually build Grand Prix engines for Coventry Climax and Jaguar's fantastic V12.

The new engine, with six cylinders and double overhead cams, was mainly supposed to power the planned luxury car Mark VII (MK Seven), but landed first in the sports car XK 120. Speed was the biggest advantage of the XK 120, but it grew all the more popular as it was cheaper and more reliable – and demanded less service – than juggernauts like the Aston Martin and Ferrari. It could also easily be trimmed by

whoever wanted to compete with it.

With the XK 120, England found the sports car that the country needed. This model earned solid export money, especially from the USA, and through it Jaguar acquired an enduring status. Nor, to be sure, did the production of different versions – the XK 140 and 150, from 1948 until 1960 – make the basic model any worse.

The XK 120 clearly illustrated how a host of odd circumstances might converge to create an epic chariot in the motoring world. Over 50 years since its premiere, it holds such a lofty class among sports cars that it is still surprisingly competitive. ■

1950
–1960

The first modern Grand Touring car, a Lancia Aurelia 1953 coupé. Racing numbers and absence of hubcaps are among the evidence that this is a competition version. Like all contemporary Lancias, it still had the driver's wheel on the right. But its design was classic: A compact 2.5-litre V6 engine, a four-speed transaxle and mid-mounted rear brakes. Even in standard form it could do nearly 170 km/h (105 mph), and on the autostrada it cruised at 145–155 km/h (90–95 mph). Although the model continued for eight years and won countless rallies, only not more than 5,000 were made.

THE KOREAN WAR BREAKS OUT WHEN NORTH KOREA uses Soviet weapons and supplies to attack South Korea. The USA intervenes immediately to help the latter country, and the former is called an aggressor by the United Nations. Price inflation in the West grows as an effect of the war. Modern democratic elections are held in India.

West Germany, after its defeat in World War II, is making a surprisingly fast recovery with United States aid under the Marshall Plan. The Soviet Union warns of German rearmament. The French author André Gide, a Nobel Prize winner, dies. General Douglas MacArthur, who led the American troops against Japan and later the U.N. forces in Korea, is dismissed by President Harry Truman for pursuing a private foreign policy in the Far East contrary to the U.N.'s intentions. King George VI dies and Princess Elizabeth becomes the Queen of Great Britain. Sir Winston Churchill is awarded

Between October 1948 and 1970, over 1,600,000 examples were built of the Morris Minor designed by Alec Issigonis. The Traveller estate car was introduced in 1953, and 204,000 of this type appeared. It got a radical face-lift in 1956, with a new grille and an arched one-piece windscreen. But by 1966 it began to seem old-fashioned and cramped. It had used four different engines, from a 27-horsepower side-valve of 918 cc to the current overhead-valve with 48 hp and 1098 cc, increasing its top speed from 60 to 80 mph (100 to almost 130 km/h). The wood on these cars was genuine, and also essential to their structure – a problem for enthusiasts who restore the model (it became very desirable in the 1980s).

the Nobel Prize in literature for his historical writings.

Relations between the Soviet and Western states deteriorate due to the Russians' unreasonable foreign policy, which takes forms such as shooting down airplanes that come near their territory. Stalin dies at last, succeeded by Nikita Khrushchev. In Egypt, Colonel Gamal Abdel Nasser seizes power. Austria, divided into four zones by the Allies since 1945, finally obtains full independence when the Soviet Union accepts this proposal from the other occupiers. The economy of West Germany is steadily improving.

Peaceful uses of atomic energy are hailed after a conference in Geneva about scientific research on it. The world's first car-telephones are tested in Stockholm. A new type of container made from butadiene rubber is invented for storing large amounts of oil and petrol. So is a Swedish method, "Tetra Pak", for packaging milk. People are going to the cinema as never before, and Hollywood's movie industry thrives. Many films are produced in Europe, too, and Denmark has regular television broadcasts, while colour TV is inaugurated in the USA. The transistor appears, foreshadowing a technological

European family cars from the 1950s at their best. This sedan version and estate car of the Borgward Isabella were both made in 1960. They inherited an overhead-valve engine and independent suspension from their predecessor, the 1934 Hansa 1100, but the rear suspension now used spiral springs instead of a transverse leaf spring. While they naturally had hydraulic brakes, their hydraulically controlled clutch, fully synchronized gearbox, and pontoon body were technically advanced even in 1954. Such a car in other countries would have had four doors, yet Germans were satisfied with two doors, so the estate car could demand no more. The steering-column gear-shift was quite normal in the 1950s, but rather archaic by 1960. A Borgward Isabella was big (4.37 metres long and 1.7 wide) as well as heavy (weighing 1,025 kilograms empty). The TS version with a stronger engine cruised at about 130 km/h (80 mph). However, a self-supporting body was a risk for a small factory, and Borgward's money ran out in 1961 despite having sold over 200,000 Isabellas.

Sturdy German engineering craft: the 1957 Mercedes-Benz 220S. During 1954 this self-supporting structure replaced the original type with a separate chassis frame. It continued until 1959 with no external changes, but many improvements were made under the shell – servo brakes in 1955, optional automatic clutch in 1957, and the SE series with fuel injection in 1958. Though the rear swing-axle design had well-known limitations, the power from the four-bearing 2.2-litre six-cylinder engine with overhead camshaft was steadily raised from 95 to 115 hp. Few cars could compete with this one in cruising at around 135 km/h (85 mph). Its production also kept growing, and approached 30,000 per year at the end of the 1950s.

The first owner of this 1957 Chevrolet Bel Air convertible must have paid some 3,000 pounds, including the freight and other charges added in England. To European eyes it looked expensive, particularly with the impressive grille, chromed side-strips, and fins (which had not yet even reached their later sublime height). The panorama windshield and its thick posts seemed less aggressive when the roof was down. The wheels were 14-inch (a novelty that year) and indicated brake problems, not least if the car was equipped with a two-speed automatic transmission and one of the optional V8 engines (such as 4.6 litres and 220 horsepower). It was Chevrolet's only open model in 1957 (besides the sporty Corvettes), and sold in over 47,000 examples – more cars than the Auto Union factory in Germany could produce in a whole year.

revolution as it replaces the conventional vacuum tubes in radio equipment.

The biggest catastrophe in aviation history occurs when an American troop transport of the Globemaster type crashes, killing 86. Flying celebrates its 50th birthday in 1953, and can boast of having already reached twice the speed of sound, Mach 2. Record flights are now made with Cold War secrecy, but we do learn that three American B52 bombers fly non-stop around the world in 45 hours, at an average speed of 525 mph (840 km/h).

Grand Prix car races have been held since 1906, yet only in 1950 is a World Championship founded. That year's winner is an Italian, Giuseppe Farina of Alfa Romeo. The need for all kinds of motor vehicles since World War II is still great, and the car industry everywhere is working all out. A normal family car can now accelerate to 60 mph (100 km/h) in about 30 seconds and run up to 90 mph (140 km/h). Because of higher average speeds, the ever more efficient engines do not lower petrol consumption, which stays around 10 litres per 100 km (approx. 25 miles per gallon). Regular service intervals for vehicles are introduced, and owners are urged to obey them.

In 1954 Citroën presents its first car with hydropneumatic suspension, the six-cylinder type 15CV Six. Next year brings the entirely new Citroën DS19. To stimulate sales, even

(*Left*) "Spain is a poor country," said Pegaso's chief designer Wifredo Ricart, "so we have to make jewels for the rich." This Z102B, manufactured in the old Hispano-Suiza factory at Barcelona in 1954, is really exotic. It had an aluminium 3.2-litre V8, four overhead camshafts, four carburettors, a five-speed unsynchronized transaxle of de Dion type, a limited-slip differential, and mid-mounted rear brakes. Saoutchik in Paris, and Touring in Milan, built suitable bodies. Shown here is a Touring body that might well have influenced both the 1961 Jaguar E-type and Datsun's 1969 Z-series. A price of 30,000 dollars was spoken of in America, which may explain why only 125 Pegasos were made between 1951 and 1958.

(*Above*) Undoubtedly the most exciting Chrysler model during this decade was the 300 coupe from 1955. Rare, too, it numbered only 1,692 examples. The idea was simple enough: Virgil Exner's new (but tardy) body form in the New Yorker hardtop version was lowered, given a grille from the expensive Imperial series, and equipped with a 300-horsepower V8, dual four-port carburettors, and two exhaust systems to create the right sound. The automatic transmission and servo steering (both standard) were perhaps not what Europeans expected in a sports car, but such "muscle cars" did not aim to compete with Ferrari and Jaguar. Soon they became a breed of their own.

The Fiat 500C disappeared in 1955 after a career that had begun already in 1936. It had hydraulic brakes, plenty of leg room, a four-speed gearbox, and independent front suspension. All other minicars had been compared with it before the war, and even in 1950 it was not ignorable due to its revised version of the old overhead valve 570-cc engine, now with 16.5 horsepower. While faster than the original Morris Minor with a side-valve engine (1949–52), it was a two-seater (lacking much rear space). Moreover, service and repairs were a nightmare for the do-it-yourselfer; everything looked accessible but tended to require abnormally small fingers.

(*Top*) The original Saab 92 from 1950 was yet another triumph of streamlining over other considerations, as could be expected by a manufacturer who was one of the European leaders in aircraft engineering. Technically, it was a refined and improved DKW. A water-cooled two-cylinder two-stroke engine of 764 cc drove the front wheels. The gearbox had three speeds and a freewheel, the steering was of rack-and-pinion type, and the brakes were hydraulic. Disadvantages were the scant head-space, poor rear visibility, and built-in rust traps in the body sides pulled down over the wheels. The choice of colour was also small, only green being offered. For nearly 30 years the body shape, though not the engine, would continue.

(*Above*) Volvo went on making variants of the original PV444 (exhibited in 1944) until the mid-1960s, still with the same sloping rear end. But in 1957 the model started to look old, with lines from American cars of 1942 (mainly inspired by Ford) and a three-speed gearbox whose long, angular shift-lever was most reminiscent of 1935. However, there was a good deal of news under the bonnet: The cylinder volume had grown from the original 1414 to 1583 cc and, with two carburettors, generated 85 horsepower for a top speed of 145 km/h (90 mph). That it was a sound and sensible car could not be denied, as this model initiated Volvo's series of successes on the difficult U.S. market.

Kaiser-Frazer's Henry J of 1951 was a rather small car, 4.2 metres long with a 2.5-metre wheelbase. Intended as a "farmer's car" like the Model A Ford in the distant past, it had a very conventional structure – independent front suspension with spiral springs, semielliptic rear leaf springs, and hypoid rear axle. The engines were simple side-valves bought from Kaiser's future partner Willys-Overland, namely the famous Jeep engines: a 2.2-litre four-cylinder and a 2.6-litre six. Inside the unimaginative body, early examples lacked even a baggage compartment. As fate decreed, the American public wanted more car, more power and more acceleration, since cheap gasoline was still flowing. It took nearly four years to sell 120,000 of the Henry J, whereas some 200,000 Valiants were sold in their first season alone.

European factories begin making year-model changes. With suitable designations, and the U.S. concept of "styling", very slight alterations can give a naive car-buyer the impression of phenomenal improvements. Inspiration from aircraft is borrowed especially by American designers; the bonnet acquires rows of holes to imitate a plane's exhaust pipes, the instrument panel becomes a maze, and the body's rear end has fins of sometimes stratospheric size.

True innovations during the 1950s are disc brakes – first developed in England and tested by Jaguar in competition – as well as motor oils. Thanks to additives, the oils' better qualities lengthen the interval for changing oil, and virtually eliminate the need to decarbonize engines. Tubeless tyres are introduced, as are radial ones which can turn even a car with dubious wheel suspension into a road-hugger. The Wankel engine arrives. Production ceases for the last car with a straight eight-cylinder engine, the Russian luxury ZIZ. Ford's latest model, the Edsel, is unveiled and called the company's

The 1960 Plymouth Valiant was important, being Chrysler Corporation's first compact car. But it is also remembered as the first mass-produced model with an alternating-current generator. Further, it symbolized a transition in engines; from the old-fashioned long-stroke side-valve six (made with few changes since the 1930s) to a new, and not too large, overhead-valve design that was mounted at a 30-degree angle in the frame. The exterior was fairly reserved as well, apart from the "trash-can lid" stamped on the trunk top, supposedly representing an outdoor spare wheel. The 2.8 litres of cylinder volume were not enough for fine performance, but a Valiant with automatic transmission did 90 mph (145 km/h), and took just 12.6 seconds to accelerate 0–50 mph (0–80 km/h). In sum, it performed like a big American straight-eight from 1939. And by European standards, its length of 4.7 metres made the Valiant another big car.

The 1951 Mercury Club Coupe anticipated the new look of U.S. Fords. It had independent front suspension with spiral springs – not until 1949, which is hard to believe – and a hypoid rear axle. Its cross-braced chassis frame, though, was more Lincoln than Ford. The divided windshield and the bulging fenders already appeared somewhat obsolete. In fact, when GM and Chrysler had short-stroke V8 engines with overhead valves, Mercury's engine was still an antiquated side-valve with 4.2 litres and only 110 horsepower. GM had used automatic transmissions for eleven years, but this was their first season in Fords and Mercurys.

"only new car in ten years", but it turns out to be a huge fiasco. In France a train sets a new railway speed record of 330 km/h (205 mph).

Physicists mourn the death of Albert Einstein. A political crisis in Argentina topples Juan Perón. Soviet troops invade Hungary to crush a popular uprising for freedom. Egypt causes a widespread conflict by closing the Suez Canal and nationalizing its company, which Great Britain partly owns. This results in an oil crisis, until it is found that oil deliveries can

continue by sailing round Africa. The planned economies in the eastern states become less shaky, whereas the West faces problems with increasing inflation.

The USA and the Soviet Union propose new disarmament plans to the U.N. General Assembly. Hungary's secret police, BACS, is executing freedom-fighters. Women's right to vote in Egypt is supported against Nasser's regime by the organization "Daughters of the Nile", but its chairman Doria Shafik is deposed. The second Soviet satellite goes into orbit, this time

M.G.'s first modern shape, and the first model to sell in six figures, this is an MGA 1600 from 1959–61, with BMC's four-cylinder B engine of 1588 cc. Its top speed was 100 mph (160 km/h) and it did a quarter-mile (400 metres) in 19.3 seconds from standstill. Fuel consumption was around 10 litres per 100 km (25 miles per gallon). Independent front suspension had existed on M.G. sports cars since the 1950 model TD. Yet the T-series had a quite unsuitable aerodynamic design, and the engine needed lots of tuning to get past 80 mph (130 km/h). This example went to the United States – no English or European buyer would have given it white-sidewall tyres.

The original Bentley Continental R-type (1952–55) is probably the most coveted classic car of the 1950s, after the Mercedes-Benz 300SL. Only 207 were made, almost all of them with H.J. Mulliner's lovely fastback two-door body. It was equipped with the renowned 4.6-litre six-cylinder Rolls-Royce F-head engine, and had an excellent four-speed synchronized gearbox, whose gear lever was placed at the right on right-hand drive cars (l.h.d. ones, sadly, used a column lever). A final drive ratio of 3.08 gave it a top speed of 115 mph (186 km/h), cruising at 100 mph (160 km/h). If driven cautiously, it drank at most 13.5 litres per 100 km (18 miles per gallon). But the price – about 5,000 pounds before sales tax – was paralyzing in 1953.

carrying a dog named Laika. In Little Rock, Arkansas, racists try to stop ten black students from entering a school, and Federal airborne troops are sent to restore order. The Finnish composer Jean Sibelius dies.

Large data-processing machines are built in various places, mostly in the West. The former Hungarian chief of state, Imre Nagy, is executed. General de Gaulle is elected President of France after political upheavals and government crises. Fidel Castro appoints himself head of Cuba's government, and all private property is nationalized. The British "Hovercraft" makes its first trip across the English Channel. A moon rocket is launched by the Soviet Union; another in America explodes during ground tests, and the USA frets at its rival's lead in space technology. The Tibetan revolt against China is beaten down and the Dalai Lama flees to India; his country suffers a socialistic reform with the Panchen Lama as a puppet faithful to the Chinese.

A four-power conference – initiated by Khrushchev, hosted by France, and including the USA and Great Britain – collapses because the Russians and Americans argue about violations of air space. In Japan, socialists and communists demand a rejection of U.S. military aid and a neutral foreign policy. The Soviet Union shows strong interest in Latin America, but the United States warns both the Soviets and Chinese not to interfere in the West. John F. Kennedy is about to become the next American President. A new capital city, Brasilia, is founded in the interior of Brazil. ■

The Great American Norm, or one of the 128,582 Chevrolet Bel Air Hardtop Coupes from 1956. Such a high figure would have been striking for a European manufacturer's entire production – in Germany it was exceeded that year only by Volkswagen and Opel. The V8 engine of 4.3 litres was not very strong (165–170 hp, or 205 with all the power-raising accessories), and the basic specifications still included a six-cylinder engine and three-speed manual gearbox. You could, however, "load" your Chevy with an automatic transmission, servo steering and brakes, electrically controlled seats and windows, air-conditioning and (for the first time this year) safety belts!

Mercedes 300 SL

WHY SOME CAR MODELS BECOME MORE PROMINENT than others is often a mystery. Seen at a distance, they may not appear to deserve such success. Those that are remembered as superb creations can become boring with the years – and yet they excite an admiration hard to set aside.

Such a model is the Mercedes 300SL. It stands firm in history as the "gullwing", a nickname derived from the doors which swung upward and, in open position, recalled a pair of silver seabird wings. This construction was not entirely new, but necessary on a car whose tubular frame required a truss structure in the sides, so wide that it simply left no space for ordinary doors. The only option was to make the doors move vertically.

Naturally, though, the gullwings were not the end of the originality that made the 300SL a classic. For its time, it was in many ways a result of innovative thinking, which also paid off frequently at races. Moreover, its lines were so beautiful that the American market, in particular, demanded that it be produced as a convertible or roadster – a further source of its popularity and renown.

While it did better in competition than any previous Mercedes, the 300SL maintained some respect for tradition. It was based on many components from the usual models, and had the same fundamental philosophy as most other fast cars of the period: a large engine that guaranteed power, and rear-wheel drive.

The engine came from the standard 300 sedan, but was sloped 40 degrees toward the left, to lower the centre of gravity and to allow closing the low bonnet top. It was a heavy straight six-cylinder engine, and not completely vibration-free. To lessen this problem, a big vibration damper was mounted forward on the crankshaft.

At first, the engine had a relatively mild power of 115 hp from 3 litres. But gradually its output increased, finally reaching 240 hp – with fuel injection instead of the earlier three carburettors.

When Mercedes resumed automobile manufacture after the war, there were no plans to try again for the great competition triumphs of the pre-war years. Most effort was concentrated on making the factory profitable so as to ensure its survival. Developing a new Grand Prix racer was unthinkable mainly for economic reasons. However, a sports car might be built from the standard model components, and this is what happened. The 300S engine, front carriage and rear axle went into a very low truss frame that was both light and strong. As the 300S engine was fairly easy to tune up, 175 horsepower were extracted with a different camshaft, other carburettors, and various lightenings or polishings.

The new sports model was called 300SL because SL meant "Sport Light". Its debut in the 1952 Mille Miglia won second and fourth places. The Bern Grand Prix brought a triple victory, and three cars entered Le Mans that year. One of

these dropped out, but the other two took first and second places. This feat was repeated at the grueling Carrera Panamericana in Mexico, drawing attention to the car in the USA – which sealed its success. The 300SL had fulfilled a purpose: to show that Mercedes was still among the world's best auto makers.

Next the company began to consider building a real Grand Prix car, but it was postponed. Max Hoffman, the Mercedes agent in New York, took such a liking to the 300SL that he ordered 1,000 for America, and all hands went to work on series production.

First shown at the New York exhibition in 1954, the series model differed substantially from the preceding competition 300SL. Its body shape had become a bit rounder, although the basic gullwing shape persisted. Both the body and frame were strengthened, increasing the weight by nearly 400 kg (850 lbs). But this was compensated with more power, so the performance remained similar. The added power was due, among other things, to replacing the three carburettors with fuel injection, yielding lower fuel consumption and greater reliability as well. Mercedes had used fuel injection in the aircraft engine industry, but in petrol engines it was new to the car world.

As a sporty conveyance for daily use, the 300SL never earned true popularity in the United States. Its single-jointed rear axle was capricious and could cause problems with handling for an unaccustomed driver. Sudden, unintended skids were possible due to the track-width change at the back with this construction. The roadster model's handling was improved

by a transverse compensation spring, which did not allow the two rear-axle halves to wobble as much.

Neither were the gullwings suitable for city traffic. In cramped parking spaces, they could not be opened without hitting adjacent cars. The doors also had such high thresholds that women who climbed into the car risked exposing "plenty of leg", which was too much for the prevailing morality and led to loud protests from American housewives. In 1957 the 300SL gave rise to a roadster model that gained quite a following in the USA, but its sales were less significant than the reputation it has acquired as a classic.

Viewing a 300SL in reality is an experience indeed. The logic of its lines and their harmonious impact on the eye can fill one with joy. The driving experience, by contrast, is dubious. When I first tried a 300SL in the early 1960s, it was an old – or at least a used – sports car that did not feel very fresh. Consequently, I never tasted the sensation of power to which so many people lost their hearts when the model emerged. For me it was mostly a thing of the past.

Several years later, I had the chance to test one of Mercedes' own totally renovated 300SLs on an airfield in Germany. Again, it was not as thrilling as I expected. It resembled a big, uncomfortable home-build with a lorry engine that groaned in pain under the bonnet. Acceleration provoked an intake sound like the belching in a local heavyweight restaurant.

For all that, I can understand why those who encountered the new 300SL in the early 1950s found it astonishing. One should hardly permit one's belated impressions of a relic to tarnish the image its worshippers once beheld. ∎

BMW V 8

What distinguished the BMW 502 from a 501 were the foglamps built into the wings, and a chrome strip along the sides.

THE BMW 502 WAS GERMANY'S FIRST CAR AFTER THE war that came with an eight-cylinder engine. It was sorely needed, as the earlier six-cylinder engine in the BMW 501 gave only 72 horsepower and was too weak for this rather heavy car.

Except for its V8 engine, more chrome and some small changes, the 502 was basically identical to the 501. But it proved to handle very differently and, with 100 horsepower from 2.6 litres, it was something of a power-pack for the time. Even so, its output did not strain the engine much.

BMW was one of the German auto manufacturers that suffered most after the war. When the country was divided up by the Allies, the BMW factories in Eisenach landed on the wrong side of the Iron Curtain – in the Soviet zone. When production resumed, it was thus controlled by the Russians. BMW's plant in Munich was governed by the Americans, but got under way considerably later.

The first postwar BMW cars, then, came from the Soviet sector, and not until 1952 were they renamed EMW, for

Eisenach Motoren Verk. On the whole, these cars were just adaptations of previous BMW models to the austere conditions after the war. There was a scarcity of raw materials, especially metals, so the initial quality of "Russian" BMWs left a great deal to be desired.

Such limitations did not face BMW in the West. American money was pumped in to start manufacture and stimulate employment. Several prototypes of new models were made – among them a smallish car that actually ended up with the general agent in Sweden, although it never went into production. BMW decided to take a step forward in size, and greeted 1952 with the medium-large 501.

This model's style dated to before the war: no modern pontoon body, but relatively conventional lines with sweeping wings in front and back, only partly integrated with the body. Despite its old-fashioned look, the 501 was a handsome car with a classic look. It was, however, much too heavy for the old six-cylinder engine.

What the 501's lines recalled most were BMW's pre-war sports models. Hence the buyers expected performance, but found it quite sluggish. This was a worry, leading to quick work on a model 502 as well as a V8. The new engine's original 2.6 litres and 100 hp, while hardly comparable to an American V8, were a definite improvement on the 501's pitiful 72 hp.

Der persönliche Stil

BMW 502 V 8 Zylinder

Warum fahren erfolgreiche Geschäftsleute und kultivierte Frauen BMW?

Weil sie wissen, daß die dezente Eleganz der Karosserie ihrer Persönlichkeit und ihrem Lebensstil angemessen ist.

Technische Vollkommenheit, Sicherheit und Fahrkomfort sind bei BMW selbstverständlich.

Es ist daher ein Vergnügen, einen Wagen zu fahren, der so gut aussieht wie ein BMW.

 **501** | 2 Liter 6 Zylinder | **502** | 2,6 Liter V 8 Zylinder

BAYERISCHE MOTOREN WERKE AG MÜNCHEN

Entirely built of light metal, the V8 was better known for its smooth running and primitive strength than for sprinting qualities. It could move the 502 in a single gear from 20 to 160 km/h (12 to 100 mph). That was certainly a drivable machine!

For the Frankfurt auto show in 1955, a larger rear pane was added, and the 501 could be ordered with a bigger V8 of

3.2 litres and 120 hp. Top speed increased to 170 km/h (105 mph), ruling out any complaints about BMW's performance.

The 502 was built with a classic frame of beams with transverse stabilizing tubes. Everything was well-overdimensioned, more like a lorry's than a passenger car's frame. The front suspension was independent and the rear axle was live, both the front and rear being sprung with longitudinal torsion rods. The gearbox, placed beneath the front seat, was linked to the

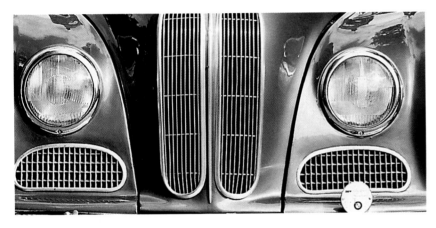

clutch case and engine by a short cardan shaft. This design was made chiefly to distribute more of the car's front weight backward, thus improving the overall balance.

Generally called the BMW V8, it was a comfortable car to drive – not a racer, but feeling solid almost to the point of clumsiness. Its weight also gave an impression of moving like a flatiron along the road, which it did. The fine balance meant excellent handling in contemporary terms.

Besides, it was spacious and the first models had full-width seats front and back. In later, more luxurious cars, the front seats were separate and the rear seat's back-rests were cupped for three passengers, who also had three arm-rests. The big panes allowed the driver very good visibility, and further

aids were the hanging pedals and steering-column gear-shift.

In 1958, BMW replaced the figures 501 and 502 with a designation according to the engine size – such as BMW 2.6 for the smaller V8 and BMW 3.2 for the larger, while 3.2 Super had a V8 with dual carburettors and no less than 140 hp. Still later, the system was revised to 2600 and 3200, indicating the models' engine volume.

Already during the early 1960s, safety thinking surrounded BMW's bigger models. Safety-belt fastenings existed since 1962, the body formed a protective cage around the passengers from the outset of the 502 model, and the strong frame opposed side-collisions. Windscreen washers were standard.

In the summer of 1962, manufacture stopped for the two basic models 2600 and 3200, although the more expensive 2600L and 3200S continued until 1964. The last BMW cars with the V8 engine of the Fifties were the coupé and a few cabriolets, built until 1965. But the engine itself survived in a marine version until 1968.

These had been among West German's most interesting, if also somewhat outdated, cars – yet their rapid demise was due to financial problems at BMW. The V8 models simply did not pay off, being too complicated and therefore costly to build. A shadow of bankruptcy passed back and forth over BMW throughout the 1960s, and it was rumoured that Mercedes would take over.

By a close margin, however, the company endured and managed to turn loss into profit. This it achieved with a quite different and much more modern design than the old V8 models. ■

Citroën DS 19

You might see it coming along on three wheels – the fourth having been removed, together with the covering wing. But this was no trick: the Citroën DS did not need the usual number of wheels. One of them could easily be removed by raising the car to the highest position of its hydropneumatic suspension. The wing came off simply by using a wrench on a bolt at the back edge, being held in front only with a flange. Here indeed was a remarkable automobile. 🚗

In 1955 more than two decades of production had gone by for the Traction Avant model, and the Citroën company was widely expected to come up with something rather special in its new model.

Nor did anyone find cause for disappointment. When the latest Citroën was presented at the Paris show that year, it drew standing ovations from the motoring journalist crowd, and soon the public's approval signified a real success. Nothing as delightful, modern and elegant had even been imagined.

The road to this achievement, though, was far from straight and smooth. It all began with a little black notebook, carried by the man who was then head of Citroën. Pierre Boulanger always jotted down every idea that might prove useful for the new car, which went under the provisional name VGD – meaning *voiture de grand diffusion*, or "car with a

large spread". His vision was that the wheels should be well separated, implying a long wheelbase, to give the best handling and comfort.

When Boulanger was killed in an auto accident, the new chief summoned André Lefebvre, who had helped to create the B7 model during the 1930s. Many fresh ideas, more or less "crazy", were combined with Boulanger's notes to lay the foundation for the VGD. The car's main features were to be an aerodynamic shape, a low centre of gravity, and light weight, while placing as much of the weight as possible at the front. This would ensure stability in driving.

Already in 1948 there was a test chassis, with pressed beams of sheet steel that formed an enclosure like a bathtub. Above it, a strong cage was made of pressed steel sections, to surround the passengers. On the outside were hung the wings, bonnet and rear hatch. A basic intention was to facilitate undressing of the chassis, with nothing but a screwdriver and a wrench.

Problems faced the choice of engine. A low position was desired, preferably with a boxer engine at the far front end of the body. An attempt was made to couple three air-cooled engines from the 2CV, but the result had too little power and

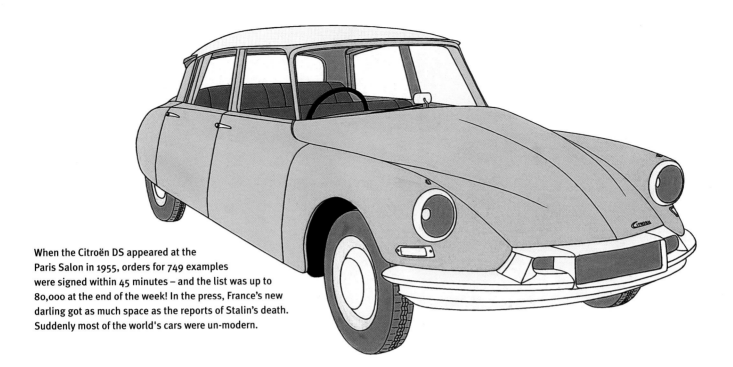

When the Citroën DS appeared at the
Paris Salon in 1955, orders for 749 examples
were signed within 45 minutes – and the list was up to
80,000 at the end of the week! In the press, France's new
darling got as much space as the reports of Stalin's death.
Suddenly most of the world's cars were un-modern.

was given up. After several other strange proposals, an engine from the B11 was selected, with a new cylinder head.

The brakes were located next to the gearbox. In fact, they could be nowhere else, as the front-end design ruled out any brakes at the wheels. Inspired by Jaguar, which then had disc brakes on its racing cars, the Citroën people developed their own disc-brake system, and this worked perfectly. Citroën was among the first series-produced cars to have disc brakes in front.

One advantage of the loosely hung wings and hatches was that these parts could be painted separately, and mounted in the final stage of the car's assembly. Thus, they avoided small damage during the process of manufacture – and a customer could deal with serious damage by ordering a painted part in the right colour. However, this system worked badly, since it is almost impossible to mix paint with exactly the same shade twice. Consequently, the colours often varied between the car's parts. Moreover, reserves of pre-painted wings, bonnets and doors were difficult to maintain.

The most important and technical innovation, though, was the new suspension system. It replaced metal springs with compressed air, as if using several balloons – besides the tyres themselves – to soften the car's wheel impacts. The pneumatic pressure could also be regulated by adding hydraulic pressure, which led to the term "hydropneumatic".

This system took quite a long time to develop, and many ideas arose about exploiting it for further purposes. The brakes were coupled to it, with excellent results. Braking worked faster than in an ordinary system, and no actual brake pedal was needed – just a small valve that opened and closed.

Hence, the first DS models had a little "button" on the floor to serve as a brake pedal. But the customers did not like this device and, from 1962 onward, the brake valve was hidden with an ordinary pedal.

The hydropneumatic system also came to be used for regulating the car's height, and for steering. Yet in the latter case, a full servo effect could not be employed, as it made the steering too sensitive and caused negative reactions when, for

Citroën DS 19 with open body by Henri Chapron.

this helped to make up for the relatively weak engine.

As for styling, the car was brilliant. It looked like a thing of the future, and resembled no other vehicle on the road. Giving a very low and long impression, it seemed to be speeding even when parked. The body sides were smooth, with no stiffening folds – and the front wheels were farther apart than the rear wheels, as if the whole car tapered backward.

New materials were used, too. Lefebvre tried all sorts of novelties, and naturally the DS acquired a plastic roof, plastic instrument panel, and foam-rubber seats with nylon covers.

Twenty years of successful sales awaited the DS, and just over 14 million were produced. The related ID models also had hydropneumatic suspension, but were simpler and lacked servo assistance of the clutch, gearbox and brakes.

The DS – a term pronounced in French as *déesse*, meaning a goddess – has definitely been an object of worship. Clubs now do their best to keep it alive, especially in the face of corrosion, which was one of the problems overlooked by the designers. The car rusted badly and often disappeared prematurely. Despite this, many drivers even in other countries would rather retain a crumbling DS than buy the best modern car.

A statement attributed to the German motoring journalist Alexander Spoert may sum up this story: "The Citroën DS is not the future's car, but today's. All other cars are from yesterday." ■

example, swerving. The driver was simply unable to keep up with it, so the effect was restricted to keep the car under human control.

The gearbox, while basically a normal manual one, had hydraulic manoeuvring and a fully automatic clutch. It thereby wasted much less power than did ordinary gearboxes, and

Austin-Healey

WHEN LEONARD LORD, OF THE NEWLY FOUNDED British Motor Corporation (BMC), saw the prototype of Donald Healey's sports car, he instantly adored it and knew what he wanted to manufacture.

Austin Healey 100S

Automobile history can be grateful for the fact that, while most people do not survive airplane accidents, a few have lived through more than one – and these included Donald Healey. Subsequently working as a Royal Air Force administrator, he grew interested in cars and motoring sports. After becoming a designer for Riley and Triumph, he got bored and began to construct his own cars, using components from other makes.

Among the initial Healeys was a sedan in 1947. Powered by a 2.4-litre Riley engine, it was then the world's fastest series-produced passenger car, with a top speed of 105 mph (168.5 km/h).

Next came the Healey Silverstone, a two-seat sports car that was manufactured in 105 examples. Its most remarkable features were the headlamps built into the grille, and the spare tyre that stuck out of the rear end – thus also serving as a bumper.

Healey collaborated with Nash in America, and this led to the Nash-Healey in 1950, a two-seat sports car with a Nash Ambassador engine of 125 hp. Its aluminium body was built in England, but given a Nash grille that was not very pretty. Only 504 were made.

In the early 1950s, Healey planned to create a sports car that would be cheaper than the previous Silverstone model. Now he decided to use the same four-cylinder 2.6-liter engine that sat in the Austin A90 Atlantic.

The new car was christened the Healey Hundred, due to a conviction that it would do over 100 mph (160 km/h). Its prototype was presented at the 1952 London Motor Show and caused a small sensation. Sir Leonard Lord of BMC was as thrilled as the others, and proposed with no hesitation to make the car under the name Austin-Healey 100. Before the exhibition was over, he and Healey reached an agreement.

Instead of the plan to build five cars per week in Healey's old airplane hangar, production was located at Austin's works in Longbridge where a hundred cars per week would be made. The price was fixed at an astonishingly low level of 750 pounds.

As it turned out, only the engines came from Longbridge and the manufacturing took place at Jensen in Bromwich. In 1957, operations were moved to the M.G. factory in Abingdon, where they proceeded alongside the MG A and B – something that Healey purists do not like to be reminded of.

The Healey 100 was a success from the very start, and already in 1953 the goal of a hundred cars weekly was fulfilled. That same year, the car made its racing début at Le Mans, finishing second and third in its class. During the next two years it set a number of speed records, such as running for 24 hours at an average 132 mph (212 km/h).

Austin Healey 3000

The Austin Atlantic engine that went into the car's initial version was a pushrod type, with 2660 cc giving 90 hp at 4,000 rpm. The gearbox had three speeds, and overdrive on the top two. Actually there were four gears, but the first was blocked because it could hardly be used. At the rear was a live rear axle with spiral bevels. A hypoid rear axle was installed in 1955.

A box-beam chassis was used, the body being welded directly onto it. In complete form, the car weighed 1,900 lbs (865 kg) and had a maximum speed of 105 mph (170 km/h).

Besides the standard model 100, a trimmed model 100M was available, with a high-compression cylinder head that raised the power to 110 hp. Finally, there was the racing version 100S with a light-metal body, 132 hp and a top speed of 145 mph (230 km/h). The standard model was made in 14,012 examples, but the 100S in only 50.

AUSTIN-HEALEY 300

In 1956 appeared the first big change. The Austin-Healey 100-6 was presented, with Austin's six-cylinder engine of 2639 cc (also used, for instance, in the Austin A90). To accommodate this large engine, as well as a double seat for children, the wheelbase was extended. But a two-seat 100-6 could also be bought. Production totalled 14,436, and in 1959 the cylinder volume was increased to 2912 cc.

At this point, the model was renamed Austin-Healey 3000. It proved to be an ideal rally car, and during 1960–64 it brought home many trophies. Among the great Healey drivers

1958 Austin Healey Sprite

were the brothers Morley, Pat Moss (sister of Stirling Moss), Ann Wisdom and Timo Mäkinen.

A full list of such victories would take long, but worthy of note were the 1960 and 1964 Marathon de la Route, the second women's championship won by Pat Moss and Ann Wisdom, the Alpine Rally in 1961 and 1962, and class wins in the Monte Carlo Rally. Even on courses, the Healey beat the rest of its class and team in the Sebring and Mille Miglia races..

Until production stopped in 1968, the Austin-Healey 3000 changed little, except that its engine power rose steadily. In the end, the Mark III had 148 hp and could do 120 mph (195 km/h). Totally 41,534 were made of the Mark I, II and III.

What Austin did not achieve with the Atlantic was done to excess by the Healey models. And these were embraced whole-heartedly in the United States, where many of the cars were imported and are now prized by collectors.

AUSTIN-HEALEY SPRITE

During the mid-1950s, Sir Leonard Lord asked Donald Healey to design a small Austin-Healey that would correspond to M.G.'s earlier Midget models. The result was the Sprite, a little two-seater with independent suspension. Only 11.5 feet (3.5 metres) long, it used BMC's A-engine with 948 cc and 43 hp.

The Sprite's front end could be swung up entirely, for easy access to the engine. Most characteristic were its headlamps, which stuck up from the bonnet and inspired the car's nickname "Frog-eye" in England. Originally, the Sprite was capable of 85 mph (135 km/h) and cost only 678 pounds. Considering its performance, this was a bargain, and Sprite had no real competitors in England except the two-cylinder Berkeley, although the Triumph Spitfire arrived in 1962 as a strong challenger.

Soon there were trimming sets for the Sprite, and they often increased the speed to over 100 mph (160 km/h). A specially trimmed car driven by Graham Hill reached 133 mph (213 km/h) on a motorway in Belgium. With such resources, the car was naturally soon raced, and it paid off well. A class victory was won at Sebring in 1959, and English club competitions made the Sprite very popular.

In May 1961 came the Sprite Mark II, with the same body as the M.G. Midget, and disc brakes in front. However, its grille was unlike the Midget's and it had no chrome strips along the sides. Next year, the "Spridget" models – a common term for the Sprite and Midget – acquired a new engine from the Mini Cooper. This had 1098 cc and 60 hp, raising the top speed to 90 mph (145 km/h).

In December 1970, the agreement with Donald Healey expired. The cars' name became Austin Sprite, but deliveries ceased in July 1971. Production of the Sprite amounted to 38,999 and, needless to say, many collectors now wish there had been one more. ∎

The Doghouse

IN MARCH 1957 CAME ONE OF THE MOST CRUCIAL decisions in automotive history. Building was to begin for the "Doghouse", which then had the working name ADO 15.

The choice to make a reality of what would be the ancestor of all modern small cars is attributed to Sir Leonard Lord, who was later entitled Lord Lambury. An engineer himself, he had complete faith in a Greek-born employee, the talented engineer Alex Issigonis.

After working on various detail designs, Issigonis was given the task of designing the postwar period's first modern small car for Morris – the Minor. But although he earned great praise for it, the fact is that he never became satisfied with the Minor. His constant dream was to go further, and plan a truly advanced small car with driving qualities, interior space, and technology that suited a modern automobile.

This "Gordian knot" was eventually untied by Issigonis. He discovered that such a car's engine must be placed transversely, not lengthwise, so as to leave more room for the passengers and baggage. The rest of his smart ideas followed more or less by themselves.

Besides putting a transverse engine above the gearbox, and letting the two share the same lubricant oil, Issigonis created a whole new suspension system for small cars. The rear end had longitudinal link-arms which, via a trumpet-like lever, pressed on rubber elements that did the actual springing.

These elements were replaceable to adjust the ride's hardness, and the car's height could be varied by the "trumpet" length.

The latter invention also proved to be valuable when the car was lowered for competition purposes. A similar device existed at the front end, yet its trumpets and rubber elements stood upright. Ordinary telescopic shock-absorbers were mounted all round.

Not just a wheel at each corner, but front-wheel drive, was the new small car's basic principle. The engine and gearbox gave its front end an advantage of weight, helping to stabilize the direction of movement. Almost regardless of how the car was driven, it held the road as long as you turned and throttled.

The first series-produced examples were a smash hit when released in the autumn of 1959. Buyers shouted for the micro-miracle, which had enough space for four people and some baggage even though it was barely 3 metres (10 feet) long.

Its engine was the only old feature: Austin's classic A type, with overhead valves and four cylinders in line, now enlarged to 848 cc and 34 horsepower. Due to the car's low empty weight of 635 kg (1400 lbs), the resulting performance was excellent for that time. Some users, perhaps more enthusiastic than exact, described the acceleration as "breathtaking".

The car's nickname arose when an English journalist, at the 1959 presentation, remarked that it was the size of a doghouse. This term pre-vailed forever after, despite its official names – "Seven" in the original Austin version, and "Mini" in the Morris. Of these, the gradual winner was "Mini" for examples of either Austin or Morris make.

A trimmed version arrived in 1961. John Cooper, a well-known racing driver, enlarged the engine to 997 cc and, with double SU carburettors, got no less than 55 hp from it. The next year, BMC (British Motor Corporation) began to compete with the Mini. Many inter-national rallies were thus won by drivers such as Ranuno Altonen, Paddy Hopkirk and Timo Mäkinen. Still more triumphant was the Mini-Cooper S, unveiled in the spring of 1963 with a 1071-cc engine, followed a year later by a version with 1275 cc and 76 hp. The classic Monte Carlo Rally was won by Minis in 1964, 1965 and 1967.

If the transverse engine and front-wheel drive made a

perfect recipe for small cars, it also meant that success was not permanent. Other manufacturers took over the concept, even refining it, and by the early 1970s the "Doghouse" was quite old-fashioned. A novel version named "Clubman", with a nose 10 cm (4 in) longer, never sold well and was given up.

The "Doghouse" came at the right moment. It had some

1964 BMC Mini in the Morris version

thing fresh that the public embraced immediately, but there were defects too. Its quality was not very high. Cooling problems – the engine overheated – were almost as frequent as electrical problems with a system designed by Lucas, and rust was bad after only a few years.

While a new one can still be bought today, the model is now hopelessly obsolete. But its status as a forerunner of the modern small car, with a crosswise engine and power to the front wheels, will surely live on. ∎

Lotus Elite

COLIN CHAPMAN IS COUNTED AS ONE OF THE greatest designers of cars. He made a large number of innovations that are found today in everyday automobiles. In spite of his premature death, the Lotus company still produces fine cars as well as helping many other manufacturers to solve their technical problems.

Among Colin Chapman's early achievements was the use of plastic in building cars. The Lotus Elite can thus be called a turning point in automobile history. Until then, no one had tried to series-produce a car in which both the chassis and body were made of glassfibre-reinforced plastic.

Chapman had previously designed and built several small, fine sports cars such as the Lotus Seven and Eleven, but he had not yet made a real touring car. His creations were more like racing cars and met with considerable success.

Work on the Lotus Elite began in 1956, and the first prototype was presented at the 1957 London Motor Show. But production of the model started only two years later because, at that time in England, there was little experience of using plastic reinforced with glassfibre.

Another problem was that Lotus simply did not have

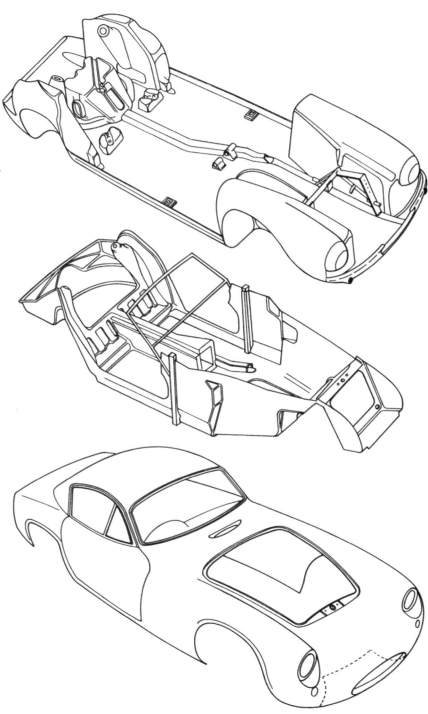

The Lotus Elite was a combination of glassfibre-reinforced plastic and self-supporting structure. It had three main moulded parts (shown here from top to bottom): the lower section with wheelhouses, a front "framepiece" to hold up the front wheel suspension, and an attachment for the differential; the inner body panels, drive shaft, engine-room sides; and the upper body section with the roof and wings. The doors, bonnet, and baggage-compartment lid were separate units. Only the front "framepiece" and the windscreen-arch tubing were made of metal.

A milestone in the motoring world, the Elite was the first Lotus designed for highway use and made entirely of glassfibre-reinforced plastic. Many people thought it one of the loveliest GT cars ever built.

enough factory space for building the new model. Consequently, the self-supporting design was manufactured by Bristol Aircraft, and delivered to Lotus where the engine and suspension were mounted. Initially, the structure consisted of 60 separately cast parts, but these were reduced to three – the floor section, midsection and body (as illustrated here).

The Elite had a four-cylinder engine with an overhead camshaft. Its cylinder volume was 1216 cc, and it gave 85 horsepower at 6,300 rpm. The gearbox had four steps and the top speed was 120 mph (195 km/h).

A sophisticated wheel suspension was used, reflecting Chapman's experience with racing. It was fully independent, with triangular links and spiral springs in front, while the rear had spiral springs and transverse links – known as Chapman struts. There were also disc brakes, and on the rear wheels they were mounted internally.

In competition, the Elite did extremely well. Between 1958 and 1964, it took home a class victory at Le Mans every year. The results were equally striking at club races in both England and America.

For all its triumphs and its beautiful looks, the Elite did not sell widely. It was much too expensive, and the buyers were mostly racing enthusiasts. To improve matters, Chapman offered customers the option of building an Elite from a kit.

This lowered the price and saved them a sales tax of 33%, which was not charged on kits. Even so, Lotus is said to have lost 100 pounds on every Elite it sold.

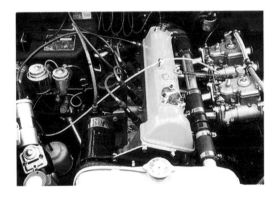

Chapman was now in desperate need of a profitable car, and in 1964 came the Lotus Elan, whose spinal frame was also a technical landmark. Production of the Elite, however, stopped in 1963 after a total run of 988 cars. Many of these survive today, and are rightly admired wherever they appear. ∎

Porsche 356

THE ORIGINAL SKETCHES FOR WHAT WAS TO BE A leading sports-car classic, the Porsche 356, date back to July 1947. They show something like a fat cigar, with a rear engine approximately in the middle, followed by the gearbox. An open model, it has no roof. The rear hatch

1958 Porsche 356

apparently opens backward for easier access to the engine, and there is only one seat – a sofa that might accommodate three bold humans.

The chassis technique was based on Porsche's own design for Volkswagen: suspension with torsion rods at both the front and rear. This primitive Porsche was a pretty gifted conveyance, granted that it had disadvantages. In particular, its intended production had become too expensive.

Nonetheless, the first Porsche was built according to the 1947 design, and was ready in May 1948 with its open stream-lined body. Displayed to journalists in July at the Bern Grand Prix, it drew immediate praise, especially for having excellent road qualities and being very easy to drive.

Porsche soon realized that, to make his own sports car, he must keep the costs as low as possible. The initial 356 had an

impossible price. A sensible solution was to exploit the Volkswagen, whose manu-facture had unexpectedly begun in the bombed factories at Wolfsburg. Basing the new sports car on parts from VW meant not only that it would be cheaper, but also that future spares could probably be supplied through VW dealers.

All this was arranged, and the engine-before-gearbox design was changed to the Volkswagen system with the engine in back. Most of the car was built with basic compo-nents from VW. Evil tongues said that a Porsche was not a distinctive car but a Volkswagen with tougher spark plugs, which could be pushed harder. Yet nothing could have been farther from the truth.

For while the Porsche 356/2, the model with the engine in back, did rest upon a Volkswagen foundation, it had unique characteristics in both driving and other respects. The VW engine's volume of 1131 cc was soon decreased to under 1100 cc, so that the car could compete in this class. The valves were enlarged and the compression raised. Suddenly the engine felt gigantic – not least due to Porsche's light body, made of

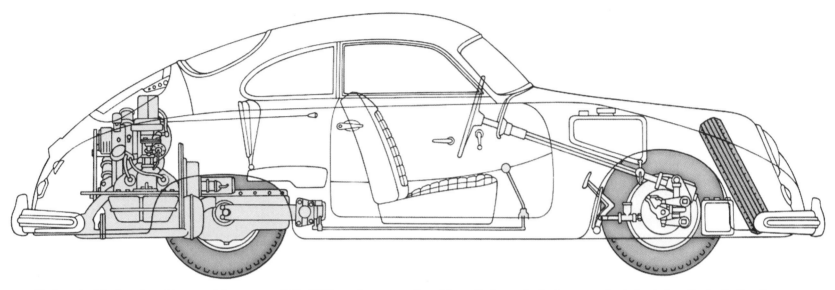

The innards of the Porsche 356 have much in common with the VW Type 1 (see page 146), and the earliest examples took many mechanical parts from the Beetle. Even the front suspension obeyed the same principle of torsion bars and backward-turned supporting arms. But this system was far older in origin, deriving from Auto Union's famous 16-cylinder racing cars, which Ferdinand Porsche had designed.

hand-beaten aluminium in a coupé shape. During 1948, a series of 150 cars was planned, but it ran into obstacles.

Such a method of making bodies was arduous and definitely unsuited to mass production. There were also problems with manufacturing the bodies, and other factors that distracted Porsche: for example, being Volkswagen's retail agent in Switzerland, and more business in the Porsche design company.

A body shop in Switzerland agreed to build some cabriolets. One of these was shown in March 1949 at the Salon in Geneva, and numerous fascinated buyers signed up for it. Without this success, Porsche would probably have stopped making cars. History, though, had different aims.

The production went ahead slowly, and not many cars came out. When Porsche moved the operation to Germany in 1951,

only about 60 had emerged from the original factory in Austria. To avoid the difficulty of hand-beating, he ordered 500 coupé bodies from the German carriage-maker Reutter. Thus the manufacturing process was set right, and Porsche's name began to earn fame as a car make.

Countless victories, in both track races and rallies, contributed to the 356's renown. Its engines were improved and given more power. When its last specimens were built in August 1955, to be replaced by the 356A, nearly 8,000 of them had rolled forth, ensuring a bright future for one of the world's greatest sports-car manufacturers.

The subsequent 356A, and the later 356B which continued until 1963, were distinctive in their own ways – but essentially the same car as the 356/2 which had been put together with VW pieces. ∎

Ferrari 250 GT SWB

1959 Ferrari 250 GT SWB

Enzo Ferrari was born on 18 February 1898, in a little house at Via Santa Caterina 136 in Modena, Italy. His father Alfredo, who ran a workshop, came from nearby Carpi and was the son of a delicatessen owner. It has thus been said that Enzo fulfilled the destiny of a family of gourmets by making the most appetizing of automobiles. He died in 1988.

FERRARI IS UNQUESTIONABLY THE WORLD'S MOST PRESTIGIOUS sports car make. Others have indeed produced equally fine cars, but none can match the renown of this name. Here is one of the best models Ferrari ever built.

When young, Enzo Ferrari was not technically inclined, but he learned a good deal about cars in his father's auto repair shop. After World War I, he tried to get a job at Fiat but was refused, despite his letters of recommendation. He found work with a couple of small firms, one of which was owned by a racing enthusiast. Enzo was given a chance to compete, and his fortune was made.

In 1929, Enzo established a legendary racing team – the Scuderia Ferrari, which was based in Modena. Eventually he managed to persuade Alfa Romeo to take it over. This was his occupation until 1938, when Alfa decided to start competing again by itself. Then Ferrari had to move his cars and personnel to Milan.

At this point he felt tired of racing and left the team in 1939. His thoughts turned to building a car of his own, and in the old Scuderia Ferrari premises on the Viale Trento Trieste, he founded a company called Auto Avio Costruzioni. It could not be named Ferrari because, on leaving Alfa Romeo, he had agreed not to use his name on any racing car for a period of four years.

He now received an order for two cars, to be ready in time for the 1940 Mille Miglia. One of the customers was a debutante, Alberto Ascari, who would become World Champion twice after the war in a Ferrari. The cars that were built had a simple designation: Tipo 815.

PEACE BRINGS THE FIRST FERRARI

In 1946, Ferrari commenced the construction of a car with his own name. It was the Tipo 125, equipped with a V12 engine –

The most desirable of all Ferraris – 250 GTO from 1962

something that later amounted to a synonym of the Ferrari make. A steady series of successes followed, and the road to riches lay open. Until 1955, when the Ferrari 250 GT emerged, Enzo's red rockets won innumerable races for both Formula 1 and sports cars.

Already at an early stage, Ferrari went into building sports cars for road use. The first, appearing in 1948, was the neat little 166 Inter, with a body by Touring of Milan. Its small V12 engine of 1995 cc yielded 110 horsepower at 6,000 rpm.

Next came several superb models such as the 195 and 212 Inter, the 340 and 342 America, the 250 Europa and the 410 Superamerica. But the arrival of the Ferrari 250 GT in 1955 marked the birth of a definite classic.

This was the first true GT (Gran Turismo), which meant a fast long-distance touring car. Its type of body was known as a berlinetta, indicating in Italian that it was a small sedan. Illustrated here is a 250 GT from 1959, which had the additional designation SWB (Short Wheel Base). Many observers regard it as still one of the most beautiful creations in automotive history. Its harmonious lines are comparable to those of, for example, the Lotus Elite and the M.G. TC, described elsewhere in this book.

The Ferrari 250 GT contained a welded tube frame. In this sat a 3-litre V12, giving 220/240 hp at 7,000 rpm – or 260/280 hp in the competition versions. Of the 163 examples built, 74 were for racing.

With its four-speed gearbox, the car could reach between 203 and 268 km/h (125–165 mph) depending on the trimming and gear ratios. Its acceleration varied accordingly, but was at least as good as 7 seconds from standstill to 100 km/h (60 mph).

The bodies, produced by Pininfarina, were made of either sheet steel or aluminium. Wind-tunnel tests showed that the design gave extraordinarily low air resistance, to a degree not matched by many cars even today.

These cars saw frequent use on race tracks, and Enzo Ferrari is said to have remarked: "They can be driven on the road during the week and in competition during the weekends." That was just what he wanted. But a glance at the SWB should be enough to reveal that it is not a mere "street racer". This is a racer liberated from all but the bare necessities.

Once during the late 1980s, I stopped at a traffic light in Italy, on my way to a competition for historical racing cars in Mugello. Suddenly a 250 GT, itself prepared to compete, drove up behind me. Through my window I could hear the growling of the V12 engine. The ground was shaking, and my son looked at me in terror. "Papa, what's that?" I replied coolly, "Why, it's a Ferrari 250 GT."

I stretched my arm out of the window and stuck up a thumb. Then the light turned green. After a couple of metres, I heard the Ferrari's sound rise to a roar, and a second later it passed. The driver gave me a V-sign and the car vanished into the distance. ■

Ford Edsel

EDSEL, THE SON OF HENRY FORD, WAS A CAPABLE industrialist who unfortunately had to work in the shadow of his powerful father. But he held on, and influenced the old man already during the 1920s to replace the Model T with something new, as well as to bet on the Lincoln Zephyr which did very nicely in the 1930s.

> It has not been unknown for a car project to collapse even though everything looked quite good on paper. Some of the makes involved have become synonymous with failure, such as the Mercedes A-Klasse which was nicknamed the Flip-class after turning over in steering tests. No less notorious was the Ford Edsel, predicted to be a success and put down after only three years. 🚗

Edsel had many merits as both a businessman and a human being, so his name carried weight in the Ford company. When he suddenly died, his oldest son, Henry Ford II, became the natural successor to Grandpa. It was also natural to name a car model for Edsel as a token of esteem.

America's auto industry in the 1950s was largely based on the fact that customers were faithful to their makes. This was partly due to the country's financial system. People continually bought new cars and, as long as they kept to the same family of makes, their credit went on rolling. One could buy anything at all – it was only a matter of moving up in size when one wanted to change models.

General Motors offered a whole spectrum of cars to choose from. Chevrolet was low-priced, then came Pontiac and Oldsmobile, but Buick and Cadillac were there too. The same could be said of Chrysler, starting with a Plymouth and exchanging it for a Dodge or Chrysler, and next for a De Soto or Imperial.

At Ford, the model range was narrower: Ford meant cheapness, followed by Mercury and Lincoln. That was all. When more expensive models began to sell better during the mid-1950s, Ford woke up and started designing a finer car in the medium-price class. The whole project was called the E-car, partly because it had been decided to name the new series for Edsel Ford.

At first, Edsel's widow and children were opposed to the decision. They did not look forward to seeing his name on hundreds of thousands of hubcaps. But after many other proposals, and a contest that brought in 18,000 more, the Ford people resolved that "Edsel" was not such a bad prospect. Once Henry Ford II was persuaded, this became the new car's official name.

The intention was to sell Edsels on a grand scale. Before their introduction on 4 September 1957, as the year model of 1958, Ford invested enormous sums in spreading the car's image. Hired stunt-men performed dangerous manoeuvres for the press and public, fashion shows and competitions were

The 1959 Edsel Ranger 4 Four Door Sedan cost $2,684 and was made in 12,814 examples.

held, and movie stars were engaged to encourage a warm response from the wondering market.

Interest was infinite, but when the car did emerge, buyers were not as eager as expected. It was just terribly ordinary, like any other American car of the late Fifties. Perhaps a bit too much chrome, and a softer ride – yet these were not seen as advantages at the time. Rather the contrary. Besides, the initial model's automatic gearbox had a pushbutton system in the middle of the steering wheel, which seemed exciting but was fairly foolish and impractical while driving.

Many thought that the Edsel's design was exaggerated. It had lines and chrome features which were not logical but looked crude. Neither was the front view appreciated. One person compared the oval, vertical grille with the yoke of a horse, while it reminded another of a toilet seat. Evil tongues – presumably competitors – even suggested a resemblance to female genitals, which was too much for the puritanical society of those decades.

The Edsel was potent enough, as it used Ford's strongest engine of 345 hp. Still it proved to be a flop: in 1958 only 63,110 were made, on a market of more than six million cars. During the second year, production fell to a mere 44,000. For the model's last year, 1960, the figure was barely 3,000.

Several models of the Edsel existed under names such as Citation, Corsair, Ranger and Pacer. All of these designations were to be used later by other manufacturers in the USA. But Ford never again dared to repeat its disappointing experience with the Edsel. ■

Cadillac 1959

1959 Cadillac Eldorado De Ville

SOME CAR MAKES HAVE PRODUCED YEAR MODELS THAT became classics with time and are always regarded reverently by motoring enthusiasts. They need not love the car in question, but they respect the fact that it marked a special moment in automotive development – rather like connoisseurs of wine who bow to the bottles of a distinguished year.

The 1959 Cadillac is such a car. Few vehicles characterize their period as clearly as this one. For 1959 brought the "fin hysteria" of the fifties to its peak. The practice of adding fins to a car's body style might well have meant, for instance, that drivers felt ever more like fish in a growing sea of traffic. But actually it reflected the rising image of rapid, including supersonic, airplanes.

Streamlining and speed in the air were symbols of success in the late 1940s and early 1950s. Flying had been a useful tool in World War II, but now it became popular and pointed the way to a future full of potential. Emblems of aircraft pervaded the auto industry – in the names of makes and models, as well as in decoration – so why not give the whole body an appearance of being airborne?

Studebaker began to do so already in the forties with a pontoon body, whose fenders were pulled in to flatten the sides. The body increasingly resembled an airplane's fuselage, suggesting not only elegance but power and velocity. Fins were adopted to some extent by almost every manufacturer, mainly in America and spreading to Europe. Obviously, fins could not be put on a Volkswagen Type 1 body – yet even the conservative Mercedes had a temporary hint of fins on its rear.

The 1959 Cadillac was the pharaoh of fins. Nearly nineteen

feet long (5.72 metres), it weighed 2.2 tons and needed a big engine. This was normally Cadillac's V8 of 390 cubic inches (6.4 litres) and 325 horsepower. The Eldorado had an additional 20 hp, due to a different camshaft and three dual-port carburettors instead of one four-port.

Impressive though it was, the car's design reveals surprising vulgarity to a modern observer. How can such a thing have been built at all? That the men bent over a drawingboard would fall for its beauty is understandable, but to imagine the chairman of the board standing for it requires a great deal of fantasy.

The grille consisted of a number of shiny buttons mounted on shafts. Offshoots of the grille wrapped around the corners onto the fenders. Dual headlights, parking lights and turn lights were framed or ringed in chrome. There were eyebrows over the headlights, and a chrome detail over each front fender running backward – with a little fin sticking up.

The panorama windshield was angled back at its upper edge. Only a press fold at the front fenders interrupted the clean body sides. The body tapered backward to a chrome strip where the enormous tailfins protruded. These held two rear lights, like squeezed-out rockets, with reverse lights in the middle and ringed by chrome. The grille pattern was repeated in the chrome between the trunk's lower edge and the rear bumper.

An old topic of speculation is how the 1959 Cadillac would have looked without its fins. Apart from the grille and front end, it might have presented a really harmonious shape. But the car's lack of logic can also be accepted in its own terms and leave us admiring the original design. Today we should be grateful that Cadillac dared to make history with it.

In spite of its size, the car was not hard to drive. Servo steering and an automatic transmission enabled it to almost drive itself. A governor was standard and brought the car up

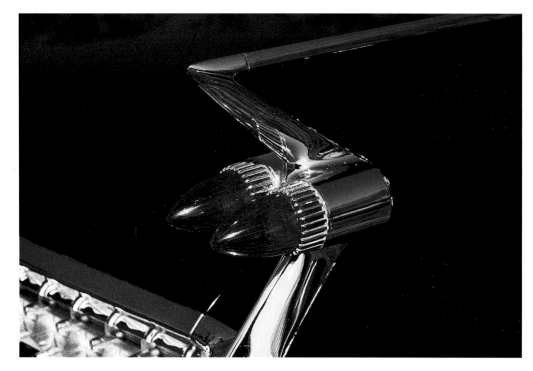

to the previously set speed after braking.

Test drivers often complain of inability to see all four corners of a car when sitting at the wheel. But the opposite was true of the 1959 Cadillac. Never has a car displayed its extremities so well, and a finfanatic could be excused for seeing nothing except the corners.

The wide front seat did not provide perfect comfort: It tended to bulge at the sides and make the passenger's body lean. But it had to be a sofa, and it added softness to the ride. One seemed literally to float along the road in this car.

Cadillac used chrome in 1959 to define the differences between many of its models. Their chrome strips were of varying width, thickness and location. Keeping track of which model had which chrome is a Cadillac expert's nightmare. Anyhow, the 1959 programme offered four models with the same wheelbase of 130 inches (330 cm): the Series 62, the 63 De Ville, the 60 Special Fleetwood, and the 64/69. A longer wheelbase of 150 inches (380 cm) belonged to the Fleetwood 75 and Series 67. All had the same style, though with slightly distinctive bodies.

Simplest was the Series 62, but even this model carried elaborate equipment – including servo brakes, dual rear lights, and electrical adjustment of the windows and front seat. The 63 De Ville cost more and was available as either a sedan or a coupe.

Series 64 was the Eldorado. It could be a two-door hardtop or a convertible, named the Seville and Biarritz respectively. There was also a four-door hardtop, often called the Brougham. The 60 Special Fleetwood had an elongated chassis, allowing wider doors that were advertised as increasing the comfort of stepping in or out.

For those unfamiliar with the make, a Cadillac may be just an ostentatious limousine. Nonetheless, the company has been responsible for many technical innovations over the years. Things that we think natural in a car have frequently started in a Cadillac. While the 1959 range did not go far in this direction, it was surely a kind of breakthrough to create the world's most extravagant flasher of fins. ■

1960
−1970

The Ford Thunderbird had become one of the usual large American two-door cars by 1963, available as a coupe or convertible – but it lacked the elegance of, for example, its rival the Buick Riviera. This year an odd version was the above Sports Roadster, with spoked wheels and streamlined headrests in racing style. The latter were actually just a glassfibre panel covering the rear seat, and most buyers were not amused to pay 650 dollars extra for it. The standard engine was a 6.4-litre 300-horsepower V8, and a manual gearbox was not offered.

IN AUSTRALIA, SIX PEOPLE PERISH DURING A HEAT wave, with temperatures up to 52°C. Albert Camus, the 1957 Nobel Prize Laureate in literature, dies in an automobile accident in France. President Charles de Gaulle's liberal policy toward Algeria causes violent riots there. The largest passenger ship ever, named *France*, is launched. Newspapers around the world publish the first picture broadcast via the moon. The city of Agadir in Morocco is totally destroyed by an earthquake.

Piracy at sea still occurs, and a pirate captain with 70 men hijacks a cruise liner with 560 passengers off the Caribbean island of Curaçao, but eventually he has to give up.

South Korea is in an uproar – the autocratic president Syngman Rhee resigns. An earthquake in the Pacific Ocean wreaks great damage in Hawaii, Japan, the Philippines, Australia and New Zealand. The famous opera tenor Jussi Björling dies. Nikita Khrushchev attacks the United Nations

From this angle it is hard to see that the 1964 Chevrolet Corvair Monza holds a rear engine, and that the "bonnet" is reserved for baggage. Ralph Nader has not yet launched his crusade against this development of the Volkswagen theme, with independent suspension all round and an air-cooled six-cylinder boxer engine. But it was already quite clear that the Monza was not just a simple compact car like others. The same year, Chevrolet also took a step toward future improvements – by using the exhaust to drive a turbocompressor. Such a device had previously been used only in heavy diesel lorries, and its widespread use in passenger cars would not begin until the 1980s.

and its general secretary, Dag Hammarskjöld, with a display of uncivilized behaviour at the U.N. General Assembly in New York. De Gaulle's policy gains ground and Algeria wins independence. Experiments with artificial insemination give rise to scientific and religious debates in Italy.

Adolf Eichmann, a main Nazi persecutor of Jews during the war, is brought to trial in Jerusalem, sentenced to death and executed in 1962. The Soviet Union sends an unmanned rocket to Venus, and Yuri Gagarin becomes the first human being in space. France undergoes a political crisis, facing De Gaulle with wild demonstrations. The Swedish royal flagship *Vasa* begins to be raised at Stockholm, having capsized on her maiden voyage and sunk 333 years earlier. East German

communists, supported by the Soviets, build a wall across Berlin, effectively cutting the country off from West Germany. At Cape Canaveral in Florida, the Americans send their first man into space, Alan Shepard. President John F. Kennedy meets Khrushchev in Vienna.

U.N. General Secretary Dag Hammarskjöld dies in a mysterious airplane crash near Ndola in Northern Rhodesia (later Zimbabwe). President Kennedy reveals that Cuban bases have Soviet rockets pointed toward the United States; a serious crisis erupts. After American threats, Khrushchev backs down, promising that the weaponry will be dismantled and returned to the Soviet Union. An American nuclear submarine, *Thresher*, goes to the bottom in 2,800 metres of water,

The 1968 Jensen, an Anglo-American product, had servo assistance for most purposes. As early as 1936, Jensen built a luxury car with Ford's V8 engine. This Interceptor, designed by Vignale, is equipped with a 6.3-litre Chrysler V8, three-speed automatic gearbox, dual-circuit brake system with discs all round and double master cylinders, electrically powered side-windows, and heating coils on the rear window pane. Servo steering, however, would not be included until 1970. It is interesting to note that Jensen now had a full steel construction, whereas glassfibre bodies were used during 1954–66. The price of 3,472 pounds was a lot to pay for a car in the late 1960s, even if the fuel consumption of 22 litres/100 km (about 11 miles per gallon) was no worry as long as petrol remained cheap and abundant. Still, the top speed of almost 200 km/h (125 mph) and the comfortable ride enabled 4,500 of these cars to be sold between 1967 and 1973.

and 129 men die. Southern states in the USA suffer racial violence and the black pastor Martin Luther King campaigns for Afro-Americans' civil rights.

German cars achieve international successes at the expense of some British makes, which cannot quite match the quality that comes from careful production, thorough inspection and good service, demanded by growing worldwide competition. Automobile technology in the 1960s is ever more attentive to safety. Europeans begin to realize that rear-engine cars such as the Volkswagen, Renault 4CV, Škoda and Simca 1000 and others, with a rear suspension of the swing-axle type, have a dangerous tendency to oversteer as the power of engines is increased. An inexperienced driver may be surprised and lose control – just as a well-trained one can use the same tendency for fast driving on curves and corners, as shown by Porsche's successes in racing. In the United States, a Chevrolet model emerges, the Corvair, with a six-cylinder "boxer" engine; it offers definite understeering as long as one is careful about the tyre pressure. But the pressure is often ignored, and some fatal accidents provoke the consumer champion Ralph Nader

Every line betrays its beauty: Even when standing still, the 1968 Lamborghini Espada looks as if it is doing 240 km/h (150 mph), as it certainly can. This was the company's best-seller and 1,277 had been sold by 1975. Since the aim was a four-seater, the engine lay in front: a 3.9-litre V12 with four overhead camshafts, and six carburettors fed by two electric fuel pumps. The five-speed gearbox had Lamborghini's peculiar synchronized reverse. Here was a car for owners who could and gladly did drive, so it did not even offer servo steering as an extra, let alone an automatic transmission. But electric side-windows and air-conditioning were standard, like the centre-lock wheels.

to write a controversial book, *Unsafe at Any Speed*. This deals the final blow to the Corvair, and ultimately to all family-type passenger cars with the engine placed behind the rear axle.

In California, air pollution becomes a gloomy problem, and 1965 brings compulsory testing of car exhausts. Two years afterward, NSU's Ro80 is presented, the world's first series-manufactured automobile with a Wankel engine, a compact triangular rotating-piston design. Sweden introduces right-hand traffic, as does Israel a year later. Direct fuel injection, instead of a fuel system with traditional carburettor, is adopted in series production by several car makes. Americans increasingly regard the automatic transmission as a natural feature in a family car. This decade does not display any other revolutionary technical innovations in cars, but their speed is now being measured by police with radar equipment.

The West German chancellor since 1949, Konrad Adenauer, resigns in 1963 and is replaced by Ludwig Erhard. America receives a shock, and a mystery of its own, when President Kennedy is shot in Dallas. The St. Bernhard Tunnel – Europe's first road passage through the Alps, with a length of 5.8 kilometres (3.6 miles) – is inaugurated. Regular passenger traffic by hovercraft across the English Channel shortens its travel time radically. The French-British supersonic passenger airliner Concorde is unveiled at Sud-Aviation in Toulouse. Back at Cape Canaveral, now named Cape Kennedy, the world's first commercial communications satellite "Early Bird" is sent into space. The United States, Great Britain and the Soviet Union agree to a ban on nuclear weapon tests in the atmosphere, in space and under water. History's biggest train robbery is committed in Buckinghamshire, England, costing somebody

American Motors tried during the 1960s to throw off its image of pragmatic platitude. The Marlin – originally a Rambler in 1965 – was an attempt to enter the "personality" market, and this 1966 version had a suitably strange shape. But it was a big car (wheelbase and length 9'4" and 13'3", or 2.85 and 4.05 metres) compared with, say, the Ford Mustang. The standard engine, as expected, was a dull overhead-valve 3.8-litre, although an optional 5.4-litre V8 could give it impressive speed. The public did not appreciate its whale-like looks, resulting in ever lower sales figures and only 17,500 buyers in three seasons.

several millions of pounds. The Vaiont Dam in Italy collapses, wiping out six townships.

Greek and Turkish inhabitants of Cyprus approach open war with each other. Sir Winston Churchill dies from a blood clot in the brain. Lyndon Johnson is sworn in as the next U.S. President. American astronaut Edward White takes a 20-minute "space walk" from the satellite Gemini 4, which circles the earth 62 times. Race riots occur in Watts, a black district of Los Angeles. Indira Gandhi becomes the new Prime Minister of India. The Berlin Wall passes its fifth birthday and Walter Ulbricht, the East German head of state, declares that it has maintained peace and prevented "the adventurers in Bonn" from starting a war.

Israel wins a blitzkrieg known as the "Six-Day War" in June

(*Top*) The sluggish but dependable Peugeot 403 sold in more than 1,100,000 examples between 1955 and 1967. There were many model variants, such as the 403/Sept (with the old 1290-cc engine from the 203 model), a diesel, a cabriolet, an estate car and a series of light transport vehicles. Although rust took a toll in the end, the 403 was a tough car; among other things, it managed a victory in the 1956 Ampol Trial in Australia, and did well in the African Safari rally – where the subsequent 404 was to succeed strongly. Pininfarina designed the bodies of both the 403 and 404, but he preserved their French character. This disappeared on later models, which could as easily have been Fiats or Austins from the same drawing-board.

(*Above*) Not yet the ultimate in conventionally built Ferraris for road use – the Daytona was still to come – but the best available in 1966, this is a 275 GTB/4 berlinetta with the short wheelbase of 2.4 metres (7 feet 10 inches). Servo disc brakes and dual circuits were almost standard for supercars, but Ferrari had now adopted independent rear suspension and a five-speed transaxle with limited-slip differential. The V12 engine had the renowned cylinder dimensions (77 x 58.8 mm) giving 3286 cc of volume, but now there were two overhead camshafts per cylinder bank, and six Weber carburettors with dual ports. Its 300 horsepower meant a top speed of 250 km/h (155 mph), and a quarter-mile (400 metres) in 14.7 seconds from standstill. Despite only two years of production, 280 were sold.

(*Top*) After 1963 no genuine sports cars were in the Mercedes-Benz model range, but a series of well-developed and lovely roadsters had a six-cylinder engine with overhead camshafts. The original 230SL was refined into this 250SL (2.5 litres, seven-bearing crankshaft) from 1967, and finally into the 280SL. Fuel injection was standard, and the redesigned rear swing axle eliminated the road-holding problems of older versions. All the models had servo steering and automatic gears. Top speed was nearly 200 km/h (125 mph), and these luxurious open cars sold in great numbers: 44,312 between 1963 and 1971.

(*Below*) Brutal strength in Euro-American style: The AC-Shelby Cobra 427 from 1967. Its body came from the 1954 AC Ace and it had the same chassis frame with two sturdy steel tubes. But now spiral springs, both front and rear, replaced the earlier system of transverse leaf springs, and the wings were widened due to the necessarily wider wheel-rims. It did about 100 mph (160 km/h) with AC's aging six-cylinder engine, or 150 mph (240 km/h) – matched by great acceleration – with the American Ford's finest V8 of 7 litres and 425 horsepower. Some 1,500 Cobras of various types were produced during 1962–69, earlier ones having engines of 4.3 or 4.7 litres). The model also became a favourite of replica builders in the 1980s.

The problems of mid-engine cars were obvious in the 1966 Lotus Europa. You could, of course, lift off the panel over the rear to get at the carburettor, battery and oil filler. The original version had a Renault R16 engine with push-rods, reaching 185 km/h (115 mph) and accelerating in 10.4 seconds from 0 to 100 km/h (62 mph). This is a later example of 1971, as shown by the cut-down upper body sides, the wheels and the two fuel-filler pipes. It then had a Lotus-Ford engine of 1588 cc with double overhead camshafts. Of the different Europa types, 9,230 were made, the last in 1975.

1967 against Egypt, Syria and Jordan. Martin Luther King is shot in Memphis, Tennessee – soon followed in California by Robert Kennedy, the last President's brother. The democratic "Prague Spring" movement in Czechoslovakia comes to a bitter end when Soviet, Polish, East German, Bulgarian and Hungarian troops invade. This is condemned by the world, termed a threat to international order and morality by the U.N., and seen as a great setback for efforts to relax tension between East and West. Richard Nixon manages to win a presidential election. In Spain, the decrepit dictator Franco chooses Prince Juan Carlos as his successor. The war in Vietnam, two decades

old, reaches a climax and, in Washington, massive protests confront the White House. In France, President de Gaulle dies.

The world's first heart transplant is performed by a South African doctor, Christian Barnard. Soviet achievements in space have almost ceased to embarrass the United States, and in 1968 an American manned vehicle travels around the moon. Next summer, this trip is made by the rocket Apollo 11 and an ancient dream comes true. Neil Armstrong's soaring pulse echoes on global television as he becomes the first mortal to step on what everyone is suddenly calling "the lunar surface". ∎

Chevrolet Corvette Sting Ray

A Sting Ray from 1963

THIS IS THE SPORTS CAR THAT HAS BEEN BUILT for a longer time than any other. It began in 1953 and is still as popular as ever.

The Chevrolet Corvette arose because General Motors' design chief Harley Earl, himself a sports-car enthusiast, wanted the company to make something that could compete with Jaguar's XK120, which was very popular in the United States.

As usual in America at that time, the Corvette started out in the role of a "dream car". Such mesmeric machines were exhibited at the national automobile shows to test public response. This one became the world's first series-produced automobile with a body made of plastic reinforced by glassfibre.

But the dream was not fulfilled, for the car contained Chevrolet's old 3.8-litre cast-iron six-cylinder engine, as well

as a two-speed Powerglide automatic gearbox. The latter was enjoyed least of all by American sports-car fans. Sales were bad and, at the end of 1954, the retailers had 1,500 unwanted examples. It seemed that the ambitious project would meet a sorry end.

In 1955 came Chevrolet's new V8, which changed the situation. This engine had 210 horsepower, and the car was given a manual gearbox. The standard engine yielded a top speed of 120 mph (190 km/h). An optional four-port engine offered 225 hp, and 1957 brought a fuel-injected engine with 283 hp. Now the car could do about 135 mph (215 km/h), on a par with the contemporary Jaguar XK140.

The power increased constantly in the capable hands of Zora Arkus-Duntov, and in 1962 he extracted 360 hp from

what was then a volume of 5358 cc. Annual production had passed 10,000 cars in 1960, and at last the company began to profit from the model.

Triumphs on the race track were also commencing. Between 1958 and 1963, Corvettes won every year in Class B of the SCCA championship. In 1960 they finished eighth and tenth at Le Mans, a considerable achievement in the face of such competitors as Ferrari and Aston Martin.

THE STING RAY ARRIVES

For a true Corvette enthusiast, the name hardly existed until the Sting Ray was introduced in 1963. Apart from the engine, this was a completely new car, even in the body design with its retractable headlamps. For the first time there was a fastback coupe with a "split" rear window – a model that is highly desirable today.

The road-holding was improved by giving the Sting Ray independent suspension on all four wheels. In front were link-arms and spiral springs, while transverse leaf springs and lower crosslinks were in back.

Among the several engine options, the strongest had 360 hp. The gearbox was either a four-speed manual or a two-speed

Powerglide automatic. With a 250-hp engine, the top speed was 145 mph (235 km/h).

During its first year, the Sting Ray sold extremely well, and more than 21,000 cars found happy owners – the best Corvette sales figure until then. Totally, 118,964 of this original model would be built.

In 1964, the split rear window disappeared, and in 1965 disc brakes were added on all wheels. Five engines were now available, the strongest having 6490 cc and 425 hp.

However, the horsepower craze required even bigger engines, and in 1968 came the L88, with 6997 cc and 435 hp. The "theoretical" top speed of a Sting Ray – which the model was then no longer called – was 170 mph (275 km/h) with an L88 engine. In racing form, this engine generated 560 hp, a fantastic feat for a pushrod motor.

The car's design underwent some changes, inspired by the experimental car Mako Shark II. In 1969 the name "Sting Ray" returned, but was spelled "Stingray" – and here ends our story. As already indicated, the Corvette line continues to thrive. ∎

1961 Chevrolet Corvette

NSU Wankel Spider and Ro 80

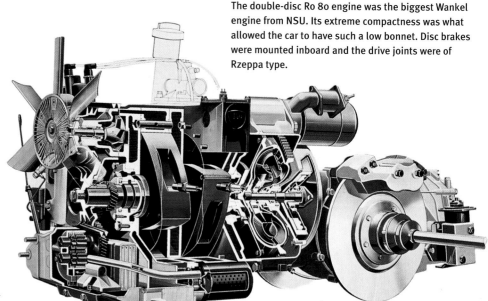

The double-disc Ro 80 engine was the biggest Wankel engine from NSU. Its extreme compactness was what allowed the car to have such a low bonnet. Disc brakes were mounted inboard and the drive joints were of Rzeppa type.

NSU WAS THE FIRST AUTO MANUFACTURER to put a Wankel engine in a series-produced car. But the design was unreliable and, ironically enough, it was Mazda in Japan that would bring the Wankel engine to perfection.

Felix Wankel, born in 1903, was an inventor – and a truly ingenious one. In 1924 he began to work on a rotary-piston engine. Such engines had been built previously, but all the experiments had failed because of their problems with sealing.

As it happened, sealing problems were Wankel's specialty, and in 1934 he presented a new type of sealing to Daimler-Benz. However, their enthusiasm was mild to say the least.

Infuriated, Wankel took a job at BMW in the engine design department. He was given complete freedom, but met

NSU's 1963 Wankel Spider was a descendant of the Bertone-designed Sport Prinz.

with little understanding when he proposed the Wankel concept again. So he left BMW and went to NSU (Neckarsulmer Fahrzeugwerke), which showed greater appreciation of his advanced ideas.

NSU began its activities in 1901 by making a small one-cylinder motorcycle, and was to become even better known in this field than as a car manufacturer. In 1906 appeared its first car, the Neckarsulmer 6/10 PS.

Then followed a long list of autos and motorcycles. NSU also competed often, notably with motorcycles that enjoyed much success all the way into the mid-1950s.

In 1957 the first rotary engine was test-driven. It had 125 cc and delivered 29 hp at 17,000 rpm. During the spring of 1960, two NSU Prinz III cars were exhibited with rotary engines. These had a chamber volume of 250 cc and gave about 30 hp.

Wankel's rotary engine now aroused enormous interest, and patent rights were sold to many companies. Curtiss-Wright in America bought the right for making airplane engines. Numerous firms also purchased the manufacturing right for

NSU Ro 80

petrol powered Wankel engines in various size classes.

At the Frankfurt auto show in 1963, NSU created a minor sensation by unveiling the NSU Wankel Spider. This pioneer in the series production of rotary-engine cars had a single-disc engine with 500 cc, yielding 50 hp. Its turning speed was supposed to go no higher than 6,000 rpm, but could easily be wound up to 8,000 rpm, which often led to serious consequences.

The Wankel Spider, though, was a model hard to sell, as it soon acquired a bad reputation for so many engine break-downs. Moreover, it was expensive at 8,500 marks, compared with 5,135 for the Sport Prinz. Totally, only 2,375 examples were built between 1964 and July 1967 – and not until the next October were the last cars sold.

Another sensation occurred at Frankfurt in 1967, when NSU presented the Ro 80 – a vehicle far ahead of its time, just as in the case of the Citroën DS 19 (see the article on that car). The Ro 80 not only challenged BMW and

Mercedes, but had a double-disc Wankel engine. Its chamber volume was 995 cc, equivalent to around 2,000 cc for a two-litre piston engine. The output was 115 hp at 5,500 rpm.

With its wedge-shaped body, the Ro 80 could reach a top speed of 180 km/h (110 mph). It had front-wheel drive and many technically sophisticated details.

Unfortunately, the Ro 80 carried a crushing price, which at first was 14,150 marks, compared with 11,800 for a BMW 2000. It sold well to begin with, but shared the Wankel Spider's unreliability. The saying was that a Ro 80 received three new engines before it had even done 65,000 kilometres, and that the owner next installed a Ford engine.

Thus, according to Gunnar Elmgren, a famous Swedish motoring journalist, "...when Ro 80 drivers met in traffic, they would raise one, two or three fingers to show how many times they had changed the engine."

Despite improvements in the engine, and plans for a larger version (with 180 hp), the production was stopped in March 1977. By then, NSU had long ago ceased to operate as an independent company, for in 1967 it was taken over by Audi. And once the Ro 80 line came to a halt, the name of NSU passed into history. ■

Thanks to its low front, the NSU Ro 80 had a CW-value no higher than 0.355.

Porsche 911

A cutaway view of the 3.3-litre Turbo from 1989. In front were triangular link-arms, and the almost vertically mounted shock absorber acted as a spring-leg. The rear wheels were suspended in drag-arms. Under the wing lay the intercooler, which lowered the fuel-air mixture's temperature.

ORSCHE PRESENTED A WHOLLY NEW CAR AT THE Frankfurt exhibition in 1963, with the model designation 901. This was to follow the successful 356. Behind its rear axle and gearbox lay a six-cylinder boxer engine, with 2 litres of volume and 130 horsepower.

The car went into series production next year, but now labelled 911. Peugeot had protested against Porsche's use of a model name with a zero in the middle, which the French company had "patented". But the resultant change of name was not important. It was the essence of the car that evoked such feelings in drivers as to transform their view of what an automobile should be. Its low lines were like nothing else on the road. Comfort was superb, and the performance seemed heavenly – though the first 911's abilities, compared with what would come later, were almost laughable.

When the 356 began to be manufactured, the idea was to make a more enjoyable car from Volkswagen parts, mainly for the sake of cheapness. The new Porsche did not have even a bolt in common with the old VW, its only debt being to the concept of an air-cooled engine at the rear. Torsion-bar suspension came from VW as well, but was made very differently in the Porsche. The rear had transverse torsion springing as in the VW, but it was provided with an obliquely mounted swing-arm that guided the movements on the double-jointed axle. The rear-axle construction was much less prone to skidding than the VW's.

That the Porsche tended to skid anyhow – primarily due to

the high power on the rear wheels and the great rear weight – was another matter. This behaviour was predictable and consistent in all circumstances, so it could be exploited by whoever wanted to drive really fast. There was no risk that a Porsche 911 understeered – tending to go straight forward in a curve – since it preferred to oversteer and slide the rear end. Thus one always had "steering" through the rear end's sliding, and this was useful to adept drivers.

The front end also had torsion-bar suspension, but longitudinal instead of transverse. Each of two separate bars held its own lower triangular spring.

The 911 was effectively a two-seater, its rudimentary rear seat being rather symbolic. Perhaps two children of moderate proportions could sit in back, but not very comfortably. Porsche

1986 Porsche 911 Turbo

did a design study for a four-seat car, with an extended wheelbase, a less sloping roof, and larger rear side-panes. But this model looked terrible and was scrapped before it even became a serious proposal.

As Porsche is one of the world's smallest car makers, and was still smaller when the 911 emerged, the body work constantly smacked of handicraft. This need not mean worse results, but it often involves welding a lot of sheet-metal parts into a unit. The aim is to avoid investing much in elaborate body-pressing tools, since the total output of cars is relatively small. Such expensive tools were replaced by more craftsman-like assembly of the bodies – a procedure yielding many joints which caused bad rusting. The problems were so grave

that Porsche had to take the radical step of galvanizing the entire body, and it solved them forever.

The first 911's maximum of 130 horsepower was soon raised. Its cylinder volume increased and more power was taken out of the engine. The brakes became more efficient and the wheel suspensions were refined, though the car's basic features were kept. The bumpers changed and, from the mid-1970s, the flashers were mounted in their middle, having been mounted above them in the wings of the original models. Simultaneously the older type of air-grating over the bumper disappeared.

Unless such details are noticed, it is difficult to tell the year of a 911. Wheel rims and various smaller items have been modified. But as a whole the car has been the same, at least until 1997 when the new 911 arrived with a water-cooled engine. The classic continues to be the air-cooled 911, which has won more competitions than any other car and is still raced today all over the world. Whether in pure racing, rally or rally-cross, it has been equally triumphant and there is scarcely any make with as high a total of victories through the years.

The Porsche 911 ought never to have succeeded, as the concept of a rear air-cooled engine was no longer modern. Yet it outlasted every criticism, and will doubtless survive well into the next millennium even if altered. This achievement owed much to its quality: although the 911 gradually became a quite advanced and expensive car, it was worth the money in qualitative terms. ∎

Mercedes 600

At the Frankfurt salon in 1963, it was time for Mercedes to demonstrate that the make still belonged to the luxury class. Model 600 lit up like a bomb in the midst of the exhibition, and many people thought it was a joke. Could such a huge car with such equipment be real? But the Mercedes 600 was very real indeed. Even though it was big, costly, and not especially pretty, it came to be symbolic of absolute luxury – the car that had everything, and still does.

MERCEDES HAD MADE A NUMBER OF LIMOUSINES during the Thirties. They included the 770 Grosser Mercedes, the 500/540, and the notorious three-axle G4 monsters that were often used at Nazi parades. In 1951, the Mercedes 300 was introduced – a large, fancy car that acquired ever more modern fenders and bigger windows, until it stopped production in the early 1960s. The 300 is best known as the "Adenauer", after the West German chancellor who loved this series and ordered several special models of it for official use.

The 600 from 1963 had a newly designed V8 engine, since Mercedes regarded six cylinders as too few for this kind of car. With a cast-iron block, light-metal cylinder heads, overhead camshafts and a volume of 6.3 litres, the engine delivered 250 horsepower. It was the first V8 made by Mercedes for passenger cars. Previously, the company had built a V8 with only 1500 cc for its Grand Prix racer, the W165, during the late 1930s. The 6.3-litre engine of the 600 was subsequently also used in the Mercedes 300 SEL 6.3, which performed amazingly well.

In its normal four-door form, the Mercedes 600 weighed just over 2,600 kg (5,730 lbs). This did not prevent it from reaching 100 km/h (60 mph) in only 12 seconds, and its top speed was advertised as about 200 km/h (125 mph). These figures would have flattered many a sports car at the time, and were fantastic for a massive luxury car. But there was a lot else besides performance – in fact, almost everything – to marvel at in the 600.

Its lines did not follow contemporary fashions, and seemed rather neutral in style. Yet it displayed more chrome than was usual for Mercedes. The body was self-supporting, but also greatly strengthened for two reasons: to carry the car's enormous weight, and to allow an extended "Pullman" version (named for the American maker of luxury railway carriages). This longer model could be obtained with three doors on each side, or could be tailored to suit the customer's desires.

The standard and Pullman versions had respective wheelbases of 320 and 366 cm, and total lengths of 554 and 624 cm.

Six and a half metres and three tons of *Grosser Mercedes*. This is a 1970 six-door Pullman Limousine.

Driving a car of this size called for maximum care at intersections. Up front, it felt like any other Mercedes – but it stretched so far back that the corners of streets often had to be cut when turning.

Neither was the ride in front very comfortable. Due to the mid-panel behind the seats, they could not be slid back very far, so the driver had the wheel at his stomach if he was taller than about 175 cm (5'9"). The front seats were originally covered in leather, and the rear ones in plush.

Technically, the car was quite advanced. It had fully independent suspension by separate air cushions, whose level was regulated so that the car kept the same height above the road, regardless of the load. This regulation also hindered the body from swaying under sharp acceleration or braking. A central pump-driven hydraulic system operated the seat adjustments, window elevators, opening of the roofhatch (or two hatches in the Pullman version), and assistance for opening or closing the doors, hood and trunk. Servo disc

brakes all round, a dual-circuit brake system, servo steering, central lock, limited-slip differential, and automatic transmission were standard. The ventilation and heating were excellent for their period, maintaining the temperature automatically.

The Mercedes 600 was wonderful to drive. In 1965, I tried one in Sweden, instructed by a German engineer. Since the car cost as much as eight Volvo Amazons, any damage was worth avoiding. Thus I hesitated when, at a speed of about 140 km/h (85 mph), he told me to jam on the brakes. However, he repeated the order and I stepped as hard as possible on the wide brake pedal. I

Obviously, nothing was lacking in a Mercedes 600.

expected the nose to dive and the tail to heel, but I simply found us suddenly standing still. The level regulation had taken care of all other movements of the body. This was an unforgettable experience.

Primarily, though, the 600 was meant for its passengers, not the driver. When riding in back, one enjoyed princely comfort and perfect sound insulation. It was as roomy as sitting at home, and the pleasure was enhanced by a little cupboardbar for drinks.

A main explanation for the car's comfort has been that all of the seats lay between the axles. Given its great length, the springing movements were finished at the front end by the time they began at the rear, and this made the ride extremely smooth.

The Pullman version's rear had *vis-à-vis* seats, in two facing pairs. It therefore resembled a conference room, despite the limited space for legs in the middle. The seats and their backs, the sunroof and the mid-panel were all adjusted by a control panel.

The Model 600 stayed in the sale catalogue for fifteen years, until 1979. After that, it could still be ordered, but disappeared for good on June 10, 1981. A total of 2,677 found buyers, including 500 of the Pullman version. All were built according to order, and the claim is that no two were identical. Customers always thought of some extra accessory to be changed or added.

As a rule, the Mercedes 600 remained a car for the wealthy. Aristocrats and presidents were among its owners, not least from countries with deserts floating on oil. Today it is a leading object for collectors, and high prices are paid even for wrecks.

There are companies that scour lands such as Saudi Arabia, Kuwait, Lebanon and Iran to find any 600 abandoned by a former potentate. The discovery is shipped to Germany for renovation, and the marvel emerges anew!

A renovated Mercedes 600 continues to attract plenty of purchasers, and the price tends to be as irrelevant as the supply is sadly short. ■

Ford Mustang

1964 Ford Mustang

EW CAR MODELS HAVE BEEN AS HIGHLY PRAISED through the years, and by nearly all age groups, as the Ford Mustang. It was intended for young people, or at any rate to have a youthful style. It would appeal to the new generation that was born during or just after World War II, and had settled down to family life in the mid-1960s. Certainly the Mustang did become a youth car, but also a smash hit among buyers in general, to an extent that puzzles automobile historians. It meant the same as having a youthful spirit, no matter how old one was. And this paved the way for a sales boom.

The man behind the Mustang idea was Lee A. Iacocca, then unknown but later legendary. Made chief of the Ford Division in 1960, he took charge of future projects. Many market studies had shown that buyers wanted a car with a youthful feeling. The 1950s and 1960s ended in body excesses such as gaudy

chrome glitter and colossal tail-fins, so there was no shortage of novel suggestions. Compact cars had been launched – they might be the next tune to play on. The notion of a sporty car for young drivers arose, and turned out to be perfect.

Already in 1962 a Mustang was presented, though hardly like what was to come. The original Mustang, an extreme two-seater, was seen at the time as very well streamlined. It had air intakes on the sides and a low body line. This style was elaborated by the design department, and Ford's directors approved with the order: "Make a youth car!"

After countless clay mock-ups, a rather angular body was decided upon – not all that advanced, even for its period. The car was launched as soon as April 1964, at an earlier stage than the usual one for releasing next year's models. Hence, the first Mustangs were designated 1964 1/2. As it happened,

1966 Ford Mustang

they differed considerably from the 1965 models. This initial model had two engine alternatives, a straight six and a V8, of 170 and 260 cubic inches respectively. The standard wheels were 13-inch, later replaced by 14-inch, and the DC generator gave way to an AC type in the 1965 model.

Success was immediate: in just four months 100,000 cars sold, and a million were built in the first two years. Talk about exploiting the immature, or rewarding their enthusiasm, or both!

As an automobile, however, the Mustang was nothing extraordinary. It had a conventional front end, and rear drive with a live axle. The body was fairly compact and the interior typically American – with chrome strips and flattish, uncomfortable seats covered in braid-like plastic. It was far from being a sports car, although performing impressively. The exhaust pipes spoke with assurance and conveyed a sense of power, at least from the V8 engines. The three basic bodies were a hardtop coupe, a convertible and a fastback. In 1966 production reached 607,568 cars, the Mustang's record. Two years later, the first model was made for the last time. Its equipment had improved, but essentially Ford had not changed much in the "winning combination".

Ford asked the legendary race driver Carroll Shelby to make a true sports car out of the Mustang. The outcome was a pair of models, 350 and 500GT, which looked like their prototype but were greatly transformed. Called the Shelby Mustang instead of Ford Mustang, they had better brakes and driving qualities, higher performance and quicker steering, as well as altered suspension or shock absorption. On the whole, they came as close to being genuine sports cars as an American automobile can come. Today they are hot stuff for collectors.

In 1969 arrived the completely new Mustang, widely thought to be more aggressive because of its "shark nose". The most exciting model was the Super Cobra Jet 428, with all of 360 horsepower. A new body change occurred in 1971 with

the famous Boss 302. There were ten engine options, three of them with six cylinders. Leading the pack was the Boss 429 with 375 hp.

Yet time had run out for the Mustang and it never repeated its former triumph. Competitors were abreast of it, and imports from Europe had grown, reducing the home market for U.S. cars. 1973 was the final year for the "real" Mustang, and in 1974 things happened that dismayed devotees. The little third-generation Mustang came out and, surprisingly, it sold quite well – perhaps mainly due to the advent of compact cars and the lower appeal of fuel-hungry ones during the oil crisis of the mid-1970s. Nonetheless, this version did not save the day for Ford, and neither could the fourth generation in 1979 match the original Mustang's sales. Now only the Mustang name lingered on, and the latest model was not regarded as a true Mustang in spite of being a pretty good car. It was more of an American Toyota Celica, which the Mustang closely resembled but had nothing in common with.

The first Mustang was one of the automobile world's greatest successes, albeit without any solid claim to brilliance. It came at the right moment, had the right looks, and aroused the right urge in buyers. How a manufacturer finds such a recipe has taxed the minds of marketers in many car companies. Some have answers – and others still seek them. ■

1973 Ford Mustang

Jaguar E-type

Alongside thoughts about making a simpler copy of the racing car D-type for private buyers, the XK-SS appeared in 1957. Briefly, this was a D-type lacking the characteristic tail-fin but with an ordinary windscreen –

Jaguar began in the mid-1950s to plan a sports car that could follow the XK series, particularly on the American market. The initial aim was to create a kind of "private" model of the D-type car that had been so successful in competitions. Racing trophies were a valuable asset as sales arguments, and carried special weight in the USA. The D-type was an advanced car and so superior that, when Jaguar last raced with a team of its own in 1957, the five factory cars won first, second, third, fourth and sixth places at Le Mans.

unlike the D-type's plexiglass around the driver – as well as side panes, small bumpers and a folding top. It was supposed to be manufactured in limited numbers as a private sports car, but a serious fire at the factory in 1957 destroyed body parts and jigs. Only 16 cars had been built before the fire, and no more were made.

Instead an entirely new design emerged, and the finished car was presented in 1961. The Jaguar E-type had many lines in common with the D-type and the XK-SS. Its long, low bonnet displayed air ports on top, and the headlamps were hidden under plexiglass, creating a very distinctive impres-

sion. The rear section was bulgy and the body completely open, befitting a genuine roadster. As usual for Jaguar, its 3.8-litre engine was a straight-six with double overhead camshafts – basically the same power plant that the XK 120 had introduced in 1949.

The engine block was of cast iron and the cylinder head of aluminium. With three SU carburettors, 265 horsepower were extracted. Such high power was absolutely fantastic for a European car at the time, and offered corresponding performance: acceleration in 7 seconds through 1–60 mph (0–100 km/h) and a top speed around 150 mph (240 km/h).

This car had no frame in the proper sense. It was built as a self-supporting sheet-metal structure, although with trussed units as front and rear frames. The latter's function was not only support, but also insulation of the body from road noise, emitted in vibrations by the wheel suspensions. From the cowl wall, a truss construction of square tubes held up the engine and gearbox, besides the whole front suspension and the bonnet.

Automobile history has seen few bonnets as big as this one. The wings' outer sides were fastened directly in the bonnet edges, so that both the wings and bonnet were lifted as a single unit. Interestingly, a new bonnet purchased as a spare part from the factory was not cut exactly in length. After fitting to the car in question, it was necessary to cut the bonnet's back edge at the proper length.

Jaguar V-12: The ultimate cat

The reason: Jaguar's new aluminum 12-cylinder engine. Quite possibly, the most exciting automotive development in a decade.

The inherently balanced nature of the V-12 configuration produces an almost uncanny smoothness. There is an absence of vibration even at low speeds. And yet the V-12 can hit 70 m.p.h. with such sinuous grace that one hardly experiences the sensation of motion.

But what's so important is not the absolute power it is capable of producing but the delivery of that power through an exceptionally wide range. Result: the ultimate cat performs as well in congested city traffic as on a wide-open thruway.

Some specifics:
(1) The engine displaces only 326 cubic inches and yet develops 314 horsepower for an efficient displacement-to-power ratio.
(2) In the V-12's flathead design, the cylinders have a large bore and the pistons a short stroke for higher potential power and longer engine life.
(3) The new transistorized ignition system employs an electronic distributor with no contact points to wear or foul. Significance: A major cause of engine tuneups is eliminated.

Additional virtues: The fully independent suspension with "anti-dive" geometry to counter front-end dipping. Rack-and-pinion steering,

power-assisted with 3.5 turns lock to lock. Four-wheel disc brakes, also power-assisted and self-adjusting.

Jaguar 2+2 with the revolutionary V-12 engine—the ultimate cat. See it at your Jaguar dealer. And, for a sight you'll never forget, look under the hood.

For the name of your nearest Jaguar dealer, dial (800) 631-1971 except in New Jersey where the number is (800) 962-2803. Calls are toll-free.
BRITISH LEYLAND MOTORS INC., LEONIA, N. J. 07605

Jaguar V-12

The front suspension was built with two triangular struts that were sprung by longitudinal torsion rods. Steering used a rack and was unusually direct, with only two and a half turns of the wheel from lock to lock. The rear section was of double-jointed type, sprung on each side with two small combined shock absorbers – a design which has subsequently given Jaguar a following. The two strong rear disc brakes were mounted next to the universal joint. This rear construction was far superior to earlier live rear axles. Starting went much faster, without any "clunk" or shaking as the universal joint moved vertically. The comfort and road-holding greatly improved, since each rear wheel could adapt to the surface independently of the other.

Naturally the E-type also had disc brakes in front. The use of disc brakes was itself a source of Jaguar's leading position, and one reason why the classic C-type won Le Mans in 1953.

An E-type coupé from 1963

There were two body variants, a roadster and a coupe. Actually the coupe was a bit faster than the roadster, due to smoother streamlining with the solid top. In 1965 the engine was enlarged to 4.2 litres, and a year later came the 2+2 model with two extra rear seats, sloping roof, and big boot in back: a sort of semi-estate car, even though this body designation did not yet exist. The rear seating was miserably cramped and, at best, accommodated two half-grown children.

The normal E-type was never intended for racing sports. Rather, it was to be a fast country speedster for daring drivers. This did not prevent it from doing well in competitions, but the successes of previous Jaguar models eluded it. On the other hand, these were not the achievements that led to its impact in the history of automobiles.

A typically British interior was provided. Instruments and control buttons were gathered in the midst of the panel, except for the speedometer and tachometer which sat in front of the driver. This arrangement facilitated alteration for steering at the left or right. Leather upholstery was standard, and the driver's wheel consisted of wood-covered aluminium with holes in its three spokes. The gear-shift was very short, suiting a sports car, and the hand-brake lay in the middle.

Enjoyable driving awaited the owner of an E-type. Its mighty engine, and the recognizable "belch" from the carburettors when accelerating, added to a feeling of speed and power. The "belch", a characteristic of SU carburettors, was caused by the air rushing freely into them for mixture with the petrol.

Compared to its contemporaries, the E-type was extremely stable on the road. Its fairly long wheelbase, low centre of gravity, independent suspension, and exact steering were all details that benefited the car's balance and handling. The only problem with its driving qualities was the violent understeering, a result of the great weight in front – it seemed to want to go straight ahead in a curve when moving fast. But this could quickly be corrected with the accelerator, since the powerful engine was able to spin the rear wheels in a slide and get the whole car to oversteer instead, so that the back end came round.

If any classic car can be hailed like a hit tune, the E-type was. It drew enormous attention, not least for its beautiful lines and amazing engine, but also because it was relatively cheap. It cost only about half of what the Mercedes 300SL did, and that of course was sensational.

Possibly the low price was a predictable fruit of the English motorcar industry's hesitation to charge enough for a good design, its vague self-doubt and fear of setting a price near those of competitors, or claiming that one's own car was best. Such steps were taken in America even if the product was inferior to others, but this business approach evidently clashed with English mentality. Here was a blunt issue of self-confidence, or perhaps of conviction that the design was more important than the money.

In the case of the E-type, Jaguar had no need for weak confidence. The car was certainly worth its cost, despite some defects. One of them was the gearbox, with only four speeds and an unsynchronized first – although normal for English cars then, and not crucial as the engine power allowed starting in second gear.

A worse situation lay in the body. Of the 72,000 E-type cars that were built, nearly 50,000 went to the USA, and often to states with a warm climate but low humidity. There the body's vulnerability to rust was scarcely noticed. But in markets with rain – England and Europe, including Scandinavia – the body construction was disastrous. Antirust treatment was still generally unknown, and not even a thorough ground coating of lacquer was applied on the body sections and framework. The surface lacquering by no means sufficed to keep out rust. Today, more E-type body parts are made than at the factory in its time, so as to restore all the E-Jags which have literally rusted away.

The chassis design, too, was debatable. With the disc brakes next to the universal joint, and two joints on each of the two drive axles, the rear end was both expensive and difficult to work on. Likewise, the front end with its triangular struts and torsion rods was very sensitive to damage. A slight collision could distort the entire front frame, which cost a lot to fix.

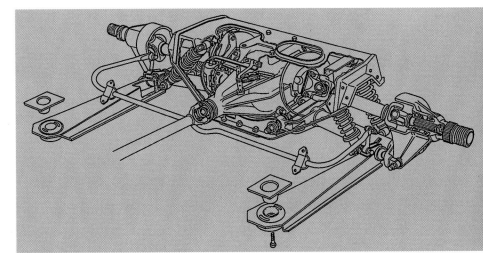

The E-type's wheel suspension was independent and hung in a separate frame, mounted directly in the self-supporting body.

In 1969 came Series II, with an offer of servo steering. The headlamps' plexiglass covering had gone, and stronger shock absorbers were placed higher, in order to meet the American safety regulations. Further, due to the USA's exhaust requirements, the engine was reduced to 245 horsepower, thereby lowering the top speed to just over 125 mph (200 km/h). This did not really please Americans, who were the primary customers. To regain the original power, a 5.3-litre V12 engine with 272 hp was introduced in 1973. The V12 E-type was identifiable by its grille with a grid pattern. ■

AC Cobra

Carroll Shelby, from Texas, had a dream – to build his own sports car. After winning the 24-hour race at Le Mans in 1959 with an Aston Martin DBR1, he was famous and admired. But his racing career ended because of a heart defect and, a year later, he was out of both work and money. Still, he had good friends, charisma and persuasiveness. The result was an automotive legend: the AC Cobra.

THERE ARE MANY TALL TALES ABOUT THE AC COBRA. One is that, in the beginning, it had to be paid for in cash, since the owners seldom survived long enough to start repaying a loan.

The obsessive idea of creating a new sports car led Carroll Shelby to a concept that was not new at all: combining a European design with an American V8 engine. However, Shelby wanted to make something even more powerful than a fast touring car. He knew that he could not do it alone – and a company like Chevrolet was hardly likely to help, for the Corvette already existed. Yet Shelby did not give up.

As so often happens in the history of cars, a chance meeting played the decisive role. Shelby had lunch with the editor of *Sport Car Graphic*. Thus he learned that an English manufacturer, AC, was going to stop production of its AC Ace, because Bristol would no longer be making the six-cylinder engine.

Shelby borrowed an Ace and realized that the car suited his idea. It had a strong chassis, plenty of room beneath the hood for a V8, and disc brakes in front. Certainly it looked old-fashioned, but he was short of alternatives. On the other hand, AC was interested in a deal if Shelby could find an adequate engine. The fact that he had won at Le Mans in a European car was doubtless significant.

As already indicated, cooperation with General Motors was unthinkable, so Shelby turned to Ford. He had heard that they were developing a new V8 of 221 cubic inches (about 3.5 litres), and he managed to borrow one through his contacts. He checked that the engine would fit into the car, although he did not drive it. The good news was telephoned to AC that he had found the right engine.

When Ford discovered what AC was up to, they sent an even newer and bigger version of the V8, with 260 cubic inches (over 4 litres). In February 1962, Shelby tested this prototype at Silverstone, and was overjoyed.

Some months later, what would become the first AC Cobra was sent to Los Angeles. It had been built according to Shelby's instructions, and within a few hours he and a friend, Dean Moon, equipped it with the new engine and gearbox. They tested it very hard indeed. "We tried to kill it," said Shelby afterward, "but it held out. So it must be a good car."

The AC Cobra 427 had a brutal look from any angle, but this oblique rear view probably does it the most justice. Top speed was about 175 mph (285 km/h) and it took 7.8 seconds to reach 100 mph (160 km/h). In other words, it was a dangerous car in the wrong hands. Note the appropriate plate-number on this example from 1967.

TEXAS CHARM AND TRUE CONVICTION

Despite lacking funds or factory space, Shelby succeeded against all odds in getting Ford to finance the assembly of 100 Cobras. He set up premises in Los Angeles, and invited motoring journalists to drive the car, since he wanted publicity. The problem was that he had only one car available, which did not seem reassuring.

Shelby's solution was to repaint the car before every test run. One day it was blue, the next day red, and so on. This trick worked, and the Cobra played to perfection. The media went wild as the car accelerated in 4.2 seconds to 60 mph (100 km/h) and reached a top speed around 150 mph (240 km/h).

Shelby employed a number of capable people for the project, but AC in England plodded along at its usual tempo. People there did not like the American mentality. Finally, a threat came from Shelby that, if they did not raise the production rate, Ford would buy their factory and shut it down. This was foolish, but had the desired effect.

The air intake was larger on the Cobra 427 than on the 289, to give the oil cooler enough ventilation. Around the intake is a chrome list that was not on the early cars, but was added later.

The first 70 cars – without engine and gearbox – arrived at Los Angeles in very poor condition. They had been damaged due to improper lashing on the ship, and Shelby was shocked. Instead of simply adding the power train, he had to hire metalworkers and painters so that most of the cars could regain their original state.

THE GROWTH OF A GIANT

Many ailments, too, affected the early Cobra. Its 260 engine tended to overheat, and the English electrical system from Lucas worked badly.

Before long, Ford announced that the 260 would be replaced by a still larger engine. It had 289 cubic inches (4.7 litres) and yielded 271 horsepower at 5,800 rpm. Moreover, it could easily be trimmed by changing the camshaft and intake,

giving 300 hp. This Cobra model was called the 289.

As the difficulty of cooling persisted, Shelby began to buy Corvette radiators from the local Chevrolet agency. Ford heard about this, and became so angry that they assigned the McCord Radiator Company to design a new radiator. The electrical problem was also solved by Ford. Without their vast resources, Carroll Shelby would never have succeeded.

Mass production was one thing, but what attracted Shelby most were races. He soon dominated the scene in America, but his aim was much higher – to beat Ferrari. Among other drivers, he engaged Dan Gurney and the Formula 1 world champion Phil Hill.

The Cobra, though, had a handicap: the body's aerodynamics. It was humorously referred to as "a flying brick". Therefore, Shelby and the designer Pete Brock went to work on a

An AC Cobra 289 from 1965, said to have belonged to the English Willment stable.

coupe version. This was a wonder, and shook up Ferrari. Nevertheless, at the end of the season, Ferrari had won the world championship for GT cars by a bare margin of 6.3 points.

AN EVEN BETTER COBRA

Carroll Shelby understood that the engine needed to be enlarged again, as compensation for the car's awful aerodynamics. Now he had his eye on Ford's 427-cu.in. (7-litre) engine, which provided over 400 hp in standard form and 600–700 hp when trimmed. But with such a powerful engine, the chassis was clearly not robust enough.

With the aid of Ford engineers, a new chassis was designed with three times the strength of that in the 289. This model became the 427. Its wings and broader tyres gave a far more aggressive impression. There were several variants, the sim-

plest having a engine with 425 hp, which could be trimmed for racing to at least 485 hp.

In 1965, Carroll Shelby got the world championship he longed for. His cars finished first at Daytona, Sebring, Monza, the Nürburgring, and Reims. The "flying brick" was at last able to vanquish Ferrari.

The final Cobra 427 left the factory in December 1966. By then, 356 examples had been built, compared to the 289's total production of 560.

The Cobra has given rise to countless replicas, differing widely in quality. But just a single replica has been approved by AC, Ford and Shelby together – the one built by Autocraft in England. Among the more prominent Cobra owners is the king of Sweden, whose car is appropriately nicknamed the "King Cobra"! ∎

Fiat 127/128

Fiat's 127 appeared in 1971, designed by Oscar Montabone. This is a 1050 CL from 1977, which was a costlier variant with, for example, more luxurious wheel rims. The 1049-cc engine delivered 50 hp.

FOR THE FIRST TIME IN 1967, FIAT WON THE COVETED TITLE "Car of the Year". It did so with the model 124, a very nice car at the time, with a longitudinal engine in front and rear-wheel drive.

A year later, the company earned second place with the 125, a bit larger than the 124 but still powered on the rear wheels. Then Fiat said farewell to the sixties, and began the next decade with two new small cars built like the classic "Doghouse" – with transverse engines, a wheel at each corner, and front-wheel drive.

In 1970, the Fiat 128 became the "Car of the Year". Two years after that, the title went to the 127. Both of these were

fine in the light of their contemporaries.

When the 128 won, second place was taken by the Autobianchi A112 – an interesting fact, as the A112 provided the basis for the Fiat 127 that won two years later. Autobianchi was Fiat's little "experimental factory", where some designs were tried out on Autobianchi models before they came to Fiat.

The Fiat 128 was a compact small car in the true sense of the term. It had a squarish shape, a width and length respectively of 160 and 390 cm (63 and 154 inches), and an angular body that gave a solid impression. Thanks to this angularity, the space inside was ample. It resulted in the use of the four-door version of the 128 as a taxi, especially in Italy.

No concessions were made to designers who wanted a backward-sloping roof. Here Fiat chose straight lines that offered good interior headroom. Nor were the passengers' legs cramped, mainly since they sat rather upright and not halfreclining.

The 128's best features had to do with driving. Its excellent balance and the front-wheel drive made it wonderful to handle. Clearly, it could do better on the road than its performance allowed.

Only 55 horsepower emerged from the 1116-cc engine. The top speed was said to be 142 km/h (89 mph) and the car accelerated in 16.5 seconds to 100 mph (60 mph). This, to be fair, was not bad in 1970.

The Fiat 128 was made between 1969 and 1984.

But Fiat committed one mistake. The production quality was not high enough when the car reached the market. Irritating minor faults and sudden visits to the workshop burdened its reputation, and there was resistance to buying it – at least for export. At home in Italy, the 128 sold like spaghetti, but due to the greater tolerance of such troubles.

With time, however, the quality improved. Toward the end of its manufacturing life, the 128 was among the best small-car bargains. It became one of Fiat's super-sellers, and acquired a range of body versions: two- or four-door sedan, three-door station-wagon, and a coupé model. The last of these, and a special version called the 128 Rally, had a 1290-cc engine with 67-75 hp depending on the model.

The 128 was also exported and made, for example, in Yugoslavia under the name Yugo. This had a three-door semi-station-wagon body that never existed on the Italian 128.

FIAT'S 127

Fiat's 127 was more or less a scaled-down 128, only 360 cm (142 inches) long, and narrower at 153 cm (60 inches). Its relatively old-fashioned engine was an ordinary four-cylinder pushrod type with 903 cc. Through the years, this engine would be used in many other Fiat and Autobianchi models.

The 127, too, held the road quite well. It had very reliable handling and, despite the short wheelbase of 223 cm (88 inches), it was not jerky. The suspension worked fine and gave it good road contact. All of 47 horsepower were extracted from the 903-cc engine, sufficient to endow the car with an admirable temperament.

If nothing else, shifting gears in a 127 afforded an enjoyable sense of speed, which was enhanced by the engine's rough tone. Acceleration to 100 km/h (60 mph) took 16 seconds and the top speed was advertised as 140 km/h (87 mph).

But most of the feeling owed to the car's sound, not power. The tiny engine was pretty helpless when it really counted. With four passengers and a load of baggage, its spryness vanished and one could tell that it was a sluggish weakling.

Unlike the 128, this model did not have any other variants. The 127 maintained its style throughout, while it did get a face-lift after ten years – with new furnishings and a partly novel front. It was then called the 127 Comfort. ■

Jaguar XJ6 and XJ12

The Jaguar V12 was first put into the 1971 E-Type and, one year later, into the new Jaguar XJ12. Shown here is the 1989 version with a swept volume of 5,345 cc and 295 bhp at 5,500 rpm.

JAGUAR BUILT AN EARLY REPUTATION WITH ITS fine saloon cars. Large, comfortable and quiet, they soon earned a general nickname – "The Big Cat".

The first example appeared in 1936, with the designation S.S. Jaguar 2.5 litre. After World War II, it was replaced in 1948 by the Mark V, a bigger car that would become the basis for several different models – the Mark VII, VIII and IX. In 1962 the Mark X emerged, an entirely new car except for the engine. This, too, was a colossal vehicle and had room for six people, its wheelbase measuring 120 inches (3,048 mm).

Yet another such model was introduced in 1968, the XJ6. With a wheelbase of 109 inches (2,768 mm), it was smaller than the Mark X – or 420 G, as this was called after 1967. The XJ6 was available with two alternative six-cylinder engines: the familiar old version of 4.2 litres, and a more economical one of 2.8 litres. The latter, however, easily overheated and burned piston rings, so it was given up in 1973.

The XJ6 had a gigantic engine compartment that puzzled many people. But in 1971 the reason for this design was revealed. The company began to provide the car with its famous V12

An early XJ6

Jaguar XJS Convertible

engine of 5.3 litres and 272 horsepower, which of course came from the Jaguar E-type V12. This model was called the XJ12, and proved to be the best-selling V12 car of the postwar era.

With the XJ6 and XJ12, two new Jaguar models were ready to conquer the world. The spacious, silent, six-seat saloon could do over 125 mph (200 km/h) and cost only a third the price of a Rolls-Royce Silver Shadow. The same models were produced as the Daimler Sovereign and Double-Six respectively, for the

Daimler factory had been taken over by Jaguar in 1960.

Minor changes were made in the XJ6 and XJ12 through the years. In 1973 they acquired higher bumpers and a more compact grille, while the 2.8-litre engine gave way to that of 4.2 litres and 170 hp. Then, too, the output of the V12 engine was increased to 289 hp. Both models could also be obtained in a very handsome coupé version, the XJ-S. It was presented in 1975 and is still manufactured today.

Finally, a replacement for the XJ6 and XJ12 was introduced in October 1986. Although superficially similar to its predecessors, this was a wholly new development and continues to uphold the proud Jaguar tradition. ∎

1970
–1980

The Datsun Sunny 120Y, new in 1973, was the third generation in a series of conventional sedan models that had first been launched in 1965. This model came with two alternative engines of 1171 and 1428 cc. Here is a 120Y from 1974.

THE MIDDLE EAST AND THE UNITED NATIONS HEADQUARTERS are the scenes of peace talks between Israel, Egypt and Jordan. Egypt's president, Anwar Sadat, inaugurates the Aswan Dam as the Soviet president, Nikolai Podgorny, looks on. Activities in space are lively – Apollo 14 takes three American astronauts to the moon, two of them landing to study the surface. Then the Soviet Union makes a trip with a rocket named Mars 3 to the planet Mars. The Soviet spacecraft Soyuz 11, carrying three cosmonauts, completes a docking with the unmanned vehicle Salyut 1, but these men die from air embolism when re-entering the earth's atmosphere. Apollo and Soyuz crews stage a meeting in space.

Another representative of the fast luxury-car class was the Aston Martin Lagonda. Though ready in 1976, it did not reach customers until 1978. On paper, the Lagonda seemed much more attractive than Bentley's Turbo R, but in reality the latter beat it for both acceleration and top speed. The V8 engine of 5.3 litres gave 309 horsepower at 5,500 rpm, bringing the Lagonda up to 220 km/h (135 mph).

In 1969 the DBS V8 arrived, with a four-camshaft V8 engine of 5340 cc. Its body had been designed by William Towns for the six-cylinder DBS.

In Paris, the famous covered market Les Halles is torn down. Chaos in Northern Ireland's capital city of Belfast comes close to civil war. The Russian-American composer and conductor Igor Stravinsky passes away, as does the American jazz musician and cornet stylist Louis "Satchmo" Armstrong. Thanks to progress in electronics, the telephone's dial can be replaced by buttons. President Nixon visits Peking in February 1972, and Moscow in May. The United States Supreme Court abolishes the death penalty, following several states such as California. Palestinian terrorists storm the Israeli village at the Olympic Games in Munich; two Israeli athletes are killed and nine are taken hostage. Israel refuses the demand for release of 230 Palestinian prisoners, and when the deadline runs out, shooting kills the hostages and five of the terrorists. In Rio de Janeiro, the renowned German-Brazilian opera singer Erna Sack dies.

Cadillac's Eldorado captured the climax of the American Dream. "If you want to be successful, buy a Cadillac" was a refrain of the 1950s, and continued into the 1970s even though this model declined. Seen here is an Eldorado convertible from 1972, then unusual for the USA in having front-wheel drive, with an 8.2-litre V8 engine of 365 hp.

Total brain death is now accepted as a criterion of death in numerous Western countries, among then Switzerland, West Germany, Belgium, Norway, Finland, the Netherlands and France. The traditional heart stoppage continues to decide the matter elsewhere. A volcanic eruption on the Icelandic isle of Heimaey destroys a third of its houses, whereas its area increases by 2.5 square kilometres. The French-British airliner Concorde for travel at twice the speed of sound is ordered by

Great Britain, France, Iran and China. But many companies prefer the Boeing 747 jumbo jet, partly due to its much lower fuel consumption. The Soviet Union also develops a supersonic passenger plane, TU144, yet it runs into technical problems when test-flown. Leonid Brezhnev, the Soviet Communist Party chief, visits America and stresses the importance of peaceful cooperation between the superpowers.

Cars are being produced and sold in unprecedented

A typical American car before frugality set in was the 1974 Lincoln Continental (top). Its huge 7.5-litre V8 engine was, however, limited to 220 horsepower by new exhaust-emission laws.

Also characteristic of the USA's rear-wheel-drive luxury sedans was the Chrysler New Yorker (middle). It sold well, especially to traditionalists who were suspicious of front-wheel drive. With a 5.2-litre V8 giving 130 hp, it was reasonably priced at $13,990. Chrysler could keep the price down because this model's tool costs had long since been paid off.

A new type of car for Cadillac was the Seville (bottom). Both smaller and more expensive than other Cadillac models, it had a standard V8 of 5.7 litres, in a much-modified version of GM's X-body. The main customers were a quality-conscious segment of the market dominated by Mercedes-Benz. The Seville was introduced in 1975 and very soon provided 15% of Cadillac's total sales, which was quite good in view of its high price.

In 1975 the Chevrolet Corvette was still made in open form, which would not happen again until eleven years later. This model had only two engine alternatives, a 5.7-litre V8 with 165 or 205 horsepower.

Alongside its true supercars, Ferrari built smaller mid-engine cars that were related to the Dino 206, which originated in 1968 and is shown here. Its V6 engine grew to 2.5 litres, so the model was later called the 246. Popular in both covered GT and open GTS forms, it had a production run of 3,761 during 1969–74, more than for any previous single Ferrari model. In 1973 came the bigger 208 and 308GT4, with new V8 engines of 2 and 3 litres respectively, as well as a body seating 2+2 on a somewhat longer chassis, the bodies being designed by Bertone and built by Scaglietti. But the Dino was entirely Pininfarina's work.

Among the strangest American autos of the Seventies was the AMC Pacer X, launched in 1975 as "the first wide small car". Meant to compete for buyers of the Pinto and Vega, it was originally assigned a GM-built Wankel engine. But this plan failed and a tired, thirsty six-cylinder engine of 3.8 or 4.2 litres landed under the Pacer's bonnet. From 1978 onward, it could also be obtained with a 5-litre V8. The semi-estate body was almost as wide as long, and few people liked its overall looks. After selling only 72,158 in six years, the Pacer was laid to rest at the end of 1980.

quantities. There are currently just 1.9 inhabitants per car in the United States, although 3.5 in France, 4.6 in the Netherlands, and 5.9 in Japan. The new Citroën GS, originally meant to use a Wankel engine, is announced in France. Later some GS are actually made with a 107-horsepower engine of this type, which receives the model designation GS Birotor. Nearly all small cars, and many large ones, are now designed for front-wheel drive. Exceptions are distinctive sports cars, still with rear-wheel drive that gives adept drivers a unique thrill. The simple, austere sports car becomes established in Great Britain, built by specialized firms such as Lotus and Morgan. Volkswagen sets a record in number of manufactured cars of

the same model, 15 007 003, the previous record having been held by Ford's Model T.

Along with their increasingly common discs, brake systems are equipped with an auxiliary unit – normally a mechanical servo cylinder between the brake pedal and master cylinder – from which the fluid pressure goes out to the wheel brakes. The servo cylinder is activated by a vacuum from the engine's intake manifold when the driver steps on the brake pedal, and greatly reduces the hard pedal pressure that disc brakes would otherwise need. It is during the 1970s that synthetic oils begin to occur widely in passenger cars, despite study and some use of such oils for military purposes already during the

The Lamborghini Espada could do a little over 250 km/h (155 mph) and was the world's fastest four-seater car when it appeared in 1968. Its 12-cylinder engine came from Lamborghini's famous Miura, and the body was designed by Bertone. Production ceased in 1978.

1940s in Germany. For ordinary passenger cars, these oils cost too much until Mobil in the USA launched its first entirely synthetic oil.

History is made by a building that lends its name to a political scandal: Watergate in Washington D.C. The Republican government under Richard Nixon proves to be pervaded with suspicion of its opponents, and combats them by crooked methods. A cease-fire is agreed upon in Vietnam, and America leaves the South after years of vain effort to vanquish the North

Vietnamese. Thus deprived of support, the South is taken over and its government goes into exile, leaving the communist followers of Ho Chi Minh to reconstruct the ruined land.

An oil crisis strikes the West when OPEC (the Organization of Petroleum Exporting Countries) slows the flow of crude oil and raises its prices. This is intended to make the West force Israel to give back the territory she took in 1967, as well as to help solve the problems of Palestinian refugees. Panic grips industrialized nations that have no oil reserves, and many of

American Motors' AMX was unusual in being a two-seat coupé, as most of the similar cars – for example, the Charger and GTO – had four or five seats. It was built on a short Javelin chassis, with the wheelbase reduced from 109 to 97 inches. The standard engine was a V8 of 4.75 litres and 225 hp, but options had 5.6 and 6.4 litres, the latter delivering 315 hp. Responsive handling and bucket seats made the AMX best on the road among all American Motors cars. Yet customers were fewer than hoped, and bought only 19,134 examples.

them introduce petrol rationing. U.S. Vice President Spiro Agnew is convicted of tax evasion and has to resign. A spectacular opera house in Sydney, Australia, sculpturally designed by the Danish architect Jørn Utzon, is inaugurated after 19 years of work; it seats 2,700 people and has cost 17 times the original estimate. The Suez Canal, closed since 1967, reopens.

France gains a new president by the election of Valéry Giscard d'Estaing, whereas America loses one with Nixon's resignation in the wake of Watergate. The oil crisis stimulates discussion of alternative energy sources – nuclear fission, fusion, coal, shale, peat, dams, wind, the sun, the sea and so forth. Wood, however, remains the chief fuel for 90% of mankind. Prince Juan Carlos ascends the throne of Spain and appoints Adolfo Suárez as Prime Minister, who repudiates

The BMW Procar M1 really looks like a winner – including a very stiff chassis, mid-engine, professionally designed wheel suspension and aerodynamic body. Both the standard and racing versions had the same straight six-cylinder engine, but their respective powers were 277 and 485 hp.

the old Franco dictatorship and quickly institutes democracy.

Margaret Hilda Thatcher is elected the British Conservative party leader. At decade's end, she will become Great Britain's first female Prime Minister. India, which was called "the world's largest democracy" after its independence 28 years earlier, grinds to a halt in the summer of 1975. Its first prime minister Jawaharlal Nehru's daughter Indira Gandhi, now in the same office, moves with amazing speed to declare a state of

emergency, imprison her enemies and silence opposition. With five weeks of mass arrests, constitutional manipulations and press censorship, she makes it clear that there can be no return to "unbridled freedom".

A breakthrough is seen by "cassette TV" (video). Warnings are heard that people tend to read ever less and watch TV ever more. The American spacecraft Viking 1, and later Viking 2, land on the planet Mars. Jimmy Carter from the

Deep South is elected U.S. President, and the dark chapters of the Vietnam war and the Watergate scandal can be regarded as closed. In Denmark, the world's biggest generator of wind power is tested, delivering 2,000 kilowatts at a wind speed of 14 metres per second. At the nuclear plant of Three Mile Island, on the Susquehanna River near Harrisburg, Pennsylvania, a reactor accident takes place and is soon said not to have done so. ■

Experimental Safety Vehicles were seldom elegant creations, as their appearance was sacrificed to crash-safety. Shown here are a Mercedes-Benz ESF-05 and a Fiat mini-ESV. The Fiat was built on a small 500 base, and its front end, though reinforced, seems very unlikely to have given any protection at all.

The wave of nostalgia that swept over America during the Seventies and Eighties gave rise both to authentic replicas with modern machinery, like the Auburn (*above*), and to so-called neoclassic cars. The latter had a Thirties look, often exaggerated and lacking any real precedent. Auburn's 853 boat-tail Speedster was a favourite of replica makers in the USA, where at least three firms built such cars – and Australia had another one.

A typical neoclassic was the Clenet roadster (*right*). Built in Goleta, California by Alain Clenet from France, it used the Lincoln Continental's chassis and machinery, but the body midsection was M.G. Midget. Production lasted from 1976 to 1982, also with a four-seat version from 1981. While hardly cheap at $83,000, a Clenet was better value than, for instance, a Buehrig which cost no less than $130,000!

American muscle-cars were at their zenith in the early 1970s. One of the most striking and speedy was Plymouth's 1970 Superbird. Strongest of all the Road Runner models, it could have either the 426 Hemi engine with 7 litres, hemispherical combustion chambers and 425 hp, or else the 440 with 7.2 litres and 390 hp. Its enormous tail-wing was developed for the NASCAR races, where Superbirds clocked up to 220 mph (350 km/h). NASCAR required a homologization series of at least 1,500 cars, but Plymouth built as many as 1,920 Superbirds in 1970.

VW Golf

In this fine cross-section one can see clearly how the Golf is built, shown here as it looked at the end of the Eighties. The basic layout is the same as when introduced in 1974.

URING THE 1960S VOLKSWAGEN HAD TROUBLE deciding which direction its technical development should take. In 1965, BMC in England had launched the front-wheel-driven Austin/Morris Mini, and was followed by several European car makers for the rest of that decade.

To Volkswagen, development seemed problematic. The factory at Wolfsburg was virtually identified with cars having an air-cooled boxer engine mounted in the rear. Such was the

original "People's Car" and it had been advertised into a virtue. The VW Type 1 saw much improvement and modernization, but its basic construction was kept. In the end, even fanatical VW buyers were forced to admit that only enthusiasm preserved the antiquated design's appeal. In the ever tougher competition for customers, this was not enough.

A completely new body arrived in 1961 on the old bottom-plate: the Volkswagen 1500. That it had a rear engine was

The first Golf convertible, presented at Saint Tropez, was built by Karman in Osnabrück. This example is from 1988.

successfully camouflaged – until the driver found out. Its sales were scarcely comparable to the Type 1's, even when the cylinder volume was raised to 1600 cc and a coupé model was introduced.

The VW 411 appeared in 1968, a rather large four-door sedan. But the four-cylinder boxer engine was still back there. Now people began to argue seriously that the factory's conservatism and stubbornness would be its downfall. For six years, only 355,200 examples of the 411/412 were produced – a disastrously low figure for a manufacturer of Volkswagen's size. Evil tongues said that the designation 411 meant "4 doors but 11 years too late".

Then something amazing happened. Volkswagen bought a finished design instead of making a fresh one. The NSU company was in economic trouble, but had a design ready for presentation. VW bought the company and started to produce

the new car in 1970, as the K70. At last, Volkswagen understood the point of a car with front-wheel drive and a water-cooled, front-mounted, in-line engine. For their part, the customers were confused. Accustomed to believing that only an air-cooled engine would do, they wondered what might become of them.

Volkswagen held its ground, and in 1973 came the next water-cooled, front-wheel-driven model: Passat. This was not a VW design either. In the meantime, VW had also bought Auto Union, and the Passat was based on the Audi 80. Initially it was delivered with Audi's engine, built by Mercedes-Benz during a short period of owning Audi!

That same year, Volkswagen ran up a loss, and a big one, not to say enormous – 807,000,000 Deutschemarks. But work was proceeding with the first independent VW design, using a transverse engine and front-wheel drive. It emerged in May

The Golf GTi was the archetype of a "hot hatch". Here is its new version from 1983. In the late 1980s its cylinder volume rose to 1781 cc, yielding 139 horsepower.

1974 and proved an unprecedented triumph: the VW Golf.

The first Golf, with a somewhat angular but quite roomy body, was unremarkable in terms of design. Its four-cylinder, water-cooled engine could have 1093 cc and 50 hp, or 1471 cc and 70 hp. The front wheels were suspended in McPherson spring-legs, the rear wheels in backward-turned supporting arms. However, the car was built with care and it soon earned a good reputation. Unfortunately it had rust problems, like so many of its competitors.

The VW Golf was born at the right moment. In 1973 the oil crisis had almost taken the breath out of Western industries, and fuel prices climbed steadily afterward. This situation suited the Golf perfectly. It was a family car with such modest

fuel consumption that the average driver could afford to run it. Those were the days when Europeans, and especially Americans, started to drive small cars.

By the two-year mark, half a million Golfs had been made – and six months later, a million. It was a phenomenal sales success, and now there was money to design the Golf in several variants. Although nearly everybody had predicted the death of open cars, a convertible appeared in 1979, built by Karman in Osnabrück. But the Golf that truly boggled the mind was the GTi model, presented in 1976.

With this model, Volkswagen created a totally new kind of car, the GTi class. These were small closed cars, whose engine power and driving qualities enabled them to get away from

1998 VW Golf

most contemporary sports cars. Before long, other manufacturers adopted them. The Golf GTi became a standard for the rest to match. VW refined it and, in 1982, an engine of 1.8 litres and 112 hp was installed. In 1986, a 16-valve engine with 139 hp arrived. The ultimate Golf for road use was probably the VR6, launched in 1991 and having a 2.8-litre engine of 174 hp.

At regular intervals, new versions of the VW Golf emerged – each time with technical improvements and novel looks, though unmistakably still a Golf. In 1978, an American factory opened at New Scranton, Pennsylvania. Golfs sold in the USA were called the Volkswagen Rabbit. The factory produced at most 400,000 of them annually.

The Golf 2, from 1983, was followed in 1986 by a four-wheel-drive variant, the Golf Syncro. In 1991, Golfs began production at Mosel, in former East Germany. The Golf 3 came in 1993, and 1997 saw the fourth generation of Golfs

presented in Bonn. During the year before this, the factory had built 17 million Golfs, and was expected to turn out 900,000 of the new car in its first year alone. The factory's own record of 22 million for the old Type 1 was well on the way to being surpassed.

Essentially, the Golf 4 employed the same techniques as its predecessors – with McPherson suspension in front, servo-assisted rack-and-pinion steering, disc brakes all round and ABS. The body was built with close attention to "passive safety", as regards not only the body's own ability to absorb external forces in a collision, but also protecting the passengers with double airbags – both in front and at the sides.

The new Golf could be delivered with seven different engines. Using either petrol or diesel, they had from 75 to 216 horsepower. ■

Renault 5

One of the best known Superminis of the 1970s was the Renault 5. It differed from the others in having a longitudinal engine. The second-generation 5 (nicknamed Supercinq), introduced in 1985, fell in line with its rivals in having a transverse engine.

THE RENAULT 5 WAS A STROKE OF ITS MAKER'S GENIUS. Renault finally had a new idea, after relying too long on design ideas that derived from the 4CV – and thus from the years before World War II, with their rear-engine models such as the Dauphine and Major. A small car with proper dimensions for stressed Parisians, the Five featured good handling, four-wheel drive, and ample space in comparison with other scaled-down automobiles of the period.

Typically French accessories like an "accordion" sunroof helped the Five to become popular. Its design was not especially advanced, and could rather be called anonymous, but the austere body lines gave it a tough appearance that appealed to both young and old. Most significantly, this elementary style was peculiar to the Five and made it conspicuous.

The only problem with its construction was that Renault chose to place the engine longitudinally, instead of following the accepted trend of a transverse engine that left more room for the passengers and baggage. Even so, there was nothing cramped about the interior. A long-legged driver sat easily in front, while in back the lesser leg-space was compensated by

1979 Renault R5 Turbo 2

more headroom due to the angular body.

The rear seat contained very thin stuffing, so the passengers' lower extremities soon became a bit numb. But the doors were wide and allowed easy entry at both the front and rear. The front seats could also be folded forward, facilitating access to the rear.

Although its driving qualities were excellent, the car varied greatly in performance according to which engine it used. The smaller engines were rather awful, yet the TS worked impressively. This model had considerable torque that provided not only fine acceleration, but also enough power to persist when passing other vehicles. The fuel consumption was surprisingly low, even if one tramped on the gas pedal for more power. In fact, it was the lowest among contemporary cars of the same class.

Four-wheel drive, and almost precise steering, endowed the Five with admirable tracking stability. Few cars could keep up with it on curving roads at really high speed. On motorways, however, it droned like a beehive. The characteristically French sound of the engine's intake, when feeding it more fuel, was a growing disturbance as the speed increased.

Throughout the Five's lifetime, Renault never tried to make it quieter. The simple truth was that French buyers wanted to hear the car as it sped up. For them, the sound was a sign of temperament.

Anyhow, the Five was a big success and sold well. It was followed by a version with a wholly new body and partly new design, but the real glory belonged to the original. Its many advantages were opposed by a single serious drawback – rapid rusting.

When the Five was designed, the engineers apparently gave no thought to corrosion. As a result, the body was full of built-in rust pockets. Untreated edges, joints, folds in the sheet metal, and dirt traps where moisture lingered, were a perfect encouragement to rust. Hence the Renault Five began to fall apart much faster than average cars. ■

1988 Renault 5 GTE

Ford Fiesta

1987 Ford Fiesta 1.1 Ghia

WITH UNDISTINGUISHED RECTANGULAR
headlamps that gave little light, wheels that were much too
small (only 12-inch, a great limit to access and tyre choice) as
well as interior heating that either cooked or chilled you, the
Ford Fiesta was no dream car. It did, however, become one of
Ford's all-time bestsellers.

This was not the company's first small car with front-wheel
drive: the Taunus 12M had preceded it. But the Fiesta did
represent a serious effort by Ford to make a small car that
was truly modern for its time.

When Henry Ford II first saw the Fiesta in England, he
reputedly said, "A damned good job, boys!" Then he went
back to America. It was a deep tribute from Ford, who could

barely squeeze himself into the little car. Besides, he was
known for being quite sparse with praise of his designers.

What chiefly paved the way for its sales success was the
Fiesta's simple construction. It followed the same recipe as
most other small cars during the 1970s: a transverse engine in
front, driving the front wheels. But in one respect it differed
from the rest. Ford had allowed his spare-parts people and
genuine mechanics to participate in the whole design process,
resulting in various simplifications – which would mean less
complicated repairs and cheaper spares.

Many were disappointed by Ford's selection of its engine
when the Fiesta appeared. It had a conventional pushrod
engine, all made of cast iron, at a time when ever more manufacturers were bringing out engines with overhead camshafts
and using aluminium at least for the cylinder heads. Yet the
old engine soon proved to be no disadvantage in the Fiesta.

1987 Ford Fiesta XR 2

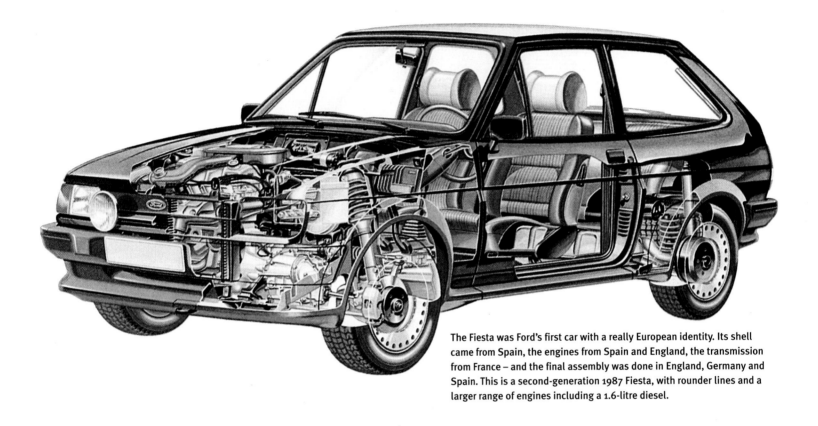

The Fiesta was Ford's first car with a really European identity. Its shell came from Spain, the engines from Spain and England, the transmission from France – and the final assembly was done in England, Germany and Spain. This is a second-generation 1987 Fiesta, with rounder lines and a larger range of engines including a 1.6-litre diesel.

Easy service, long life, and low fuel consumption were benefits. To be sure, 53 horsepower raised no eyebrows. Passing another car at 60 mph (100 km/h) was sheer torture. In fact, if the engine did not get 98-octane petrol, it knocked and could well damage the exhaust valves.

The Fiesta was very roomy by contemporary standards. It held four average-size passengers, and the rear baggage section was easy to use, its floor hiding a couple of practical pockets for small items. The visibility was good, helped by low windows at the sides, and the backward view was excellent. One needed only to aim with the rear window's lower edge when reversing, as the car ended there.

In the front were a conventional spring-leg type of suspen-sion and a rack steering without servo. The shock absorbers were a problem: Ford chose bad quality, which made for bouncy cars. But the rear end was simplicity itself, a live axle with spiral springs. The front brakes had discs with a sliding yoke that tended to rust solid, while small drum brakes were in the rear.

A Fiesta was enjoyable to drive, especially in city traffic where it really found its stride. In general it was considered spry and easy to manoeuvre, but on country roads it performed too weakly for wide acceptance. At any rate, it earned a reputation for lasting long and costing little per mile. For many years the Fiesta was among Europe's cheapest cars to own, and this did much to offset its limitations of power. ■

Lotus Esprit

COLIN CHAPMAN MANUFACTURED SMALL SPORTS cars with racing qualities in the 1950s, followed by the Lotus Elite – an advanced tourer, as we have seen in another article – and next by the pioneering Elan and Europa.

In 1974 Chapman took a further step upward, presenting a new Elite, which, at £5,000, was the most expensive Lotus to

date. A year later it was joined by the Lotus Eclat. These models could be regarded as successors of the Elan Plus Two.

But Chapman had even bolder things in mind, and in 1976 came the Europa's replacement: the Esprit. It had a mid-mounted engine and contained a good deal of Formula 1 technology – not surprisingly, as Lotus led the developments in Formula 1 at that time and was doing very well on the race courses.

The Esprit was designed by an Italian, Giorgeto Giugiaro, and had the same engine as the Eclat and Elite. It was a four-cylinder twin-cam engine of 1973 cc, mounted at 45 degrees.

There were three versions for different markets, since exhaust emission requirements had begun to hit hard. At most, the engine gave 160 hp at 6,200 rpm.

The gearbox had five speeds and the car, weighing 2,425 lbs (1,100 kg), accelerated in 7 seconds to 60 mph (100 km/h). It could do a bit over 135 mph (220 km/h), but the low-emission versions managed only 125 mph (200 km/h), a disappointment when they could hardly keep up with a Golf GTi.

Not until 1978 did work begin on an improved engine, which was to be turbo-fed. Giugiaro was also assigned to endow the body with a more daring appearance and better aerodynamics. The Esprit Turbo emerged in 1981, with the same engine but lower compression. Its novelty was that the turbo, made by Garret AiResearch, raised the output to 210 hp at 6,000 rpm. Only six seconds were needed to reach 60 mph (100 km/h) and the top speed was somewhat over 150 mph (240 km/h).

FAME ON THE SCREEN

A figure who did much to promote the model's popularity was James Bond, who in 1981 moved from an Aston Martin to a Lotus Esprit Turbo in his film *For Your Eyes Only*. As usual, the car bristled with refinements, including a ski rack on the sloping rear end.

In 1986 the next version arrived – Esprit Turbo HCPI, which stood for High Compression Petrol Injection. Its power and top speed were only marginally higher, but the car was a dream to drive. As someone has sensibly said, "The most important thing is not how fast the car goes straight forward, but how it gets round the curves." ∎

From 1986 onward, the Esprit Turbo was provided with a spoiler at each end. This helped to improve its stability, road-holding and steering characteristics at high speed.

Ford Granada

COLLABORATION BETWEEN THE GERMANS AND English has always seemed reasonable when it comes to large companies like Ford, but in practice there has been friction. The same happened on this occasion, though the fundamental design ideas were accepted by each side. Apart from sharing the Granada's shape, chassis and basic construction, each wanted differences for its home market, and each got them.

For instance, two contrasting V6 engines emerged, while they had very similar performance and fuel consumption: a 3-litre for the English market, deriving from the old English 2.5-litre V6, and a 2.3- or 2.6-litre version for the German market. In principle, not a single bolt was identical in the two engines – which did not say much for company cooperation. The German 2.3-litre was best adapted to the car, but the 2.6-litre prevailed and was increased to 2.8 litres, as well as get-

Ford in Europe was in dire need of a sales success when the Granada appeared in 1973. The company's old 17 and 20M on the German market, and its Corsair, Consul, Zephyr and Zodiac on the English, had fallen behind competitors and only something radical could win back buyers.

The solution from Ford in America was to make a large, comfortable, low-priced car, that would let people enjoy luxury without going broke. This resulted in the Granada, a global car to be manufactured in both England and Germany, and exported to much of what was then the "free world".

ting fuel injection when exhaust cleaning was introduced for some markets. Moreover, the German V6 proved to have the longest lifetime, so the English V6 gradually disappeared.

The Granada's body was reminiscent of a small American car: big and broad, with comfy seats and plush fillings. Interior space was no problem even for a long-legged driver. He could also fit in the place behind himself, and such generous leeway was uncommon in contemporary cars. But a disadvantage was the low roof height in back, notably when the car had a roof-hatch.

The body was made with attention to the period's most scientific knowledge about deformation by crashing. Due to the ample space inside, passengers had far to fly before hitting the surfaces, and this lessened injury in a collision. As for driving qualities, the Granada was much better than previous large European Ford models. Live axles and the simple spring-strut front end were gone: a Granada's front had two triangle-links with spiral springs, and a special frame that was suspended on robust rubber bushings, which superbly insulated the body from bothersome road noise. The rear end had a double-jointed axle, greatly improving the comfort and eliminating the earlier live axle's disturbing tendency to make the car hop sideways on bad roads.

Simpler models were to be called Consul, the Granada having a slightly higher price. But eventually the Consul name vanished, and all models were called Granada. From the very outset, a whole range of models was created: two- and four-

The 1985 Ford Granada 2.8i Ghia. Ford used the name Ghia for a well-equipped model. Ghia was a previously independent Italian designer, bought up by Ford in the mid-1960s.

door sedans, a two-door coupé with fastback body, and a four-door estate wagon.

There were also several different engines, gearboxes, and equipment alternatives for tailoring the car to personal desires. Nobody would be turned away because the model of his or her dreams did not exist. The watchword was: "What do you want? We'll get it for you."

This was fresh thinking for the European factories, although long used in America where the cars were produced "naked" and, on delivery, were equipped with whatever the buyer was able to pay for.

From an automobile historian's viewpoint, the Granada was perhaps not a paragon of design. Still, it became popular – mainly because it was large and roomy, pleasant to drive, and less expensive than the more established big cars. To ignore these virtues would be stuffy indeed. ∎

Saab Turbo

1978 Saab 99 station-wagon coupé

Saab was by no means the first to use a turbo. But through clever technology, it did so in a new way and broke fresh ground for the turbo's applications. In 1977 it presented a turbocharged model of the 99. This was the company's stroke of luck, for turbo then became synonymous with Saab.

Already at the turn of the century, engine designers had realized that, by pumping the mixture of fuel and air into the cylinders under pressure, the coefficient of fullness could be raised, and with it the power. One might say that a fan blowing air into the cylinders is enough, as more fuel can be added for burning, thus boosting the output.

A more sophisticated system is a pump that feeds air into the engine, so that more fuel can be accepted. If the pump is mechanical, we speak of a compressor – since that is what it does to the air – or a supercharger. Its disadvantage is that, being driven by the engine, it drains away power.

The problem was solved by letting the outflow of exhaust gases drive the air pump – the principle of the exhaust turbo.

These gases turn a blade wheel (rather as in a water mill) and its axle rotates a pump that blows air into the engine. Almost no power is then lost, and the energy comes from gases that would otherwise simply be released.

This type of exhaust turbo was used in competitions, also appearing on some production cars. Normally, the turbo was engaged to give the engine extra strength if its ordinary power curve was reached.

Yet Saab chose another approach. The turbo started when the car accelerated, regardless of the engine's current output level. Consequently, you got a virtually immediate boost as soon as you stepped hard on the gas in a Saab Turbo.

Saab was thus able to use a relatively small engine as the basis: a four-cylinder 2-litre machine, which performed like six cylinders with the turbo coupled in. If you avoided the extra power and went easy on the accelerator pedal, the usual 2-litre behaviour yielded very low fuel consumption. This was the novelty – more power only when you needed it, not always.

Saab's station-wagon coupé came at the right moment and, thanks to the exhaust turbo, its output was increased to 145 hp, quite an impressive figure. It instantly transformed the fairly boring 99 into one of the most potent cars on the market, taking only nine seconds to reach 100 km/h (60 mph) and having a top speed of 200 km/h (125 mph) – terrific performance in 1977.

The 99 was a stout, neutral car. After its first troublesome years, it also became pretty reliable, but felt far from inspiring at the wheel. It had safe handling characteristics, due to front-wheel drive, and yet fun was beyond it. While the advent of its station-wagon coupé form made it more practical, with a big rear hatch for easy loading, the 99 remained an enthusiast's

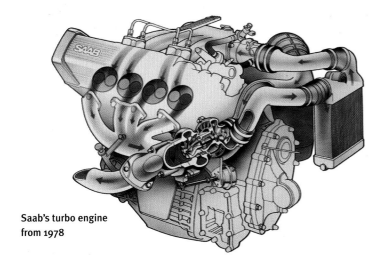

Saab's turbo engine
from 1978

car for Saab fans. It was not enjoyed for any special reason by the masses of automobile buyers.

Then the Turbo arrived, and the driving could at last be called an experience. To feel the turbo engaging when you pushed down the gas pedal, sense the rising power and watch the car passing others like what appeared to be lightning, was pure pleasure. The 99 suddenly seemed to have endless energy.

At the end of the 1970s, Saab was not a widely known make in the rest of Europe. Driving on a German autobahn and accelerating away from a BMW or Mercedes was particularly thrilling if you saw its occupants' faces, as though they were saying: "What in blazes was that?"

Once when I tested caravans in England, my 900 Turbo was pulling 1,500 kilograms and stopped at a traffic light. Beside me was a Jaguar XJ6. When the light turned green, I accelerated hard and got away faster with a trailer than the Jaguar did without one.

To be sure, the first 99 Turbo had defects. The axle between the turbo and the intake became carbonized, and had to be replaced at intervals. In the heat of the stopped engine, the oil on the common axle from the turbo to the intake wheel became a coating of coke, which wore heavily on the axle when the engine restarted. Ideally, the car should have sat in neutral

for some minutes after a drive, so that the turbo cooled off. But nobody told this to the customers.

The Bosch K jetronic injection system also caused trouble. A little distribution valve got stuck, preventing fuel from reaching the engine. The valve rusted due to the condensed water that always exists in petrol. Half a litre of oil in the fuel, every 600 miles or so, lubricated the valve and solved the problem. Neither did Saab mention this to customers, who thus often needlessly found it difficult to start the car.

The 99 Turbo was given the beautiful Inca 6-inch wheels of light metal. But given 186/60-15 tyres, there was a wide surface to drag around with the non-servo steering. It took a muscular man to park in a pocket on dry asphalt.

The 900 as a Turbo proved to be a much better car than the 99. It had better cooling of the turbo unit, an air-charge cooler, and none of the childhood ailments that afflicted the first turbo cars. By that time, however, Saab's competitors had caught up and there were turbo models from most of the major makes. ∎

1979 Saab 99 Turbo two-door saloon

Audi 100

As a model name, the Audi 100 first appeared in 1969 – but that model was quite different from what emerged in 1977. Without exaggeration, the 100-model of 1977 can be said to have laid the foundation for Audi's truly great sales successes in modern times.

Having faded away upon the breakup of Auto Union after World War II, Audi managed a hesitant comeback when DKW left the scene. The initial Audi 60 was a DKW in terms of its body, although rebuilt with the medium-pressure four-cycle engine of that period. But the 100-model soon proved to be what Audi required as an independent make. For the first time, a modern Audi was easy to drive, and offered superb performance as well as low fuel consumption.

All this sounded fine, and the customers were enthusiastic. Special praise went to the entirely new engine, a five-cylinder design which was then very peculiar. However, the choice of such a design should not have been surprising. Audi needed a bigger engine, but it would have been too big – and probably too heavy – if six cylinders were used with the existing equipment, such as pistons and connecting rods, which could be borrowed from the old four-cylinder engine. The obvious solution was to stop at five cylinders.

No less than 136 horsepower resulted, an excellent figure by contemporary standards. The car accelerated through 0-100 km/h (0-60 mph) in under 10 seconds, and could reach about 190 km/h (120 mph). To beat that, something with really high performance was called for.

All Audis were front-heavy until the 100-model arrived in 1977. Even this model suffered the same drawback, but not as seriously as did earlier Audis. The front end used spring-legs and rack steering, while the rear axle had helical coils. An aid to stable handling was the negative steering radius, which gave very reliable control if, for example, one braked with the front wheels on various kinds of surface.

The brakes were discs in front and drums in back, naturally with servo assistance. The rather hard suspension was typical of Germany, where more attention was paid to a car's stability at high autobahn speeds than to softly gliding transportation. And no complaints could be made about the Audi 100's spaciousness: it was one of the roomiest cars on the market in its day.

The body was a characteristic lightweight construction of the same sort as the old Audi 80. Computers had exactly calculated the requirements for maximum strength, so there

1978 Audi 100

was definitely no extra "fat" in any part of the body. Hence the car was very light for its size, and this had as positive an effect on its performance as on its fuel consumption.

One of the car's disadvantages was that the designers fell for a current fashion – using plastic at every opportunity in the furnishings. The whole car spoke of plastic, which did not convey a solid impression. On the contrary, it suggested the practice of "wearing them out and throwing them out". But admittedly all the plastic items were simple to manufacture and install.

Despite its length of 470 cm (185 inches), the Audi 100 was felt by drivers to be relatively small and easily handled. This assessment was largely due to the fine view from the driver's seat, with big windows and unobtrusive roof-posts.

The car was also unusually safe on the road, but had tiresomely stiff steering. There was no servo steering on the first models from 1977, though it later became standard and gave the 100 a well-deserved smoothness of handling.

Before long, unfortunately, the Audi 100 turned out to have a major problem – rust. The body's joints were so badly made that it took little time to be irreparably corroded. All too many examples have been scrapped because the rust damage was not worth fixing, even though the mechanical parts still worked perfectly.

The Audi 100 sold extremely well, and attracted innumerable customers by placing the make on the market among the best large cars. Future 100-models were thus seen as established competitors of the better-known automobiles. ■

1980
–1990

VIGDIS FINNBOGADÓTTIR MAKES HER WAY TO THE presidency of Iceland. Ronald Reagan wins an overwhelming victory in America's presidential election. The French philosopher and author Jean-Paul Sartre dies. A funeral is held, too, for Alexei Kosygin, the only top Soviet politician who succeeded in leaving his post without being either fired or fired at. More passenger cars are produced during 1980 in Japan than in the United States: 7 compared with 6.4 million. America sends up the first space shuttle, Columbia. A Soviet submarine runs aground, far inside Sweden's southern archipelago, near a sensitive military base. Fashion-dictated skirt and trouser lengths disappear in Paris, Rome, London and New York. Hot-pants and ankle-length dresses are created with inspiration from various ages and continents.

General Wojciech Jaruzelski becomes Poland's prime minister. Pope John Paul II, also Polish, is seriously wounded by gunshots during an audience at St. Peter's in Rome. Prince Charles of Great Britain marries Lady Diana Spencer. The independent trade union Solidarity opens its second congress in Gdansk, Poland, and re-elects Lech Walesa its chairman, besides proposing a total revision of the socialist system. Pablo Picasso's masterpiece "Guernica" is exhibited publicly

A selection of small semi-estate cars from the Eighties. The 1982 Daihatsu Charade (*upper left*) was distinguished by a three-cylinder engine with one overhead camshaft. British Leyland's Metro (*upper right*) followed the usual pattern with its transverse four-cylinder engine and three-door body. In 1984 came a five-door version, but a five-speed gearbox had to wait till decade's end. The Nissan Micra (*lower left*), presented in 1983, was a fairly nondescript model and had no high-performance European version. Still, its easy handling and smooth gear system helped to make it very popular as a driving-school car. During the 1980s, the Soviet auto industry progressed far, from the conventional VAZ 2106 with a Sixties look to the fully modern, front- wheel-drive semi-estate car VAZ 2108 (*lower right*). This model was called the Lada Samara in Western Europe. The 2106 derived from the Fiat 124 and, from 1969, had a 1451-cc engine. The 2108 shown here is an early example from 1987, and in 1989 the model was available with three or five doors, as well as an engine choice of 1099, 1288 and 1499 cc.

for the first time in Spain. The artist had decided that the painting should not be taken to Spain (from New York) until his homeland was free of fascism. A military council replaces the Polish government and proclaims a national state of emergency in order to crush Solidarity. The union is banned, and Jaruzelski – having become party leader as well – insists that this is Poland's last chance to solve its own problems.

Moshe Dayan, a flamboyant Israeli general and minister, dies. Two buses on the motorway between Paris and Lyon drive too closely, and cause a triple accident that kills 53 people, 44 of them children. Leonid Brezhnev dies in Moscow and a former KGB chief, Yuri Andropov, is elected to head the Communist Party. The U.S. Secretary of State, George Shultz, begins to build up a new stability in American foreign policy. Great

The engine-driven supercharger made a comeback in the 1980s, being offered by Ford and Volkswagen among the major manufacturers. This TVR 350i has a Sprintex S screw-type supercharger, which sucks in air at about 500 cubic feet per minute at its maximum speed of 15,500 rpm. Giving the 3.5-litre Rover V8 unit an output of 270 bhp, the Sprintex was not a factory option but was fitted by Haughins, the Northern TVR Centre. They also offered a supercharged Range Rover.

No other postwar car for ordinary road use had possessed what made the Cizeta Moroder 16 T unique: a 6-litre 16-cylinder engine, yielding 560 hp at 8,000 rpm. This power plant was mounted transversely behind the cabin and, via a five-speed gearbox, pushed the car up to a claimed 330 km/h (205 mph). But only one example had been produced by the end of 1989.

Britain sends a large battle fleet to the South Atlantic and reconquers the Falkland Islands from Argentina. The French film director Jacques Tati dies. At least 300 people are killed and 1,200 injured by an earthquake in southwestern Colombia, where over 3,000 buildings are wrecked in the city of Popayan.

Tens of thousands of Poles support the forbidden Solidarity union, demonstrating in the streets of Gdansk and Warsaw. The Norwegian parliament's Nobel committee awards the Peace Prize to Solidarity's leader Lech Walesa. Zhao Ziyang, the Prime Minister of China, visits the USA and President Reagan. An American astronaut, Bruce McCandless, is the first human being to move freely in space without a line – on a "space moped" driven by small rockets. The Soviet craft

Soyuz T-10 travels in space for 237 days, setting a world record. The Polish General Jaruzelski is hardly successful in his efforts to gain credence for his policy. Indira Gandhi is murdered, and the Prime Ministry of India passes to her son Rajiv.

The first operation of an artificial heart into a patient is performed. A seeing robot is invented that can remember 99 objects, and recognize a piece of work after only one second. Computers are installed at a mounting pace in company offices and production plants. Even home computers experience a breakthrough. Microprocessors control functions in all sorts of household and industrial machines, as well as in car engines.

Peugeot, which owns Citroën, changes the company name from PSA Peugeot-Citroën to simply Peugeot SA. The Peugeot

Two of the members in the "Club of Four": Fiat Croma (*opposite top*) and Saab 9000 (*opposite bottom*). This ambitious project involved sharing resources for design and production, so that many components could be made jointly and thus more cheaply. However, the engines came from the respective manufacturers. Fiat's Croma had the smallest engine, a 1.6-litre 83-hp four-cylinder, while Saab used a 2-litre four with double overhead camshafts.

The Club's two other members were Lancia Thema (*below*) and Alfa Romeo 164 (*bottom right*). Lancia offered a choice of 2-litre four, 2.9-litre PRV engine, and Ferrari's 3-litre V8, whereas Alfa had its own 3-litre V6. The fastest of all these was Lancia's Thema 8.32, with 215 hp and a top speed over 220 km/h (135 mph). All four cars had front-wheel drive and about the same suspension.

Mature British tradition and 4,950 lbs (2,245 kg) of it: The Rolls-Royce Silver Spirit. When presented in 1980, the model had a 6.7-litre V8 with around 240 horsepower. As usual, the company has never wanted to reveal this figure. On the other hand, the air-conditioning system's power was 9 kW, corresponding to some 30 refrigerators!

205 is presented and sells tremendously. Next it proves very successful on race courses, for example with the four-wheel-drive type 205 Turbo 16. Western countries are acquiring ever more laws about catalyzers for exhaust purification. Cars are filled with sophisticated technology – including refined electronic systems to control fuel injection, nonlocking brakes, and four-wheel drive. The city of Lille, in northeastern France,

inaugurates a driverless underground railway.

The Soviet Communist party has a new General Secretary: Mikhail Sergeyevich Gorbachev. He is considered more flexible than his predecessors, and the Kremlin's ruling clique hopes that he can stop the country's economic stagnation. Andrei Gromyko is chosen as President. Their troops in Afghanistan meet tough resistance from local guerrillas. Some thirty wine-

The first factory to make purely Japanese designs in Britain was set up by Nissan at Washington, Tyne & Wear in 1986. The car was the Bluebird, initially a saloon and joined by a hatchback one year later. This is a 1988 Turbo ZX hatchback with 115-mph top speed. Of the 70,000 Washington cars made in 1989, about 30,000 were exported. Other EEC countries regard them – somewhat reluctantly – as British because of the substantial proportion (by value) of British-made components.

producers in Austria are discovered to have sweetened their wines with antifreeze fluid. The mountain Ayer's Rock, in the Australian desert, is returned to the aborigines who traditionally own it. Reagan and Gorbachev meet in Geneva, mainly to resume the disarmament talks started long ago between the superpowers – but they achieve little. The American space shuttle *Challenger* explodes after a launch. In the Philippines, Ferdinand

Marcos is deposed and Corazon Aquino becomes president.

Early in 1986 the Swedish Prime Minister, Olof Palme, is shot and the assassin gets away. Two months later, a reactor explosion at Chernobyl in the Ukraine causes the worst accident in the history of nuclear energy. East Berliners celebrate their Wall's 25th anniversary, while in West Berlin wreaths are laid in memory of about 80 people who have died trying to

Among the more advanced cars of the Eighties was Porsche's low series model 959. Externally related to the 911 series, it was a far more sophisticated design in all ways. The engine, with 2850 cc and double turbos, gave 450 hp that were transmitted via a six-speed gearbox and variable four-wheel drive. The second turbo began to operate only when accelerating sharply. Other refinements included electronic adjustment of the shock-absorber level, nonlocking brakes, and servo steering.

Lancia's absolutely top-notch model in the Delta series was the HF Turbo 4WD. Not just a rally winner, it was also a very impressive road car in both summer and winter-time. The four-wheel drive system had both Ferguson viscous coupling and a Torsen differential. In standard form, 200 horsepower were available, while the rally cars used 295 hp at 7,000 rpm.

climb westward over the Wall. Margaret Thatcher is successful, in spite of certain crises, as British Prime Minister. The aptly named *Herald of Free Enterprise*, an English channel ferry, leaves Zeebrugge in Belgium without closing her gates, and sinks with a loss of 209 people. Further Soviet-American disarmament negotiations succeed, and an initial agreement is signed by Reagan and Gorbachev. A 19-year-old aviator, Matthias Rust from West Germany, flies a small plane from Helsinki to Moscow and is noticed only when he lands in Red Square.

Gorbachev, influenced by the weak planned economy and by Polish pressure for freedom, makes efforts to promote *glasnost* (openness) and *perestroika* (restructuring) throughout the Soviet Union. As a result, both the environmental and nationality problems in the Soviet-dominated East European states become widely recognized during 1988. Gorbachev also outmanoeuvres Gromyko and replaces him as president. Naguib Mahfouz of Egypt is the first Arab to win the Nobel Prize in literature.

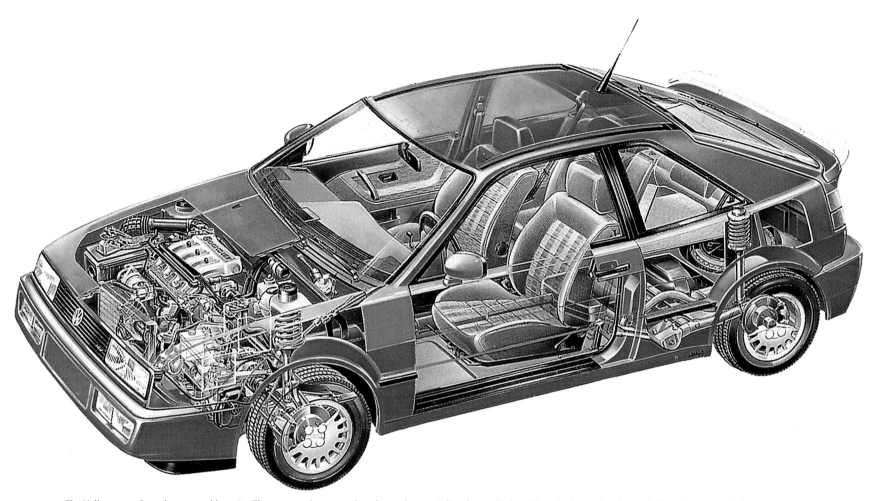

The Volkswagen Corrado emerged in 1989. There was only one engine alternative, a 1.8-litre four-cylinder with a single overhead camshaft and a mechanical supercharger. Its power was 160 hp.

In the late Eighties a number of technically complex, expensive supercar projects appeared. Jaguar's XJ220 had a 6.2-litre 48-valve V12, giving over 500 hp at 7,000 rpm, with four-wheel drive and a five-speed racing gearbox, as well as a central viscous coupling. Only one example of this kind was built, but a series of 350 cars with turbocharged V6 was manufactured – and sold for dizzying prices, amounting to over half a million dollars each.

Mercedes-Benz's open SL models were made with almost no changes between 1973 and 1989, though different engines were used during these years. They varied from a 2.8-litre 185-hp six to a 5-litre 245-hp V8. A good example was the 500SL in 1985 (*left*). An entirely new SL series began in 1989, with a fresh body and further engines: a 3-litre six and 5-litre V8, the latter allowing a top speed of 250 km/h (155 mph). The new SL had numerous safety innovations, such as an automatic roll-over-bar that popped up if the car leaned too far, and belts that stretched themselves if it collided. The "puncture-safe" tyres could be driven for 300 kilometres at speeds up to 50 mph (80 km/h) after a puncture.

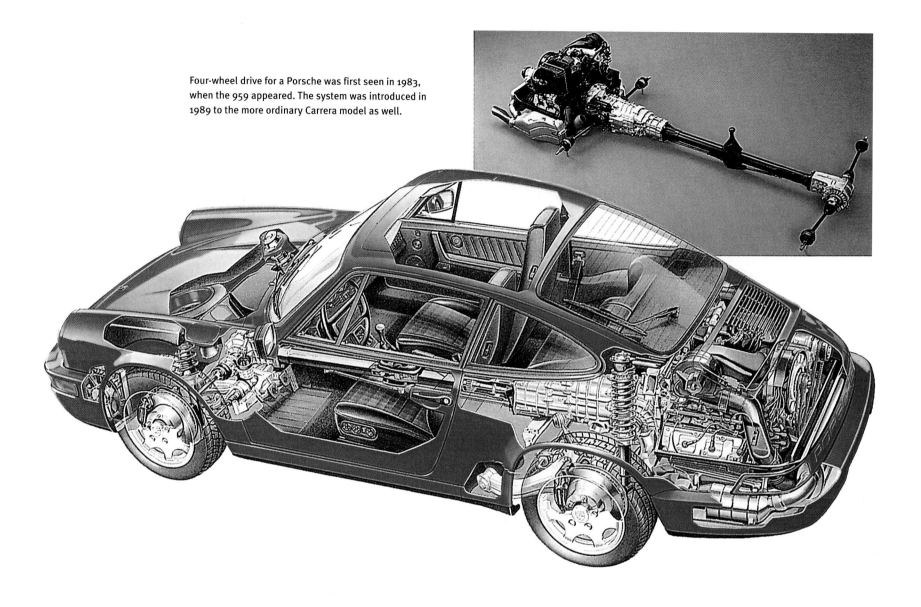

Four-wheel drive for a Porsche was first seen in 1983, when the 959 appeared. The system was introduced in 1989 to the more ordinary Carrera model as well.

All the nuclear-armed submarines in the Baltic Sea will be scrapped, Gorbachev promises. Troops are reduced, too, for example in the Leningrad military region. The democratic revolution in Eastern Europe, accelerated by *glasnost* and *perestroika*, brings the fall of communist regimes in Poland, East Germany, Hungary, Czechoslovakia and Rumania. Yet when such demands are raised in various parts of the Soviet Union itself, Gorbachev has to attempt a slowdown. The Berlin Wall tumbles and the Iron Curtain of barbed wire between East and West Germany is razed. Democratic elections are held in nearly every East European country – whereas similar demonstrations in Peking are squashed by the army. The Russian physicist Andrei Sakharov, once a "father" of the hydrogen bomb and later a dissident champion of human rights, dies at the end of this decade, having been detained at its beginning and released by Gorbachev. ∎

The top European model from General Motors in 1989 was the Opel Senator, which took the name Vauxhall in Great Britain. It made a worthy rival for the Scorpio, BMW and Rover's 800 series, besides being faster than any of these. The Senator shown here has a 3-litre six-cylinder engine with 177 horsepower.

Bentley Turbo R

The best impression of a car's character is seen from a certain angle (as noted on page 227). In the case of the Bentley Turbo R, it is an oblique front view that reveals the car's power. Almost aggressive, this beast could actually do at least 155 mph (250 km/h) and accelerated to 60 mph (100 km/h) in less than seven seconds.

WHEN W. O. BENTLEY WAS FORCED TO HAND OVER Bentley Motors to Rolls-Royce in 1931, an era came to a close and, from then on, the Bentley was known as "The Silent Sports Car".

As time went by, the Bentley products became ever more like those of Rolls-Royce. In the end, only their radiator masks distinguished them, besides the fact that a Rolls always cost an extra £130. Indeed, Rolls-Royce considered stopping the manufacture of Bentleys in 1980, when the latter's sales

were only four percent of the former's total.

Luckily this was not done, and the company decided to re-establish the once proud name of Bentley. Thus emerged the 1980 model, which replaced the Bentley T2. It was called the Mulsanne, after a small village at the race course of Le Mans, where Bentleys had harvested so many victories during the 1920s.

In 1982 came the model that would emphasize that Bentleys were no longer a cheap version of their big sister

Rolls-Royce. This was the Bentley Mulsanne Turbo. It had the same 6.7-litre V8 engine as the Rolls-Royce Silver Spirit and Silver Spur, but was provided with a Garret AiResearch turbocharger.

As usual, Rolls-Royce revealed no power figures, but did announce that the power was 50 percent higher than in the other models. Or, as it was diplomatically expressed, "sufficient at a sufficient number of revolutions". Presumably the truth was around 330 horsepower, as calculated by the Swiss magazine *Automobile Revue*.

The car's top speed was 135 mph (217 km/h) and it accelerated to 60 mph (100 km/h) in just 7.5 seconds – an astonishing achievement for a car that weighed nearly 5,000 lbs (2,250 kg). But the difference between the Mulsanne and the Mulsanne Turbo was marginal. The first had a chromed radiator mask, while the second had the radiator lacquered in the same colour as the rest of the car.

July 1984 brought the Bentley Eight, a somewhat simpler model that cost about £10,000 less. This was supposed to appeal to more youthful(!) customers, and its price was "only" £49,497.

At the Geneva salon in 1985, the fastest Bentley until then was presented – the Turbo R. It had modified springing, wider tyres and reinforced stabilizers. Hence the letter "R", which stood for road-holding. The car did over 140 mph (230 km/h).

As might be expected, the furnishings in the Turbo R were

The registration number 1900 TU is one that the factory used for many years on its "works demonstrators".

magnificent, including seats made from Connolly leather of the highest quality. The leather usually came from Scandinavian cows, as their hide is relatively undamaged by insect bites and barbed wire. A complete interior used eight hides. It was said that the appearance reminded one of an English gentleman's club. Inside the cabin, the silence was so profound that the engine's activity could be detected only by the twitching of the tachometer.

The front seats, of course, were electrically adjustable, and an electronic memory could keep track of four settings per seat. This was helpful if several different people drove the car. However, I cannot believe that the owner of a Turbo R loaned it to anybody. At most, his wife might have used it to get from the estate into London for a shopping visit at Harrods or Fortnum & Mason.

In that case, he could be forgiven for watching over her in a helicopter. So would the spirit of W. O. Bentley, puffing with pleasure at the sight of the Turbo R. ∎

Audi Quattro = four-wheel drive

Audi's Quattro dominated the rally scene during 1981–84, with Hannu Mikkola winning the World Championship in 1982 and Stig Blomqvist in 1984. The first Quattros for rally use had 285 hp under the bonnet, but the power was raised gradually to almost 500 hp.

Few motorists realize how little contact with "Mother Earth" they actually have. The fact is that it amounts to only four surfaces the size of a hand's palm – where the tyres touch the road.

This is obviously a reason for ensuring that the tyres have as good a grip on the ground as possible. The tread pattern, air pressure, tyre balance and wheel alignment should be correct. But the contact force has to be transmitted by the wheels. If the wheels spin, or are not powered, the contact is easily lost.

And here begins the gripping tale of four-wheel drive!

Powering all the wheels of a vehicle is nothing new. It was attempted as early as the 1910s, although often in vain because the wheels did not cooperate – especially when at least two of the wheels had to turn horizontally as well as axially. To make a driving joint capable of transmitting the power was simply impossible.

Some fairly successful experiments were done in England during the 1920s, including four-wheel steering associated with four-wheel drive. But they led to no extensive practical use in car production.

Lorries had power on more than one pair of wheels, but this commonly involved a bogie arrangement, with several axles coupled to the drive wheels for greater mobility. Very seldom did these vehicles also have power on the wheels that steered.

There are always arguments about which came first, but as a whole it can be said that genuine four-wheel drive did not arrive until the United States Army wanted a "general purpose" (GP) vehicle for all-round use. This is described in the article on the Jeep. For terrain vehicles and working cars of various kinds, four-wheel drive became universal after World War II. Yet for ordinary cars, it was still unusual.

Audi Quattro standard coupé from 1980

A RALLY SENSATION

In 1981, Franz Wittman of Austria drove an Audi with four-wheel drive in a rally competition and won solidly. The Audi Quattro was soon a legend, taking just about every rally prize available during that decade. Personally I recall how, at the Swedish rally in the early 1980s, the Audi cars gained about 10 seconds with every start. Instead of standing and hopping to get traction for a few seconds, like the two-wheel-drive cars, Audi's four-wheel drive got it instantly and the cars rocketed away. Further seconds were gained with the acceleration after each braking. The Audi's superiority was thus not surprising, and brought the Rally World Championship to Hannu Mikkola in 1982, followed by Stig Blomqvist in 1984.

But this was competition. Could a run-of-the-mill motorist need the sophistication of four-wheel drive?

It may be true that the majority of motorists, in most situations, can do without four-wheel drive. However, under extreme conditions, the technique might be what saves you from a disaster. This is certainly enough to justify it.

Four-wheel drive provides an active kind of safety, ensuring that more wheels have the right contact with the road surface – a property well worth the attention of many motorists. A conventional car design, with the engine in front and rear-wheel drive, requires an extra distribution gear – an axle that goes forward for the driving wheels, and an axle that goes backward for the powered rear wheels. If the engine is transverse, an angular gear is also needed to distribute the force in different directions.

According to Audi's concept of a longitudinally mounted engine, the gearbox was modified to have an intermediate differential that distributed the force forward and backward. In this device lay the unique "torsen" differential. The latter term refers to "torque sensing", and means that wheel-spin on one axle is sensed in advance, so as to transfer the force from that axle onto the other axle.

The torsen differential plays a role when huge standing rockets are transported from their assembly plant to the launching pad. Any wheel-spin under the supporting carriage might cause the rocket to topple over, at vast expense. With torque sensing, the trip becomes smooth and safe. Much the same smoothness is valuable in a car.

This rare Quattro Sport had a wheelbase 12,5 inches shorter than the standard Quattro. Only 200 of these were made in 1984/85.

By using a torsen differential in the Quattro system, no limited-slip differential was needed between the front and rear axles. The torque was varied automatically on the front and rear wheels, so as to match the road traction that was possible for each axle.

Braking action did not lock the torsen differential in any way, and was therefore not adversely affected by it. Otherwise, all limited-slip differential functions can have undesirable results when braking, since the wheels or axles are already braked and cannot be controlled as easily.

Audi's Quattro system could be connected with an electronic limited-slip differential for all four wheels. In this technique, if any wheel tended to begin spinning at the start, it was slowed with the disc brakes, so that the force was transferred to the wheel having better traction.

There are other systems of four-wheel drive: for example, through an intermediate differential without any limited-slip function, or through a "viscous" coupling. The latter contains a silicon fluid that thickens when differences in rotation rate arise between the front and rear axles. In practice, this system

can be regarded as two-wheel drive, but with gradually engaged four-wheel drive as the spin increases on the normally driving wheels. Plain four-wheel drive with manual engagement is also used.

The Quattro system, though, was superior. It provided excellent course stability, better adhesion of the tyres on the road surface, and less influence by sidewinds.

Laws of nature were not broken by four-wheel drive even in its Quattro form. Friction was essential in order to give the wheels something to push against. But the problems of poor or low friction were eliminated, as far as possible, by the Quattro's systems – including anti-spin regulation, electronic stability, and electronic brake-force distribution. What more can be wished for?

SOME TECHNICAL DATA ON THE AUDIO QUATTRO

The five-cylinder engine of 2144 cc, yielded 200 horsepower at 5,500 rpm. The competition cars had 285 hp at first, then 370 hp and finally almost 500 hp. Top speed of the standard model was 220 km/h (135 mph). ■

Lamborghini Countach

Lamborghini Countach Quattrovalvole 25 Years Anniversary Model from 1989

CAR MAKES THAT HAVE ARISEN FROM THE founder's dissatisfaction with his new car are often met in this book. It is, of course, not enough to be dissatisfied – one needs capital as well. This was no problem for the industrialist Lamborghini, who had grown rich on products such as tractors. Whether he really disliked his new Ferrari, as the myth goes among Lamborghini lovers around the world, would be difficult to prove. But probably he did have an early intention of making a good Grand Touring car to help advertise his business activities.

That he chose a bull as the radiator emblem was no co-incidence, for Lamborghini was born under this astrological sign. According to the myth, though, he displayed a fighting bull to mark his rejection of the rampant horse that sym-bolized Ferrari.

His first prototype, the Lamborghini 350 GTV, was unveiled at the car show in Turin during 1963, but it led to no headlines. Especially criticized was the body, designed by Bertone. So another coachbuilder, Touring, redrew the body and then the

Ferruccio Lamborghini was born in 1916, and began making tractors in the fifties. A couple of years later, he added oil-burner units and air-conditioners to his repertoire. It is said that he first made a car because he was disappointed with a Ferrari he had bought, and thus decided to build the perfect sports car.

car began to be manufactured, as the 350 GT.

Not surprisingly, the model had a V12 engine. It came from Bizzarini and generated 280 horsepower from 3.5 litres. A total of 118 cars were made.

THE MIURA

Already in 1964, design work commenced on the model that would bring Lamborghini fame and praise. It was named after Don Eduardo Miura, a Spaniard who raised fighting bulls.

Without Lamborghini's knowledge, three men – Gianpaolo

Dallara, Paolo Stanzani and a New Zealander, Bob Wallace – devoted their free time to developing the new car, which was to have a transverse V12 engine. They hoped to convince Lamborghini to start racing.

When they revealed their ideas to him, Lamborghini agreed to exhibit a chassis at the Turin car show in 1965, where it rightly aroused interest. Just a year later, the chassis was supplied with a very beautiful body designed by Marcello Gandini at Bertone. The car became a great success.

There were no definite plans to manufacture the Miura, but many potential customers asked about it. Ferruccio Lamborghini gave way at last. The first Miura was delivered in March 1967, and that year 108 examples were made. A total of 615 would result, including a single open car.

The Miura was not Lamborghini's only model and, until the Countach arrived, he created others such as the Espada, Isolero, Jarama and Urraco. However, these did not have the same charismatic image as the Miura.

COUNTACH!

In the early 1970s, Lamborghini became worried about the situation on the Italian labour market and sold his shares to two Swiss investors.

Meanwhile, work proceeded on a successor to the Miura. It is said that, when one of the employees first laid eyes on the prototype, he burst out, "Countach!" In the Piedmontese dialect, this meant "Fantastic!"

With a body from Bertone, the prototype appeared at the Geneva salon in 1971 and was greatly admired. Yet the motoring journalists thought it only a design exercise, and were thus astonished when the Countach went into production three years later.

While the prototype deserved attention, it was nothing compared to the series-made car. This had a body designed by

Lamborghini Countach, prototype

Gandini that was very extreme, almost brutal in shape. Quite long and wide, it had giant air intakes to the motor behind the small rear windows. One could hardly see to the rear, although this mattered less because nobody was likely to overtake the car.

A spectacular detail of the Countach was that the doors opened upward and obliquely forward at about 45 degrees. They gained the adoration of most photographers when illustrating the new model. The present author himself has also fallen for this temptation.

THE GEARBOX IN FRONT OF THE ENGINE

The frame was a complicated "birdcage" of welded tubes. It was made by Marchesi in Modena, then strengthened at the factory with aluminium and glassfibre panels. The body was manufactured in sections of aluminium, and all bodies were individually produced. Hence, if one crashed in a Countach, one could not simply visit the retailer and order new parts. They had to be remade, and that was not cheap!

The Countach was a genuine mid-engine car, with the engine placed in front of the rear wheels' centres. To provide room for the enormous V12, it was necessary to put the gearbox in front of the engine. As a result, the driver and passenger were separated by a substantial housing for this purpose. On the other hand, the car acquired perfect weight distribution.

The engine in the first Countach, designated LP 400, had 3929 cc. In 1982 came the larger LP 500 with 4754 cc. In the last Countach version, the engine was a QV (for Quattro-Valvole, meaning four valves per cylinder) with all of 5167 cc giving 455 horsepower. This brought the top speed to 295 km/h (185 mph) and the time down to five seconds for accelerating through 0–100 km/h (0–60 mph).

On July 5, 1990, the final Countach left the factory. All of the Countach models added up to 1,851 cars.

PHENOMENAL ACCELERATION

I once had the privilege of accompanying one of the factory's drivers during an ordinary test on the roads around Sant'Agata Bolognese, where the Lamborghini was manufactured.

Before we left the premises, the driver hung the classic black "Prova" (test) sign on the rear. Then we went out on a long, straight road edged by pine trees. For the first kilometre, we had to stay behind a big trailer lorry, and I relaxed in the comfortable seat. But a shock awaited me.

Giving no warning, the driver shifted and stepped on the gas. An indescribable effect followed, like nothing else I have experienced in cars. A few inches behind me, 455 horsepower howled as if a jet plane were lifting with its afterburner on. The lorry vanished faster than a mirage, and the pine-tree alley felt ever narrower. Towards the end of the stretch, we had reached 260 km/h (160 mph). And, as I say, it was only an ordinary test before delivery. ■

Ferrari Testarossa

From the rear, a Testarossa is amazingly impressive with its width of nearly two metres.

WHEN THIS CAR WAS FIRST PRESENTED AT THE end of 1984, it happened not at the Paris auto show, but in high-class surroundings at the fashionable Lido nightclub on the Champs Elysées.

The name Testarossa goes back to one of Ferrari's most famous competition models, Testa Rossa. This meant a red head or hood, and referred to the camshaft covers, which were painted with bright-red frost lacquer.

The Testa Rossa had a classic V12 engine with three litres of volume, giving about 300 horsepower at 7,200 rpm in its final form. Only nineteen of these cars were built, between 1957 and 1962. Today, they are among the most sought-after of all Ferraris, and change owners at astronomical prices.

Nothing but the name was inherited by the new Testarossa. This did not even have a V12 engine. Its boxer 12-cylinder engine with five litres, two overhead camshafts, and four valves per cylinder, developed 390 hp at 6,300 rpm. Beneath the engine lay a five-speed gearbox.

The chassis was a square-tube frame reinforced with steel, aluminium and plastic in various proportions. All the wheels were independently suspended. Each end had double triangular links, spring-legs (double at the back) and stabilizers.

Servo assistance was provided for the rack steering. The car needed only five seconds to reach 100 km/h (60 mph). Ventilated 31-cm disc brakes were required in order to stop it from the theoretical top speed of 295 km/h (185 mph).

AN ELECTRIFYING DESIGN

Pininfarina created the Testarossa's design. Its most novel and fascinating features were the big intakes on the sides, feeding cold air to the twin radiators. On the preceding model, Berlinetta Boxer, the radiators sat in front, and could cause

The Ferrari Testarossa in about 1986. Among its most typical details were the vertical pressings on the doors, ending in the radiators' air intakes. Created by Pininfarina, they set a trend followed by others. Another striking feature was the large rear-view mirror. The wheel rims came from Campagnolo, long the supreme supplier to most quality sports-car makers.

insufferable heat in the cabin if the weather was warm. The Testarossa was also equipped with air-conditioning, which worked perfectly.

This was quite a large car, and as startlingly wide as it looked when seen from the rear – 198 cm (78 inches) compared with, for instance, 175 cm (69 inches) for a contemporary Volvo 740. The wedge-shaped body with its upturned back-

side had a length of 448 cm (14'6"), and a height of only 113 cm (3.7 feet)!

Opinions differed enormously about the Testarossa's appearance. Some thought it was the most beautiful thing ever made on four wheels, while others considered it a pompous symbol of greed in the eighties. But whatever the gossip, it was still a Ferrari. ∎

Ford Escort 1981

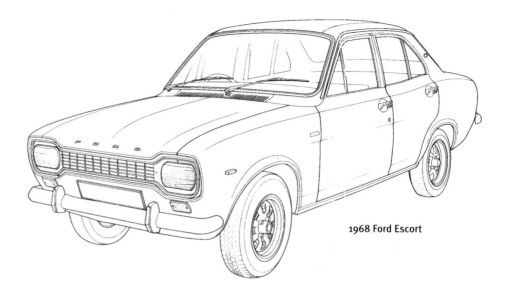

1968 Ford Escort

For many years, the automotive giants Ford and General Motors have produced models that directly competed with each other. Such pairs are the Opel Record and Ford Granada, the Ford Taunus and Opel Ascona, and the Opel Kadett and Ford Escort.

Early in the 1980s, GM abandoned the conventional style of small cars with rear-wheel drive, and presented the Kadett with front-wheel drive. This innovation left Ford no peace, and it soon responded with the new Escort, also front-wheel-driven and with a large rear hatch opening into a practical semi-station-wagon body.

The Escort was intended to sell worldwide, being manu-factured in both Europe and the United States. It would be made in quantities large enough to repay the investment quickly. Preceding the car was an enormous public-relations campaign, and expectations were heightened on every side.

In this storm of attention, the car itself was like the eye of a hurricane. Appropriate press leaks added implausible claims: the car used very little fuel, had an engine that would never wear out or need service, and much else. But these

efforts proved superfluous. The Escort came, saw and con-quered. Immediately it won the support of small-car buyers.

Handsome, fast, easy on petrol, and comfortable, it had quite different handling qualities than the old rear-wheel-drive model. On the other hand, the new Escort was less reliable than competitors like the VW Golf and Opel Kadett. For Ford chose a divided rear axle, instead of a live or semi-live one as on several other small cars.

This axle certainly increased the comfort, but it also meant a change in the track width, which led to unsteady handling – especially with a full load or in a sudden swerve. However, such details did not worry Escort buyers and the car realized all Ford's dreams of success.

Why? At least on paper, the Escort did not look much better in technical terms than its competitors. But it satisfied whoever did not want either an Opel or a VW Golf. Compared with these "senile" cars, it seemed rather bold and youthful.

Then, too, it had a completely new engine that was sensa-tional in a small car. The engine was Ford's pride. No com-promises were made, and Ford took no half-steps in introducing

1985 Ford Escort

a power plant which was ahead of its time for the general public. There were hemispherical combustion chambers, hydraulic valve-lifters, and a breakerless electronic ignition system – technical solutions that once had existed mainly on race cars.

A suitable combustion space was not necessary for extracting maximum power. It could also be used to make the combustion as efficient as possible, thus reducing the petrol consumption and the exhaust emission. The hydraulic valve-lifters were self-adjusting, and required no service if the engine oil was changed regularly.

The same advantages applied to the ignition system. Some service needs disappeared entirely – such as spark timing, fixed forever at the factory – and others shrank greatly. Due to this and the low fuel consumption, the Escort was a lot cheaper to own than competitors.

The engine had four cylinders, one overhead camshaft, and two valves per cylinder at an angle to the cam. Its volume was 1597 cc, yielding 79 horsepower. And it turned out to be the pearl that was promised, with a long lifetime, little thirst and few service costs.

Unfortunately, Ford also offered Europeans an Escort made in Brazil, to profit from the poor wages of workers there. This model, called the LX, had an old Renault engine – used in the Volvo 343 as well – and virtually no rust protection, so it corroded badly, unlike the Europe-built cars. After some years in the mid-1980s, it vanished from the European scene.

But the Escort endured, with some alterations: a more stable rear axle, new body shapes, and far better safety in collisions. Its popularity began to wane only in the late 1990s, when the new Ford Focus emerged. Numerous versions have been produced, such as the semi-station-wagon with three or five doors, a cabriolet and a sedan. Ford even tried to update the car as an exclusive Orion sedan, with more equipment and a higher price. Yet Escort buyers rejected it, and the Orion died as a separate model name. ■

Peugeot 205

I
T IS NO EXAGGERATION TO SAY THAT THE PEUGEOT 205
saved Peugeot. For the company was in a deep economic crisis at
the beginning of the 1980s. But the neat little 205 appeared like
an angel of salvation, and today Peugeot stands on solid ground.

The company is now also the oldest family-owned auto
manufacturer in the world, and only Daimler-Benz has

existed longer.
Yet Peugeot was
a family firm
well before cars
started to be
made. Its
founder, Jean-
Jacques Peugeot,
founded a cotton spinning mill in the early 1700s. Later
members of the family produced tools, clock springs, umbrella
ribs, crinoline frames and other items.

The lion in Peugeot's emblem represents the Lion of Belfort, a monument to the brave defence of the city of Belfort against the Germans in 1871. Bartholdi, the sculptor of the lion, also made the Statue of Liberty in New York. Peugeot chose this symbol because some of the company's factories are located near Belfort.

In 1885, Armand Peugeot turned to making bicycles, and
the company still does so. A couple of years afterward, he built
two steam-driven three-wheelers that were designed by Leon
Serpollet. His first car with a combustion engine emerged in
1891, with a two-cylinder engine of 565 cc and two horsepower.

One of Peugeot's abundant models deserving of mention
is the Bébé from 1912. Designed by the famous Ettore Bugatti,
it had a four-cylinder 855-cc engine giving 10 hp. It was a very
small two-seater with a total length of only 2.5 metres (8'2").
A total of 3,095 cars were made between 1912 and 1916.

A ZERO IN THE MIDDLE

At the Paris salon in 1929, the Peugeot 201 was launched.
From then on, all the company's models have had a central
zero. The first figure stood for the size class, and the third for
which place the design occupied in the order within that
class. The use of a zero in the middle has been patented by
Peugeot.

These numerical series are not entirely logical. For instance,
no models have 1 as the third number, and it was never the
first number until 1972, when the little Peugeot 104 began to
be made. As far as I know, there has not been any 102 or 103.
However, the missing numbers may stand for projects that
did not bear fruit.

1985 Peugeot 205 Turbo 16, with Timo Salonen at the wheel

Model 205 replaced the 204, which was the first Peugeot with front-wheel drive. The 204 was produced in 1,334,309 examples from 1965 until 1980.

WIDESPREAD BUSINESS

Peugeot expanded strongly through the years, and had many factories abroad as well as in France. In 1974, it bought 38.2 percent of Citroën, and in May 1976 it completely took over that company. In 1978, it bought Chrysler's European organization – whose cars, called Simca in Europe, were now renamed Talbot.

The gigantic concern eventually became insolvent and was in desperate need of a big-selling car. This proved to be the

Peugeot 205, which set the company upright again.

The 205 was a pleasantly compact vehicle, though it did not have a remarkable design. Like its competitors in that size class, it carried the engine transversely and was driven by the front wheels. However, it ranked among the quickest in its class, and no fewer than five engine alternatives were gradually developed, ranging from 904 to 1905 cc. The GTi version's engine generated 130 hp and its top speed was just over 200 km/h (125 mph).

What contributed greatly to the 205's popularity were its looks. They were partly the work of Pininfarina, and the 205 had unusually harmonious lines. One of the most successful variants was the cabriolet CTi.

COMPETITION TRIUMPHS

In 1984, Peugeot introduced the rally model 205 Turbo 16. It was equipped with a turbocharged engine of 1775 cc, which in standard form yielded 195 hp. With 2484 cc, the power went as high as 430 hp. The Turbo 16 resembled an ordinary 205, but it was specially designed throughout. For example, the engine sat in back where a passenger seat would normally be.

The car's initial World Championship victory came in 1984 at the Thousand Lakes Rally in Finland. Despite Ari Vatanen's participation in only the last three races, Peugeot won third place in the Rally World Championship. But in 1985 and 1986 it finished first. Then the so-called Group B cars were banned in the competition, since they were growing ever more powerful – usually with over 600 hp..

Peugeot's breadwinner 205 was manufactured until late 1998, and today the corresponding model in that size class is the Peugeot 206. ∎

1990
-2000

Two representatives of German technology from the late nineties. (*Top*) A four-door BMW 328i Limousine. The number of models in the 3-series was remarkably large and in 1998, BMW offered no less than 31 versions, which could be equipped with a four- or six-cylinder engine. The output varied between 90 hp and 321 hp.

(*Below*) The Mercedes-Benz C-Klasse was the middle-class model from the Stuttgart-based company. In 1998, the in-line six was replaced with a new V6 engine, which had three-valve technique and dual ignition. The C-Klasse engines generated from 95 to 197 hp, but if you wanted something really hairy you could order a specially built AMG version with Mercedes' new 4.3-litre, V8 and 306 hp. Shown here is the station model T.

ABOUT 90 PEOPLE DIE IN A VIOLENT STORM that crosses Great Britain, the Netherlands and France. The impoverished Rumanians are promised Soviet gas and oil to help them through an awful winter. Their country's secret police, Securitate, is found to have been aided by doctors in faking certificates of natural death for torture victims, and Rumania seems morally as well as economically bankrupt. France's president François Mitterand approves its sale of nuclear technology to Pakistan. The Soviet Parliament passes a law giving, for the first time, individual citizens the right to own factories and employ workers. Georgia, one of the USSR republics, asks to negotiate with Moscow for independence.

Two interesting newcomers from the second half of the nineties. At top the little Ka from Ford, which was a brave move in a time when Ford was losing market shares in Europe. Ka was based on the Ford Fiesta, but 21 cm shorter and thereby a competitor to Renault Twingo. Ka had a four-cylinder 1.3-litre engine of 60 hp.

Another new car on the market was Kia from South Korea. Kia was already in 1995 second to Hyundai in terms of manufacturing. The most popular model was Kia Pride, mostly based on Mazda technique. One version of Pride was the Pride Shout from 1997, which aimed at a younger and more fashion-conscious public.

On the fifth of July, 1990, the last Lamborghini Countach left "Linea Montaggio No. 1" at the Lamborghini factory in Sant'Agata Bolognese. On the same day, the first series-produced Diablo took shape on a temporary assembly line. The yellow Diablo in the picture was the prototype shown at many of the great motor shows. When the Diablo hit the world it was the strongest and fastest of all supercars. The output was 492 hp and top speed 325 km/h.

In Lithuania, the new parliament supports a proposal for return to the independence this republic enjoyed during 1919–40, and Vytautas Landsbergis is elected president. The Latvian popular front, in multiparty elections, immediately wins 108 of the 170 parliamentary seats. Greta Garbo dies in New York at the age of 84, having hardly been seen off-screen for half a century. Li Peng becomes the first Chinese head of state to visit Moscow in more than a quarter-century. Boris Nikolayevich Yeltsin, the Soviet Union's reform politician, is chosen as the new president of Russia.

Soviet leader Gorbachev signs the "Start" agreement for disarmament of strategic nuclear weapons, together with America's president George Bush, in Washington D.C. The Iraqi president Saddam Hussein – who claims to be an heir of the Prophet Mohammed's cousin Ali – invades Kuwait and declares it the nineteenth province of Iraq. This sparks a crisis, and the United Nations tries to mediate. Presidents Bush and Gorbachev agree at a summit conference in Helsinki that the Iraqis must leave Kuwait. Lech Walesa, the head of Solidarity, is elected president of Poland. A tunnel being built under the English Channel makes a breakthrough. East and West Germany are reunited. Gorbachev is shaken by the strong calls for freedom in Eastern Europe, and worries about their effect on the Russian people.

For many years, Citroën stood for technically advanced solutions. Since 1974, Citroën, together with Peugeot, has been a member of the PSA Group. Over the years Citroën had lost much of its avantgardism. At the end of the nineties its models looked like most of its competitors'.
Shown here is a Xantia Break. This model came in 1993 and 1998 it was supplied with a new 1.8-litre engine which generated 90 hp, but the top model could be made with a V6 engine of 190 hp.

Forces from around the world gather in the Persian Gulf to liberate Kuwait. The United States contributes most, followed by Turkey, Saudi Arabia and Great Britain. Even Honduras and Argentina each send a hundred men or so. The Gulf War proves short, despite fears of Iraq's armament and voices of appeasement in some countries. Before the losing Iraqis retreat, they set fire to over 900 oil wells. In Italy, everyone has lost confidence in the political system – the economy is

terrible and the Mafia becomes ever more ruthless. Yugoslavia is officially dissolved with the recognition of Slovenia, Croatia and Bosnia-Herzegovina as independent states, but Serbia and Montenegro form a new federation with the old national name. Much of the former country slides into a civil war that threatens Balkan-wide conflict.

The invention of laser beams is creating an invisible empire, ranging from CD players and bar code readers to tele-

The year 1996 saw the introduction of the new sports car XK8 from Jaguar. It was a success from the beginning and in the first seven months 9,539 XK8 Coupés and Convertibles were sold, most of them on the US market.
Jaguar XK8 had lines similar to the classic E-Type and the car had a new 4-litre aluminium V8, which generated 294 hp at 6,400 rpm. In the middle of 1998 the Coupé model also could be equipped with a supercharged engine. The output was 370 hp and the top speed touched 250 km/h.

When Volvo in 1991 introduced the new 850 model, one realized that Volvo had changed course. Though it had a look similar to its predecessors, underneath the bonnet was new technology in the form of front-wheel drive and a transverse five-cylinder 2.4-litre engine of 170 hp. After a while the model changed name to S70 and from 1997 there was also a four-wheel-drive version called V70 AWD. That model had a turbo engine generating 193 hp.

communications. California introduces the world's strictest requirements for exhaust-clean cars. Crowding on the roads and in the air seems to offer railways a chance of recovering lost territory, and high-speed trains are developed in Europe, led by France. As for numbers of cars per thousand inhabitants in 1993, the USA is ahead with 288, followed by Australia with 193 and Canada with 173. A German law now says that all parts of an automobile must be recyclable. The hunt intensifies for fuel-saving methods and alternative engines to reduce the stress on the environment. Many companies try to produce hybrid vehicles, for instance by combining petrol with electrical

or gas power. Daimler-Benz's new small car, the Mercedes-Benz A-Klasse, which is meant to run also on batteries in its floor, turns over during a test drive in Sweden. An astonishing medium of communication arises: Internet.

Women's situation in Islamic societies is criticized in the West, whose values are relatively liberal. The gap between Arab lands and the industrialized world is thus widened. Neo-Nazis attack refugee houses in the German city of Rostock. An economic depression spreads across Europe, causing unemployment, interest-rate jumps, currency chaos, and crises in all areas. At the same time as East European states regain

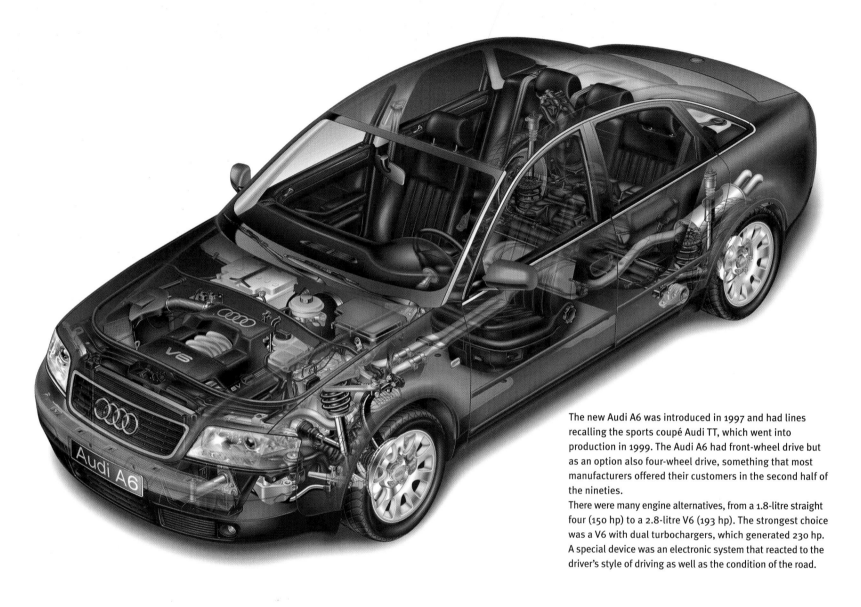

The new Audi A6 was introduced in 1997 and had lines recalling the sports coupé Audi TT, which went into production in 1999. The Audi A6 had front-wheel drive but as an option also four-wheel drive, something that most manufacturers offered their customers in the second half of the nineties.
There were many engine alternatives, from a 1.8-litre straight four (150 hp) to a 2.8-litre V6 (193 hp). The strongest choice was a V6 with dual turbochargers, which generated 230 hp. A special device was an electronic system that reacted to the driver's style of driving as well as the condition of the road.

independence and thereby split up, Czechoslovakia, for example, dividing into Czech and Slovak republics, the West Europeans are striving to establish a centralized union.

The United Nations organizes a grand environmental conference in Rio de Janeiro. It ends in many compromises, but ever more attention is paid to environmental issues. Research faces problems of human and animal survival, ecology and the impact of catastrophes due to nature or man. Experts increasingly argue that we are spending the world's

capital and living at the expense of our future. Sustainability becomes a concept to save from the fate of fashions. An unprecedented amount of oil has been spilled through the Gulf War in the Persian Gulf region: 816,000 tons, of which 300,000 burned up.

Edward Shevardnaze is elected president of his native Georgia, now a breakaway republic, after resigning as Russia's foreign minister. Cuba enters an economic crisis when Soviet aid shrinks, and Fidel Castro promises concessions to the people

After 34 years in production a new Porsche 911 arrived. It was twenty centimeters longer than the old 911 and for the first time the engine was liquid-cooled instead of air-cooled. With the help of four-valve technique and four camshafts the output was exactly 300 hp. The top speed was 280 km/h and 0–100 took 5.2 seconds. If you weren't satisfied, you could buy the 911 Turbo with an air-cooled engine that generated 408 hp.

on the 40th anniversary of his revolution. In Haiti, the military accepts demands for a return to democracy, and allow U.N. personnel to supervise respect for human rights. Former Yugoslavia's combatants stop U.N. aid convoys, so the USA begins "food bombing" instead. Georgian forces shoot down a Russian fighter plane over the breakaway republic of Abkhazia, worsening the tension between Russia and Georgia.

Tansu Ciller in Turkey, and Kim Campbell in Canada, respectively professors of economy and of law, are elected as their countries' first female prime ministers. The Palestine Liberation Organization (PLO) recognizes the state of Israel, with a document signed by PLO leader Yassir Arafat in Tunis. Norway's foreign minister Johan Jörgen Holst, acting as a peacemaker, takes the document to Jerusalem. By signing it, Prime Minister Yitzhak Rabin recognizes the PLO as legitimate representative of the Palestinian people.

King Baudouin of Belgium dies, succeeded by his younger brother Prince Albert. Civil war starts in Algeria, and violence escalates as the militant group GIA leaves the Islamic Front,

to pursue a struggle through terrorism against foreigners and Algerian liberals. The murder victims include local journalists, and even young girls who refuse to wear veils. In Russia, the process of democratization takes some steps backward when President Yeltsin sends troops into the breakaway republic of Chechenia. The Estonia, an Estonian-Swedish ferry enroute from Tallinn to Stockholm, sinks and nearly 900 people die in the worst ferry disaster in Europe since the Second World War.

Three Scandinavian nations – Norway, Sweden and Finland – each hold a referendum on joining the European Community. It yields "no" in Norway, but "yes" in Sweden and Finland. The battle against apartheid in South Africa has paid off, and former life prisoner Nelson Rolihlahla Mandela is elected to the country's presidency. A major earthquake in the Los Angeles area kills 40 and renders 20,000 homeless. In Paris, Jacques Chirac becomes President and announces that France will resume its nuclear weapon tests in the Pacific Ocean; many people abroad react by boycotting French wines. Israeli prime minister Rabin is murdered.

In the beginning of the nineties it was time for MG to make a comeback. Then Rover introduced the new MG RV8, which strongly resembled the old MGB that was put out of production when the MG factory was closed down in 1980. The RV8 engine was a 3.9-litre aluminium V8 which generated 190 hp.

Four representatives from the late nineties. **A**. At Frankfurt 1995, Audi presented a design study in the form of the sports coupé Audi TT. The car was much appreciated and was mostly made in aluminium. Audi decided to put it in production in 1999. **B**. The new Volkswagen "Beetle" was for sale at the end of 1998 but many customers already queued for the long-awaited car in the spring of 1998. **C**. In the beginning of 1999, Peugeot made a come-back in the Rally World Champion Series. The new rally car was called 206 WRC and had a four-cylinder turbocharged engine of 300 hp. The WRC car was based on the new Peugeot 206, which made its debut in late 1998. **D**. At Geneva Motor Show in 1998, Peugeot presented a concept car based on the forthcoming 206. This model was called 20❤, a French rebus meaning "Vainqueur" ("Winner").

A new American president is elected, Bill Clinton, and his wife Hillary plays a controversial, powerful role in the White House. Japan's economy loses stability and Southeast Asia's collapses entirely. Saddam Hussein, doing his best to frustrate the U.N. weapon observers in Iraq, provokes the United States, which prepares for more war in the Persian Gulf. A famous terrorist, the "Jackal", is caught napping and brought to trial. Pope John Paul II visits Cuba for the first time. The "Ice Man", a well-preserved Stone Age hunter with the oldest human body yet discovered, is about to go on exhibition in northern Italy. Africa continues to suffer from massacres, famine and AIDS. Civilization is awakening to the threat of a global blackout by the "Millennium Bug", a computer programming error. In most places, however, plans are already being laid to leap with joy – or at least relief – from the past thousand years into the next. ■

At top is a Bentley Arnage from 1998. It was a completely new model, equipped with a new turbocharged 4.4-litre V8 from BMW. The output was 350 hp at 5500 rpm and the 2.3-ton mastodon could accelerate 0–100 km/h in 6.2 seconds.

Below is a Chrysler Voyager from 1998. This model, which was introduced already in 1984, then as Dodge Caravan, was an outstanding sales success. Since then, many so-called MPV cars (Multi Purpose Vehicles) have come on the market and at the end of the nineties most of the manufacturers had a "people carrier" to offer. Chrysler Voyager from 1998, or Town & Country as it is called in the USA, had either an in-line four or a V6 engine.

BMW Series 3

1998 BMW 3-series Coupé (102-321 hp)

Wᴵᴛʜ ᴀɴᴛɪ-ꜱᴘɪɴ ᴀɴᴅ ꜱᴛᴀʙɪʟɪᴢᴀᴛɪᴏɴ ᴄᴏɴᴛʀᴏʟꜱ, ʙʀᴀᴋᴇ reinforcement system and non-locking brakes, the new BMW Series 3 appearing in 1998 was a car that virtually drove itself, and actually did so better than most ordinary drivers could.

Ever since June 1975, when BMW presented the first car in Series 3, this has been the company's model which feels best at the wheel. It is, of course, an heir of the old Series 02, but also a conscious effort by BMW to give even a relatively small car enough performance and fine handling to match the larger models.

In many ways, Series 3 was a technical sensation. Several of its design ideas came from Series 5, released a couple of years earlier. Now the time was ripe for the smaller BMW to become an equally safe car. Its standard equipment included

no fewer than six airbags: two before the driver and front passenger, two at their outer sides, and two – of a "sausage" type which then was new – to protect their heads from a side collision.

BMW had previously presented the idea of an inflatable "sausage" that expands diagonally over the side windows in front, to prevent one's head from hitting the inner side of the car. This system was an optional accessory on the more expensive models, but now it became standard in a smaller car. BMW's side-collision sausage was unique for 1968, but later that year the Volvo S 80 emerged with a "curtain" having the same function.

Impact cushioning was not the only safety feature in the new Series 3. The body had also been greatly strengthened to absorb collision forces in front and back, and the passenger compartment was shielded by a steel framework that best resembled a cage around the riders.

Series 3 was still recognizable in the model despite all its novelties. But this quality was just what BMW had promoted for many years – the family feeling. People were expected to sense that they were driving a BMW and feel at home in it.

Essentially, the new Series 3 could be called a scaled-down Series 5 in both its body style and chassis. This meant a well-rounded shape and an advanced structure. To satisfy those who worried about the rear end's tendency to slide, the car came with an anti-spin system that – when engaged – made it nearly impossible to skid.

Further stability could be added with the CBC (Corner Braking Control), which opposed a skid when braking on a turn. It worked together with the non-locking brakes, slowing any wheel that gave a sign of skidding. There was also a sophisticated steering-stability system, or DSC (Dynamic Safety Control). This slowed any wheel with a faster rotation than the others by braking it and, if necessary, by throttling back the engine until all wheels rolled in unison.

The latter technique operated like the anti-skid system that kept the little Mercedes A-class car from turning over. Having coupled it in, you could drive into a curve almost as carelessly as you liked, whatever the surface. It compensated for your error. To be sure, the laws of nature were still obeyed – if you lost touch with the road, you were lost – but as long as friction remained, the system strove to save you from yourself. It was the welfare state on wheels!

Granted that it had been perfected, the fact that it could be switched off was important. Whoever wanted to be the car's sole master was free to drive this BMW with the same handling qualities as every other modern one. The new Series 3 still had rear-wheel drive and high engine power, on which BMW buyers insisted. They valued the feeling of a car on the road, not a neutral, lifeless conveyance.

All BMW models in 1998 were given the refined camshaft control that had formerly existed only on the BMW M3. The engine's torque and tenacity were thus improved. Smooth pull throughout the speed range was noteworthy, in contrast to the earlier BMW six-cylinder engines, which slumbered until you stepped on the gas and made them kick in more power. Now there was a continuous response, even if this slightly blurred the familiar BMW character.

As for figures, the 238 model had a top speed of 240 km/h (150 mph) and accelerated in 7 seconds to 100 km/h (60 mph). Actually, though, the diesel model was most enjoyable. The 230D had a four-cylinder turbodiesel with 136 horsepower and superb performance. Its consumption was only 7

BMW 3-series Touring (90–321 hp)

litres per 100 km (about 35 miles per gallon) and none of the usual diesel's sloth resulted.

Being one of the period's absolutely most forward-looking cars, the 1998 BMW Series 3 was naturally not very cheap. But did that matter? Here was a genuine BMW offspring with top-class strength as well as safety. You could smile all the way from the bank for it. ∎

Alfa Romeo 156 2.0 T

THE ALFA ROMEO 156 LOOKED VERY ADVANCED, was pleasant to drive and gave a generally charming impression. What more could be asked of the Car of the Year? Possibly a reasonable price – but this wish was fulfilled only with hesitation.

Although Alfa wanted the car to sell in the medium range, it was not spacious enough. The interior measurements were more like those of competitors in the class of roomy small cars, such as the VW Golf, Audi A3, Opel Astra, Ford Focus and earlier Escort. Anyhow, with a 2-litre engine, the car could start off with plenty of power. Its V6 obeyed the principles of previous Alfas, but had a new cylinder head which enlarged the combustion volume and thus lowered the fuel consumption. This asset turned the 156 into a "rocket" accelerating to 100 km/h (60 mph) in 7.3 seconds.

The body felt a bit cramped for a tall customer. Too much legroom was taken up by the central console, and the roof height in the rear was as low as in any modern medium-class car. Once again, Alfa presented more of a big little car than an average-sized one.

Predictably, the 156 did not break any sales records, but it was appreciated by people who simply loved to drive. And this was a growing category of buyers during the late 1990s, when many sought a vehicle with an individual style rather than a computer-designed copy of the neighbour's car.

On the whole, nothing but the engine was kept in common with past Alfa models. Normally, manufacturers did the oppo-site: both the engine and chassis were retained in a new body. Yet the Alfa's old, well-tried 2-litre engine with its four valves per cylinder, variable cam times and dual spark plugs, was quite a good machine. All that it acquired in the 156 was a way to stretch out the fuel.

By automatically changing the cam times according to the engine's load, both its power and consumption could be in-fluenced. One had only to choose between plenty of power with corresponding thirst, and moderate fuel use with less temperament. Alfa chose a "golden mean" that gave some priority to both high power and low consumption. It would have been possible to make the 156 with an engine using even less than the actual average of 8.5 litres per 100 km (about 30 miles per gallon), but Alfa refused to sacrifice more power and risk creating a mediocre, everyday vehicle.

Perhaps still more to the point, the company hoped to bear out its reputation of being a spectacular make, and decided on substantial power at the expense of more fuel. This, indeed, was acceptable to the buyers. Power was part of the spectacle and they were willing to pay for maintaining it.

The 156 had a technically refined chassis. At each end, the wheel suspensions were built to allow very exact control of the wheels' springing movements. In front, this involved double transverse links with springarms, servo-assisted rack steering, and front-wheel drive. In back, the axle was of a somewhat new type but its springing recalled a multilinkarm axle. As a slight simplification, one could say that the suspension at both ends resembled a Formula 1 racer's.

The design followed the new Alfa style that was introduced with the little 145 model and continued in the GTV and Spider. This family membership was indicated by a strongly angled

1998 Alfa Romeo 156 2.0 T

midsection of the bonnet, which culminated in an Alfa emblem as the grille.

Handles seemed to be lacking on the rear doors, since they were hidden in the back edges of the rear side windows. This, however, was thought to be silly and counted more as a design variation than as a refinement.

The engine programme included four petrol engines and two diesels. There was a 2-litre petrol model with 155 horsepower, in addition to 1600 and 1800 versions. As its leading model, Alfa presented a V6 with 2.5 litres and 90 hp. Both of the diesel engines had an exhaust turbo, the 1900 with 105 hp being of precombustion-chamber type while the larger 2.4-litre diesel boasted 136 hp and direct injection. The "T" in the model name stands for "Twinspark" (meaning two spark plugs per cylinder), not for "Turbo".

For its size, the car was unusually safe. It had two airbags in front, two at the sides, and ample deformation zones. Thus, even though neither end was very long, the passengers survived fairly violent collisions. Other standard benefits were the anti-skid system, a brake-force distributor to the wheels with the best road contact, and the non-locking (ABS) brakes as well as safety-belt tighteners.

The electronic gas pedal meant that the power was controlled without any wires or rods. Moreover, the electronic starter key had a built-in blocking device, and could also be used to turn off the right front airbag when a child's seat was mounted there instead.

In general, the Alfa 156 was a highly enjoyable conveyance. At first, problems with quality hindered the model's sales success. Small irritating defects, mainly in the electronics, plagued many owners. Solutions were found, but by then the aura of excellence had lost some of its shine. ∎

Mercedes S-class

THE RECEPTION WAS RESOUNDING WHEN THE VEIL fell at the Geneva salon in March 1991. Before the international press stood the Mercedes S-class, a breakthrough for an automobile – with even safer brakes, new suspension and ventilation and beltadjustment, filters stopping unclean air, double window-panes, seats that were set automatically, a computer that coordinated the power train, and a very fresh V12 engine.

It is, of course, always easier to add a lot of sophisticated innovations to an expensive vehicle like the S-class than to a cheap small car. The customers are not as cost-conscious at this price level, so they can be offered more, and they demand more. Today, a luxury car must go beyond comfort and provide valuable features. The S-class did just that.

In the present case, the whole was emphasized over the parts. Rather than a refined car with things like a stronger engine, it was entirely new in both matter and soul. To begin with, its safety had been increased greatly. The front was longer, and units beneath the bonnet that might hinder a deformation had been removed.

Stiffening the front was a cross-beam mounted behind the bumper. This served not as a guard, but as a deformable reinforcement, particularly for offset collisions. Similarly, the front wheelhouses were designed to spread out collision forces and distribute them to the floor beams. Neither could the front wheels penetrate the interior during a frontal crash.

The space inside also promoted safety. Longer distances to the surfaces meant less risk of passengers hitting the furnishings. Moreover, the belts were easier to use. The upper attachment was adjusted automatically on all belts – and the belts were fastened in the seats, not the body.

Quite novel, too, was the design of the front suspension. Two triangular struts controlled each front wheel's springing movements, but the lower one was fixed in an auxiliary frame, whereas the upper one and the spring pivoted directly on the body. This solution gave not only greater directional stability, but also better sound insulation, since noise from the wheels and road surface was not transferred as easily to the body.

The steering was made speed-dependent, as the servo effect increased at low speed for easier steering, and decreased when the speed rose to allow more sensitive steering.

Environmental care was the highest fashion at that time,

1998 Mercedes S-class (177–394 hp)

and Mercedes' contribution was not just that all engines had catalytic exhaust cleaning, air injection and exhaust return. The fuel injection was regulated by a computer, giving each cylinder exactly the amount of fuel it needed in relation to the air density and the actual engine load.

For the first time in automotive history, a car obtained double glass panes with air between them. The resultant insulation was superb against both heat and cold. Besides, the risk of condensation was eliminated. In addition, the S-class could be obtained with a cabin air filter that removed disturbing smells or smoke.

Automatic door-closers were something else new. If you simply pulled the door toward its frame, it would shut.

There was a wide choice of engines. The smallest six-cylinder version had 3.2 litres and 231 hp, while the big V12 had 6 litres and 408 hp. Intermediate were two V8 engines, designated the 400 and 500, with 286 and 326 hp respectively.

All in all, the new S-class was a fantastic car. The largest model, 600 SE/SEL, accelerated to 100 km/h (60 mph) in six

seconds – not bad for a giant weighing over two tons. The V12, with its four valves per cylinder and two overhead camshafts, was said to be less an engine than a precision clockwork.

The car's comfort was astonishing, and its sound level so low that a ticking clock could be bothersome. There were so many technical improvements in driving and comfort that a week of lectures on them would have been worth attending.

Although most of the items conceivable in modern cars existed in the S-class, it did not win out to the extent Mercedes hoped. Its price was definitely high and approached twice the cost of other expensive cars, but this was not decisive for customers' dislike of the car. They found its style unimpressive, without enough display of the fact that the owner was rich.

One often hears that wealthy people prefer to be anonymous, yet conspicuous in their ability to afford a fine car. Perhaps the engineers at Mercedes thought of all but this. A car with everything was spurned by those who yearned for it. If so, the car itself was too anonymous. ∎

Audi A 3

I F WE WERE TO IMAGINE THREE SIBLINGS – ONE FROM the country, one from the city, and one from the aristocratic class with its castles and mansions – these would correspond to three noteworthy cars: the Škoda Octavia, Volkswagen Golf and Audi A3.

All three were built on the same base, and have the same engines and gearboxes. But there the similarities stop. Audi's

design is of the finer sort. If the model is a diesel, its Audi version is no malodorous monster with tired handling and embarrassingly poor performance. Here is a technically advanced product that most petrol-powered small cars cannot hope to match. In addition, its fuel consumption is well below the majority's.

The Audi slogan, "leadership through technology", perfectly suited the little A3. In a total length of just 415 cm (163 inches), the company created a car with fairly ample room and, more importantly, one which was so much fun to drive that you looked forward to the next spin as you stepped out of the door.

Very up-to-date as small cars go, the A3 was practical and dependable, and it gave the passengers a good chance of staying alive even after a serious crash. Not only the four airbags – two in front and two at the sides – but the entire body construction emphasized safety. An unmistakably solid feeling was conveyed on the road.

Besides being little, the A3 was actually best as a two-seater, with the option of folding the rear seat to form a gigantic baggage-space for only two people in front. Certainly it was possible to sit in back, but the comfort of doing so was dubious. At any rate, getting into the rear seat was by no means easy, although the front seats could be slid forward. The head-room might be sufficient, but the leg-room was minimal.

While two people could ride nicely in the rear – apart from their lower extremities – the real luxury was reserved for those in front. Perhaps the main reason was that you sat low down, not upright as in a store window. Moreover, you had a direct sensation of the car's excellent handling. It behaved superbly in a swerve even when fully loaded. The driver's place was also easy to adapt, partly due to the adjustable steering-wheel.

The baggage compartment itself was of modest size, holding only two large suitcases and a small one. Its floor lay 20 cm (8

The Audi A3 was the first Audi to have a transverse engine, and its output varied from 90 to 150 hp.

inches) under the threshold, so you had to lift the bags rather far to get them in. This was deplorable, but forgivable since the threshold base served a stiffening function, to increase safety in case you were hit from behind. Within the compartment, there were smooth sides and a flat bottom, as well as two pockets at the sides. As already noted, the rear seat's backrest could be at least partly collapsed.

Of the several different engines available, the simplest was the 1600, delivering 101 horsepower. Next came Audi's five-valve engine, either with 125 hp or with an exhaust turbo and 150 hp. Two diesel versions existed, which were the same engine with turbo generating either 90 or 110 hp.

The 110-hp diesel A3 was wonderful to drive. It spread amazement that an engine could be so far from an ordinary diesel's smells and noise. Not only did its power leave many a petrol-driven car behind, but its low diesel consumption was close to setting a record: 4.9 litres per 100 km (about 50 miles per gallon). Acceleration was equally admirable, and the car was able to hold a high average speed for hours without any sign of overstraining.

The A3 represented a type of car that many older drivers bought during the late 1990s. An elderly couple, in particular, did not need a car with a spacious rear seat. More essential were security and comfort, not to mention reliability. This Audi model offered most of the qualities of a larger car, yet was still small enough to find room in the ever more crowded cities of Europe.

No doubt its supreme advantage, too, was the promise of strong protection from accidents on highways that also became increasingly crowded. Such a mixed strategy of fine characteristics has enabled the A3, in turn, to succeed over stiff competition for customers. ∎

Chrysler Viper

PORSCHE AND FERRARI WOULD HAVE NO CHANCE. Not even Chevrolet Corvette was to be a threat. These seemed lofty goals for the new American sports car of the 1990s. And a Chrysler Viper could strike 60 mph (100 km/h) in just four seconds! Admittedly, it cost as much as the cheaper Ferraris and Porsches.

Even in first gear the car did 75 mph (120 km/h), so it managed to exceed most of the period's speed limits with no more gears at all. But the comfort was slight and one sat as if in a vise, with no hope of relaxed driving.

The Viper had such breathtaking acceleration that it almost left the human being behind. Its rear-wheel drive, expected to transfer 406 horsepower down to the asphalt, was faced with a difficult task – especially in slippery weather. Since the car was more expensive than the majority of houses at that time, neither did buyers come easily.

Thus, many a disadvantage attached to this vehicle. It was nonetheless a marvel on wheels. Actually named the Dodge Viper, but called the Chrysler Viper by Europeans for some unknown reason, it began as a style study for a sports car at the Detroit show in 1989. Chrysler wanted to demonstrate that the company had futuristic ideas, which might eventually emerge on production cars.

However, this did not please customers: they wanted a Viper right away. Many American hearts saw the Viper as a way to beat Porsche and Ferrari. It was a source of pride for the industry at home to have a sports car that could compete with the classic makes in Europe. Only a year later, after several prototypes, and simply to test whether the Viper would be worth series-producing, its manufacture was approved by the legendary chief of Chrysler, Lee Iacocca.

A year after that, the car went on sale at what, for an American company, was a modest rate of 500 cars per year. Still, it had gone from a dream-car drawing to a real automobile in a mere three years, and this alone was a record.

The recipe for building a Viper was elementary: a strong

Chrysler's Viper looked quite like the successful AC Cobra Coupe, which brought home the world championship for GT cars in 1965 (see page 229).

frame, big engine and super-light body, with rear-wheel drive. Its structure displayed nothing remarkable, but the manner of building it certainly did.

Chrysler's own V8 engine was rejected as too small. Yet to buy engines from a competitor sounded bad. Dodge trucks used a V10 engine that was large, unwieldy and not very advanced, but it was powerful. This engine was shipped over to the sports-car maker Lamborghini in Italy (then owned by Chrysler, though later bought by Volkswagen) who reconstructed it. The block and cylinder head were cast in aluminium instead of iron, and suddenly Chrysler had its own suitable power plant for the Viper, with over 400 hp.

On the frame, box-built with central stiffening by the transmission tunnel, light body panels were mounted. The body was of plastic, not worked together with glassfibre in one mould as usual, but made by the so-called RTM method of pressing parts under heat in special moulds. While the method was similar to manufacture of buckets or toilet seats, this was its first use on cars.

Far from being a toilet seat, the Viper offered an unforgettable ride. If you let up the clutch and tramped the gas pedal, your cheeks were stretched back by the acceleration; if you shifted into second and kept your foot down, you could never explain away the speed violation on a normal road.

In countries with speed limits, the Viper posed a considerable risk to one's driving licence. Even when stopped, its shape suggested that it was about to fly. The driver's purely functional position did feel cramped for those taller than average, and the slipstream was more like a hurricane than wind in one's hair. But it compared well with a trip on a roller-coaster, except for its dizzying price. Otherwise I myself would have been a glad owner. ∎

Saab 9-5 S 2.0 Turbo

THE NEW LUXURY CAR PRESENTED BY SAAB IN the summer of 1997 was not comparable with a Mercedes, BMW, Audi or even Volvo. But though a bit less competitive, the 9-5 won out on other grounds – sheer personality.

Saab's hallmark, too, has always been personality. It does not mean a lack of luxury – only that the car does without the sense of planned perfection found especially in the big German vehicles. The new Saab 9-5 was a different type of car, for those who wanted to feel involved with driving rather than being transported.

Exactly what builds up such a personality is hard to define.

One can mention details like the eccentric habit of placing the starter key in the floor between the seats, or the turbo engines that went into every 9-5. There was also the extreme safety-awareness, making one confident of outliving quite a collision. Then came the small refinements: how about fans in the seats to suck out condensation?

And that was no joke. The Saab 9-5's leather upholstery had perforations to let damp sweat be whisked away by the fans. They worked wonderfully and felt terrific on a hot summer day. Everyone has experienced the discomfort of

such seats in the heat. This soothing invention is not luxury, but caring about the customer.

The new "active" headrest was ingenious in its simplicity. When the body's back was pressed backward during a collision, the headrest on the front seats pushed forward, catching the head so that a whiplash effect was arrested.

Saab's old classic, the pollen filter, which had appeared in the 1970s, could now be complemented with a gas filter that blocked bad smells from the interior. Consequently, no smelly exhaust due to passing trucks could penetrate the car.

As the company's half-owner, General Motors naturally wanted the cost of manufacturing Saabs in Sweden to be lowered as much as possible, by using components that it already had available. Hence, the Opel Vectra contributed a bottom-plate that was lengthened by six centimetres. This gave the 9-5 a multi-link-arm rear axle instead of Saab's fine old live axle, resulting in greater comfort – but also some undesirable swaying when the driver turned hard.

The car's external design was debated. It scarcely followed the prevailing fashions, and looked more like an over-yeasted bun. However, the impression varied according to taste. What did seem clear was that the 9-5 suffered from a higher initial price than both the Volvo S 70 and the Audi A6.

In terms of environmental thinking, the Saab 9-5 was well ahead. Even then, it fulfilled the European Union requirement that 85 percent of the car's weight should be recyclable by the year 2002. The lacquers were water-based, solvents and

1998 Saab 9-5 S 2.0 Turbo

freons were banned, and the exhaust emission was very low. Much of the credit owed to Saab's own Eco technology with, for example, a preheated catalyzer for lower cold-start emission. All of the plastics were marked for recycling – indeed, several parts were made from recycled plastic.

The earlier Saab 9000 was a little nicer to drive, but the 9-5 still took a respectable place on the scale of cars with excellent handling. There was nothing really dangerous about the springing movements of the rear wheels when swerving, due to the rear axle inherited from the Vectra. The new turbo systems made the engine feel smoother than before, with a less palpable turbo effect, yet the power was present.

The four-cylinder transverse engine had four valves per cylinder and exhaust turbo. The cylinder volume was 1985 cc and output 150 hp/110 kW. The top speed was 215 km/h and acceleration 0–100 km/h (60 mph).

At that time, the Saab 9-5 was among the few cars that one could calmly imagine oneself riding through a crash. It had

dual side-impact airbags, strong beams in the doors, superb deformation zones at both ends, airbags before and the new headrests behind the front passengers, and friendly interior surfaces. In sum, it was a paragon of safety.

On the other hand, Saab had deep knowledge of child safety that was evidently ignored by those who decided about the 9-5. This factor played a mediocre role from the outset. Not until 1999 would the model offer the integrated childseat that folded out of the rear backrest, which existed already on the smaller 900 and later on the 9-3. The cars with double air-bags had no attachments for a childseat in front. To disengage the airbag function was a workshop job.

At first, the 9-5 was greeted with mixed reactions and sluggish sales. But buyers soon accumulated who found that the car did possess more personality than they had thought. One needed to try a 9-5 thoroughly in order to realize how comfortable and secure it was. Once again, a special character proved typical of Saab. ∎

Volvo S80 2.9

THE UGLY, ANGULAR BUT ROBUST AND RELIABLE
Volvo "box": this image died in 1998, completely reversed by
the S80 model. The new car was rounder in forms, charming
and handsome, as well as safe to drive.

In spite of all that, it was not a luxury vehicle. But the
pleasure of driving it was enough to win worldwide attention,
so it got off to a flying start. That some of its technology was
quite old-fashioned did not matter as much. Time-tested
designs often work better than novel refinements.

The lines were bold, inspired by the hybrid car ECC, which
Volvo exhibited as a thing of the future. The S80 was wide
and gave a "squat" impression, seemingly hefty. Its rear end,
with large lights, was reminiscent of the Jaguar XJS.

In short, it caught the daring spirit of the decade.

Comfort was perfect in front: the seats were electrically
adjustable in both length and height, as was the steering-
wheel. In back, it was not so good. For once in a modern car

with a sloping roof, there was space for the head, but not so
much for the legs.

The S80 was an exceedingly silent car. Its engine emitted a
hardly audible whisper. The only real sound was a clunking
from the wheel suspensions when you drove over bumps in
the road – one of the signs that it was not in the luxury class.
BMW, Mercedes, Audi, and even the Saab 9-5 were quieter
when traversing, for instance, a railway track. In the Volvo,
you heard a confession that the wheel suspensions had been
dealt with "cheaply".

Certainly a multi-link-arm axle lay in the rear, but the
transverse spring made of composite material, which had
existed in the S90, was replaced by ordinary spiral springs.

The front end was of spring-leg type, in principle the same
as when this design appeared in the early 1960s. Such solutions
did not render the Volvo S80 especially modern from the
design viewpoint.

On the other hand, it possessed decisive advantages in
terms of safety. "The world's safest Volvo," said Volvo! They
were careful not to say the world's safest car, but just then it
was probably that too. No other car had as comprehensive an
array of safety equipment.

There were two airbags, two side-impact bags and two
impact curtains in front. The latter would immediately inflate
and prevent the passengers' heads from hitting the inner wall.
These details were reassuring if you could imagine the car
crashing at all.

The 2.9-litre six-cylinder engine was as smooth as a well-
trained panther, with more power than its competitors. Still, it
drank less than a litre per 100 km (about 25 miles per gallon).
One could drive lazily, yet zoom away when one wanted – the
ideal for any engine, responsive to the master's whims.

The Volvo S80 was introduced in 1998 in its home town Gothenburg.

An excellent anti-spin system made it impossible to skid, as long as the S80 was not provoked. Also superb was the instrumentation, though perhaps with a few too many buttons on the wheel – besides some items that are not really essential, like a built-in telephone and loudspeakers.

The S80 was then the only car in the world with a full environmental declaration. At Volvo, the whole manufacturing process was classified according to its effects on the environment – not only the exhaust emission, the parts and the material. Thus, the S80 proved that it was possible to make a vehicle with environmental awareness overall. The car was 90 percent recyclable.

Volvo continued the integration of a child's seat in the middle rear armrest, as on earlier models. This seat folded nicely out of the armrest. However, it was not standard and had to be purchased extra.

While a very fine car, among the best in its class anywhere, the S80 was by no means revolutionary. It presented no fresh

1992 Volvo ECC

visions or technical leaps forward, but rather a sense of conventionality except in its shape. A beautiful new metal box with familiar engineering, cleanly brought together – and that was entirely acceptable to Volvo's faithful customers. Also impressed, no doubt, were "suitors" of the Swedish company, among them Chrysler, Ford and Fiat. On January 28, 1999, came the announcement that Ford offered 50 billion crowns to acquire Volvo... ∎

Chrysler 300M

IN 1955 CAME THE 300A, WHICH WAS THE FIRST OF Chrysler's so-called "letter-cars". With 300 hp it was the strongest of all American-built cars. Within a year the output was raised to 340 hp.

> In the beginning of the fifties Chrysler introduced a completely new engine that started a war in the USA – the battle of horsepower. This was in 1951 when the revolutionary hemi-engine was presented. It was a 331.1 cu.in. V8 unit with hemispherical combustion chambers and an output of 180 hp. Chrysler shocked the competitors.

But Chrysler was not satisfied and in 1962 came an even bigger giant: the 300H, whose engine generated 380 hp. With a special ram-induction system the output could be raised to an incredible 405 hp.

The last of the "letter-cars" came in 1965, but with the out-put reduced to 360 hp for a number of reasons.

The oil embargo in 1974 shocked the Western world, in particular the USA, where people had got used to petrol that was almost free. The engine output was drastically reduced and in 1978 the strongest Chrysler generated only 195 hp.

At the same time, America was invaded by cheap Japanese cars which hit hard against the US manufacturers. Many of them faced severe troubles, including Chrysler.

But in 1978, the "catcher in the rye" came to Chrysler – the dynamic Lee Iacocca! What he did is nearly unbelievable and when Bob Eaton took over in 1992, Chrysler was standing on solid ground with a net profit of $723 million compared to a loss of $795 billion the year before.

New models were introduced and the people-carrier

Voyager was an immediate success, in both the USA and Europe. Other models were the Vision and Neon.

CHRYSLER 300M

The autumn of 1998 saw a new model – the 300M – whose designation recalled the "letter-cars" of the fifties and sixties.

The 300M was the second generation of the so-called "Cab Forward" concept that was first applied in the 1994 Vision.

"Cab Forward" means that the roof has been moved forward as much as possible, thus creating more interior space without elongating the car.

Though the 300M was only 4,999 mm long it had generous interior space. As standard the car was equipped with ABS brakes, anti-spin system and an Autostick function, which made it possible to control the four-speed automatic gearbox either automatically or manually.

The 300M had a brand-new V6 engine with a capacity of either 2.7 or 3.5 litres. The engine generated 200 hp and 251 hp respectively.

Chrysler 300M was a car that really reflected the spirit which Lee Iacocca had managed to create at Chrysler Corporation. ■

Mercedes A-class

From this vantage point, the compactness of a Mercedes A-class is clear.

IN THE MID-1990S AT THE FRANKFURT AUTO SHOW, Mercedes exhibited a prototype for a strikingly small car. Many eyebrows were raised: would the company really make such a tiny thing that even a Fiat seemed huge?

But the rumours proved true. Mercedes intended to enter the small-car market, with a model called simply the A-class. Despite a length of only 360 cm (141 inches), it could hold four people and some baggage. The best point about the mini-Mercedes was that it had been scaled down in size alone. Mercedes gave its passengers a degree of safety quite comparable with larger cars.

The deformation zones in front and back are always shorter on a smaller car. Yet Mercedes had "lengthened" these zones at both ends. The car's floor was a kind of sandwich construction, with two surfaces separated by absorbent material, which served as an extended deformation zone.

In a collision, the engine and gearbox were pushed underneath the car without injuring the occupants. Similarly, the rear end did not affect the rest of the body but was pressed under it.

Four different engines were available: two running on petrol, with 80 or 102 horsepower, and two diesels of 60 or 90 hp. The fuel consumption was, for example, 4 and 7 litres/100 km (about 62 and 36 miles per gallon) in the smaller diesel and the larger petrol engine respectively. As for equipment, the A-class came with non-locking brakes, double airbags in front, electric windows and mirrors, servo steering, and an electronic ignition blocker.

The story of the Mercedes A-class might have ended here with a report of great success. At least to begin with, though, it did not. Few cars have been as debated for their defects as

When Mercedes presented the A-class in 1998, great problems arose as several of the cars turned over
during tests by the motoring press, and much work was needed to correct the defects.

this one – and all because of a handful of ambitious motoring journalists in the Scandinavian jury that chose the "Car of the Year".

At the jury's annual tests of candidates in Denmark during the autumn of 1997, the A-class behaved very oddly in the usual trial of evasive manoeuvering. This procedure, designed by the present author, was meant to show a car's stability under rapid sidewise movement. Cones were placed 10 metres apart along a corridor 4 metres wide, and the car was to swerve between them – as when, for instance, swinging left to avoid a child that runs into the street, then right to avoid oncoming traffic.

All modern cars passed such a test, except the little A-class. When it swerved, it tilted up on two wheels and came very close to capsizing. This was prevented only by the test drivers' many years of experience. The Mercedes people were surprised, to say the least. But instead of facing the problem immediately, they preferred to joke about the test as needless and irrelevant.

Some months later, the first A-class test cars reached the Swedish motoring press. In no time at all, a driver did the trick – which was not very hard – of overturning one of these cars. Now there was panic at Mercedes. German newspapers and TV published pictures of this car, causing a scandal. Mercedes' little car had failed an ordinary manoeuvering test and was dangerous.

The Swedish journalist who overturned the car was interviewed on German TV. He chanced to say that swerving might, for example, be necessary to avoid hitting an elk. As a

result, the event was called the "Swedish elk test". Once again, Mercedes tried to dismiss the fact that the A-class had awful handling properties with a full load in an evasion test. They distributed "elk diplomas" and "elk pins". Yet the jokes were not enough, and finally the company understood that something had to be done if the A-class project was to survive.

Larger Mercedes models had a steering-stability programme with an anti-spin function. This highly advanced system was installed as standard in all A-class cars, and instantly they obtained the best driving qualities in the small-car field. From being a danger, the A-class became one of the safest in these terms.

The only question was whether such electronic support would be worth using, rather than dealing directly with the car's weaknesses on the design level. If one must rely blindly on automatic assistance to keep a car from overturning, this system itself is always at risk of failing. And if it does, the car is still dangerous. That was just what happened when Swedish TV tested the A-class. A contact came loose from the driving electronics, and the car's bad handling revived, so that it nearly overturned.

The idea of a small car properly designed for safety like a big car is absolutely great. However, it can be doubted even today that Mercedes should have gone into this size class. Most Mercedes buyers would certainly have voted for the make's continued focus on large, safe models, instead of tarnishing its reputation with a wobbly little car that needs electronic "extra wheels" to stay on the road. ∎

Chrysler Crossfire

At THE END OF THE SEVENTIES, CHRYSLER, WITH THEIR FI-NE OLD TRADITIONS, HAD SEVERE ECONOMIC PROBLEMS. But like a gift from heaven, Lee Iacocca came and took over as leader of the Chrysler Corporation. During his time in office the company became profitable once again. This was in most part thanks to new models - especially the Town & Country - an MPV (Multi Purpose Vehicle). It quickly became very popular on both sides of the Atlantic. In Europe it was sold as the Voyager.

With the new Town & Country, Vision and Neon models, Chrysler took the lead among 'The Big Three' when it came to fresh ideas within the conservative American automotive industry.

In a never-ending stream, Chrysler presented astonishing concept cars, which the public took to their hearts. Some of the models soon went into production and among them were Viper, Prowler and PT Cruiser. A high-level Chrysler designer has referred to it as "hiding future products in plain sight".

The next surprise came in 2001 when Chrysler, now a part of DaimlerChrysler, unveiled the Crossfire at the North American International Auto Show. Trevor Creed, then Senior Vice President of Design, said that the "Chrysler Crossfire combines classic European proportions and technology with the power and personality of an American performance car. This modern American coupe is set to excite enthusiasts throughout the world."

The Crossfire's distinctive looks were not confined to its wedge-shaped body and low side windows. The model's eccentric rear end contributed to give a tough and very personal look. With a little bit of imagination, one could see the Crossfire's rear-end as the front-end of a futuristic mini-van, giving it a "face with character".

The man behind the Crossfire design was 25 year-old Erik Stoddard. Despite his age he managed to create a car with conspicuous lines. It was not unique but it was certainly unusual in a time of generally boring, internationalised creations.

The styling was definitely retro-inspired. This was a very obvious trend at the end of the nineties. Several manufacturers started to produce models at the time that looked like derivates from the fifties and sixties. But the old-fashioned shell usually concealed a modern platform from some standard model. The retro look wasn't supposed to cost anything, but merely to create attention and thereby strengthen the company's image.

Japan was the retro-leader, but it was Volkswagen that really broke the ice with the New Beetle. It was a 'copy' of the old Type 1 without single component in common.

The Chrysler Crossfire had many retro-inspired styling details. A radiator grille, clearly derived from the 1998 Chrysler 300M, dominated the front. But the 300M inherited it from the fifties. Another interesting detail were the split screen windows at both front and rear. It was not a true split screen: it was only an aluminium rib inside the glass that 'split' the windows.

The front fenders were raised above hood level, as in the good old days, and merged (via a distinct, and somewhat upwardly sweeping waistline) with the rear fenders. The side screens were extremely low and once again I quote Trevor Creed: "As a complement to romantic shapes and sleek, athletic lines, we gave Chrysler Crossfire a unique new glass-to-body proportion. We made the body-sides tall while minimizing glass surfaces. We wanted to give the driver that special feeling of being inside the cockpit of something very sporty, serious and protective". With the long bonnet and the distinctive rear, the Crossfire definitely had a unique and easily recognisable profile.

But most notable feature was the compact rear-end with its split

From a three-quarter front view, two details are eye-catching: the large grille with ribs in classic Ferrari style and a big Chrysler emblem, and the sophisticated headlights. Please also note the low roofline and the six-spoke wheels: 19 inches at the rear, 18 at the front. These features combine to give a very sleek appearance.

screen window like Chevrolet's Corvette Stingray Coupe from the sixties. The rearmost end of the body was very special. Those who didn't appreciate the lines compared it to a dog with its tail between its legs. But this was revised in time for production. The body-type could be defined as a fastback or a boat-tail (a design folly from the twenties).

Other significant exterior details were the air outlets behind the front wheelhouses, the headlights, the taillights and the two exhaust pipes protruding from underneath the middle of a plump rear end. The bodywork was built in one piece by carbon fibre and bolted to an all-aluminium platform.

The show-cars were given an eye-catching Sapphire Silver Pearl finish with brushed aluminium accents.

You might have thought that the Crossfire, in true American spirit, would feature a mighty V8 under the hood. But instead you had to be content with a supercharged 2.7 litre, 275 bhp V6 coupled to a five-speed manual transmission. 0-60 mph was achieved in 5.8 seconds, and the top speed was estimated to be 148 mph, according to the Chrysler Press Department.

On the 19th of August 2001, a press release reached the motoring media. The headline stated: "Chrysler Crossfire Concept to Become Reality". The prayers of the enthusiasts had been answered, and in January 2002, at the Greater Los Angeles Auto Show, the 'new' Crossfire was exhibited for the first time.

The production version of the Crossfire looked more or less like the concept car, but the styling was more thoroughly worked-out and in some aspects also more sober. The front-end had lost some of its aggressiveness and the hungry radiator grille had been reduced to almost Mercedes-like proportions. Even the eccentric headlights had given way to a more conventional arrangement. The distinctive rear-end had lost much of its original charm. On the other hand it had been equipped with a speed sensitive spoiler that

In 2002 Chrysler presented the production version of the Crossfire. Although a very smart car, one could not be blamed for saying that it differed radically from the original design and took on much from the Mercedes stable in final development - 39 percent to be precise and not only under the shell. One can't help but wonder why they didn't put a nice rumbling V8 under the bonnet instead of a silk-smooth Mercedes V6

lifted at speeds over 50 mph. Gone also were the split screen windows.

But the biggest changes occurred under the shell. The original 2.7-litre engine had been replaced with a 3.2-litre V6 from Mercedes along with the transmission, the suspension and many other parts. And instead of entirely assembling the cars in the US, the Crossfire was to be made together with the well-known German company Karman. No less then 39 percent of the parts were to come from Mercedes. An indication, perhaps, of who made the decisions. Wes Brown, auto analyst said: "Sharing parts with Daimler-Chrysler AG is a balancing act. From a Mercedes standpoint they have to make sure it's not too much sharing that hurts their brand. For Chrysler, the more parts the better."

The Crossfire was the first Chrysler that was built with parts from Mercedes. It was supposed to go into production in 2003.